Marketing Luxury Services

Miguel Angelo Hemzo

Marketing Luxury Services

Concepts, Strategy, and Practice

Miguel Angelo Hemzo
Universidade de São Paulo
São Paulo, São Paulo, Brazil

ISBN 978-3-030-86072-1   ISBN 978-3-030-86073-8 (eBook)
https://doi.org/10.1007/978-3-030-86073-8

© The Editor(s) (if applicable) and The Author(s), under exclusive license to Springer Nature Switzerland AG 2023
This work is subject to copyright. All rights are solely and exclusively licensed by the Publisher, whether the whole or part of the material is concerned, specifically the rights of translation, reprinting, reuse of illustrations, recitation, broadcasting, reproduction on microfilms or in any other physical way, and transmission or information storage and retrieval, electronic adaptation, computer software, or by similar or dissimilar methodology now known or hereafter developed.
The use of general descriptive names, registered names, trademarks, service marks, etc. in this publication does not imply, even in the absence of a specific statement, that such names are exempt from the relevant protective laws and regulations and therefore free for general use.
The publisher, the authors, and the editors are safe to assume that the advice and information in this book are believed to be true and accurate at the date of publication. Neither the publisher nor the authors or the editors give a warranty, expressed or implied, with respect to the material contained herein or for any errors or omissions that may have been made. The publisher remains neutral with regard to jurisdictional claims in published maps and institutional affiliations.

Cover illustration: Cristovao@shutterstock.com

This Palgrave Macmillan imprint is published by the registered company Springer Nature Switzerland AG
The registered company address is: Gewerbestrasse 11, 6330 Cham, Switzerland

To Liliana, for all that she taught me.
To my parents, Dezso and Suzel, for everything.
Thanks to all the people at Palgrave for the support and patience.

Foreword

> *It is the ultimate luxury to combine passion and contribution. It is also a clear path to happiness.*
>
> Sheryl Sandberg (former chief operating officer of Meta Platforms)

Why write a book about marketing for luxury services? Luxury services are fascinating, magical experiences, a delightful feast to all senses. An example of this kind of experience is a dinner at the Le Louis XV—Alain Ducasse, a Michelin three stars restaurant in Monaco, Monte Carlo. Entering a palace-like interior, one sees many waiters in white gloves circulating among the tables with silver cutlery, always smiling and friendly. A typical made-to-measure menu, starting at 500 euros per person without drinks, is composed of several small courses, offering variety and quality: appetizers such as fish cubes steamed on rock, fresh local butter served on a block of marble, pre-starter snacks, personal bread basket prepared at the spot containing six different homemade breads, each one presented and described by the waiter, followed by shellfish and chickpeas, steamed green asparagus with sheep's curd in a special sauce, turbot "au naturelle" with chard and calamari, grilled pigeon breast and guinea fowl from breast cooked on open fire. The salad is prepared individually with the leafy greens selected and cut just before being served. Desert includes homemade pink pepper sorbet prepared and served by the waiter, mango and passion fruit souffle, and rum baba with Haitian rum and raspberry with verveine ice cream. There is a choice of tea, prepared out of the herbal tea trolley, where you can choose your own mix of herbs, or specialty coffee prepared at a special coffee station, freshly prepared to maximize taste.

To consistently deliver this kind of experience is akin to a painter consistently creating a masterpiece each day. This is the challenge of the marketing manager working in luxury services. Luxury has to be enthralling, bringing people closer to beauty, the best things in life. Luxury has to be exclusive and inaccessible, but universal and democratic. Managers in luxury need to explore the potential of different segments that surfaced over the last decades and develop strategies to achieve the best positioning and differentials to be offered. Their clients are demanding, knowledgeable, and used to special experiences. A luxury brand has to offer excellence, balancing the needs of being innovative but true to its roots. Managers have to find, develop, and motivate the best skilled people to serve, managing logistics in a global setting, and being equally proficient in physical and digital environments.

I first met the author, Professor Hemzo, as a fellow student at London Business School, when he lived in London for four years and developed his interest in services and luxury marketing. We met again at various conferences, and eventually Professor Christopher Lovelock and I invited him to be the co-author of the Brazilian edition of the globally leading services marketing text book, *Services Marketing: People, Technology, Strategy*. We got to know Professor Hemzo to be an enthusiastic, passionate, knowledgeable, and rigorous researcher, educator, and consultant.

I love his new book *Marketing for Luxury Services*. It is innovative and offers a solid analysis of the managerial, historical, anthropological, and economic ramifications of the challenges managers face in the luxury service sector. I learned a lot when reading his book, especially about key decisions managers in luxury services face, and the concepts and foundations we can use to analyze managerial situations and help in decision-making.

Connecting to Sheryl Sandberg's quote at the beginning, I wish you, the readers of Professor Hemzo's book, that his passionate work contributes to your pleasure and happiness!

Professor Jochen Wirtz, https://www.linkedin.com/in/jochenwirtz/.

Singapore   Jochen Wirtz

Jochen Wirtz is Professor of Marketing and Vice Dean M.B.A. Programmes at the National University of Singapore (NUS), International Fellow of the Service Research Center at Karlstad University, Sweden, and Academic Scholar at the Cornell Institute for Healthy Futures (CIHF) at Cornell University, US. He was the founding director of the dual degree UCLA—NUS Executive M.B.A. Program (ranked globally # 4 in the Financial Times 2015 EMBA rankings) from 2002 to 2014, an Associate Fellow at the Saïd Business School, University of Oxford from 2008 to 2013, and a founding member of the NUS Teaching Academy (the NUS think-tank on education matters) from 2009 to 2015.

Introduction

This book brings together two subjects that got my attention some twenty years ago, and that I have dedicated my research and teaching ever since.

First, the emergence of the service economy, dominating most of the developed economies in the world, and the fact that, behind that tendency, there was a cultural shift, a change of paradigms, from the old idea of processing raw materials with poorly skilled workmanship, to a more profitable new way of doing business and making money, based on people's skills and competences, a much precious resource.

Second, the strength and resilience of the luxury market, always growing at attractive rates, using creativity and competences to offer high-quality, differentiated products and services, based on excellence and magic experiences. Luxury turned out to be the market where the new values of this new culture were best applied, with commitment and attention to details, resulting in satisfied and loyal clients.

Contents

1	**History and Concept of Luxury**		1
	1.1 Introduction		1
	1.2 A Brief History of Luxury		1
		1.2.1 The Era of Magic	2
		1.2.2 The Era of Power	4
		1.2.3 The Era of Success	7
		1.2.4 The Era of Individualism	12
	1.3 The Concept of Luxury		14
	1.4 Evolution of Consumption of Luxury		16
	1.5 Summary		16
	Bibliography		17
2	**The Luxury Market**		21
	2.1 Introduction		21
	2.2 Pré-COVID-19		21
		2.2.1 Market Numbers	21
		2.2.2 Players	25
	2.3 Post-COVID-19		33
		2.3.1 Financial Impacts	34
		2.3.2 Digitalization Impacts	34
		2.3.3 Behavioral Impacts	36
		2.3.4 Category Consumption Impacts	37
		2.3.5 Managerial Decisions Impacts	38
		2.3.6 Managerial Opportunities and Dilemmas	39
	2.4 Summary		42
	Bibliography		42
3	**Luxury Market and the Service-Dominant Logic Paradigm**		45
	3.1 Introduction		45
	3.2 The Evolution of Marketing and Service-Dominant Logic Paradigm		45
	3.3 Luxury Services		49
	3.4 Summary		50
	Bibliography		51

4	**How to Position a Luxury Product**	53
	4.1 Introduction	53
	4.2 How to Convince Clients that Your Brand Has a Valuable Differentiation	53
	4.3 Positioning Communication Strategies	57
	4.4 Other Elements of the Marketing Mix also Position the Brand	58
	4.5 Some Differences When Positioning Luxury Products	58
	4.6 Positioning in the Luxury Cars Segment	59
	4.7 Summary	60
	Bibliography	60
5	**Luxury Consumer Behavior**	61
	5.1 Introduction	61
	5.2 Consumer Behavior	62
	5.2.1 Personal Factors Influencing Consumer Behavior	62
	5.2.2 Psychological Factors Influencing Consumption Behavior	63
	5.2.3 Social Factors Influencing Consumer Behavior	67
	5.2.4 Cultural Factors Influencing Consumption Behavior	68
	5.3 Consumer Decision-Making Processes	69
	5.3.1 Problem Recognition	69
	5.3.2 Information Search	69
	5.3.3 Alternatives Evaluation	70
	5.3.4 Purchase Decision	71
	5.3.5 Post-Purchase Behavior	71
	5.3.6 Decision-Making in Luxury	71
	5.4 Summary	72
	Bibliography	72
6	**Defining the Persona: Segmentation and Targeting**	75
	6.1 Introduction	75
	6.2 Targeting, Evaluating, and Selecting	75
	6.3 Why Target Segments and Not Attend the Whole Market	76
	6.4 How to Segment Consumer Markets	76
	6.4.1 Geographical Segmentation	77
	6.4.2 Demographic Segmentation	77
	6.4.3 Psychographic Segmentation	79
	6.4.4 Behavioral Segmentation	80
	6.4.5 Media Usage Segmentation	82
	6.5 Criteria to Evaluate Potential Targets	82
	6.6 How to Evaluate and Select Targets	83
	6.6.1 Target Market Valuation	83
	6.6.2 Target Market Selection	84
	6.7 Luxury Segmentation	84

		6.8 Summary	85
		Bibliography	94
7	**Developing Strong Luxury Brands for Products and Services**		95
	7.1	Introduction	95
	7.2	Creating Strong Brands	95
	7.3	Creating Brand Equity	96
	7.4	Evaluating Brand Equity	97
		7.4.1 *BRANDASSET VALUATOR*	97
		7.4.2 *BRANDZ*	97
		7.4.3 Brand Resonance	98
		7.4.4 Brand Equity Boosters	98
	7.5	Developing the Brand Elements	99
	7.6	Internal Branding	99
	7.7	Measuring Your Brand Equity	100
	7.8	Managing Brand Equity	100
	7.9	Branding Strategies	101
	7.10	Brand Extensions	101
	7.11	Brand Portfolio Management	103
	7.12	Luxury Branding Strategies	104
	7.13	Summary	104
		Bibliography	105
8	**Creating Competitive Products**		107
	8.1	Introduction	107
	8.2	Defining Product Strategy	108
		8.2.1 Product Levels	108
		8.2.2 Product Classification	108
		8.2.3 Product Differentiation	109
	8.3	Product Lifecycle Management	111
	8.4	Product Line Management	112
		8.4.1 Categorization of Product Lines	112
		8.4.2 Evaluation of Product Lines	112
	8.5	Product Mix Pricing Strategies	114
	8.6	Co-Branding	115
	8.7	Packing	115
	8.8	Labeling	116
	8.9	Competitive Products in Luxury	117
	8.10	Summary	118
		Bibliography	118
9	**Place Strategies for Luxury Brands**		121
	9.1	Introduction	121
	9.2	Channels	121
	9.3	Channels and Value	122
	9.4	Marketing Channels	123

		9.4.1	Marketing Channel Systems	123
		9.4.2	Hybrid Channels	124
		9.4.3	Channel Levels	124
		9.4.4	Channel Design	125
		9.4.5	Channel Management	126
		9.4.6	Integration of Channel Systems	126
		9.4.7	Channel Conflict, Cooperation, and Competition	127
	9.5	Success Factors in Ecommerce		128
	9.6	Marketing Channel Strategies for Intermediaries		128
	9.7	Retail		128
		9.7.1	Shopping Center	130
		9.7.2	Wholesale	130
		9.7.3	Logistics	131
	9.8	Location Decisions		132
	9.9	Luxury Channels Strategies		133
	9.10	Summary		134
	Bibliography			134
10	**Managing Pricing and Value of Luxury Brands**			**137**
	10.1	Introduction		137
	10.2	The Strategic Importance of Pricing		137
	10.3	Who Determines Prices in the Company		139
	10.4	The Pricing Process		140
		10.4.1	Selection of the Price Determination Objective	140
		10.4.2	Demand Determination	141
		10.4.3	Cost Estimate	142
		10.4.4	Analysis of Competitors' Costs, Prices, and Offers	144
		10.4.5	Selection of a Pricing Method	144
		10.4.6	Selection of Final Price	145
	10.5	Tactical Pricing Decisions		145
		10.5.1	Geographic Price	145
		10.5.2	Discounted Prices and Promotions	145
		10.5.3	Promotional Price	146
	10.6	Pricing Strategies in Luxury Markets		146
	10.7	Summary		147
	Bibliography			148
11	**Communication Strategies and Tools for Luxury Brands**			**149**
	11.1	Introduction		149
	11.2	Integrated Marketing Communication		149
		11.2.1	Marketing Communication	149
		11.2.2	Steps for the Development of Effective Communication	151
		11.2.3	Selection of Communication Channels	152
		11.2.4	Budget Establishment	152
		11.2.5	Decision on the Communication Mix	153

		11.2.6	Measurement of Communication Results	153
		11.2.7	Integrated Marketing Communication Management	153
		11.2.8	Creative Communication Strategies	154
	11.3	Mass Communication		154
		11.3.1	Advertising	154
		11.3.2	Sales Promotion	155
		11.3.3	Events and Experiences	156
		11.3.4	Public Relations	156
	11.4	Personal Communication		157
		11.4.1	Direct Marketing	157
		11.4.2	Interactive Marketing	158
		11.4.3	Tips for Creating Effective Websites	158
		11.4.4	Word-of-Mouth Communication	158
		11.4.5	Personal Sales	159
	11.5	Communication Strategies in Luxury		159
	11.6	Summary		160
	Bibliography			160
12	**Managing People for the Luxury Market**			161
	12.1	Introduction		161
	12.2	Managing People		161
	12.3	Recruiting		162
	12.4	Selecting		162
	12.5	Training		163
	12.6	Motivating		164
	12.7	Evaluating		165
	12.8	Dismissing		166
	12.9	Managing People in Luxury		166
	12.10	Summary		169
	Bibliography			170
13	**Process Management and Operations for Luxury Brands**			171
	13.1	Introduction		171
	13.2	The Importance of Process Management		171
	13.3	Process Mapping Techniques		172
		13.3.1	Flowcharts	172
		13.3.2	Blueprints	172
		13.3.3	Consumer Journey	173
	13.4	Process Analysis		174
	13.5	Failure Analysis		174
	13.6	Delay Analysis		174
	13.7	Process Reengineering		175
	13.8	Managing Processes in Luxury		176
	13.9	Summary		177
	Bibliography			177

14	**Managing the Luxury Panorama for Great Experiences**		179
	14.1	Introduction	179
	14.2	Managing the Panorama	179
		14.2.1 Sensory Stimuli	180
		14.2.2 Layout, Space, and Circulation	181
		14.2.3 Visual Communication Signs	181
		14.2.4 Psychological and Sociological Interaction	181
		14.2.5 ePanorama	182
		14.2.6 Phygital	183
		14.2.7 Experiential Retail	184
	14.3	Managing the Panorama in Luxury	184
		14.3.1 Luxury Panorama and Positioning	184
		14.3.2 Luxury Panorama and the Internet	185
		14.3.3 Luxury Panorama and Flagships	185
	14.4	Summary	186
	Bibliography		186
15	**Stratetgical Satisfaction Management**		189
	15.1	Introduction	189
	15.2	Avoiding Tragic Experiences, Creating Magic Experiences	189
	15.3	Resources and Productivity	190
	15.4	Pre-service	190
		15.4.1 Information	190
		15.4.2 Customer Experience (CX)	191
	15.5	Service	192
		15.5.1 User Experience (UX)	192
		15.5.2 The Seven Steps to Great Servicing	192
		15.5.3 Expectations and Experiences	196
	15.6	Post-service	197
		15.6.1 Recovering Insatisfaction	197
		15.6.2 Managing Satisfaction and Relationship	199
	15.7	Loyalty	199
	15.8	Measuring Fidelity and Loyalty	199
	15.9	Managing Strategic Satisfaction in Luxury	200
	15.10	Summary	201
	Bibliography		201
16	**Culture and Leadership**		203
	16.1	Introduction	203
	16.2	The New Paradigm of Services and Cultural Changes	203
	16.3	Leadership in Luxury	204
	16.4	Summary	204
	Bibliography		205
Index			207

About the Author

Miguel Angelo Hemzo is Professor Dr. at the Marketing Area of the School of Arts, Sciences and Humanities of the University of São Paulo, Brazil since 2005. He has been teaching since 1989.

He has a Ph.D. and an M.Sc. in Marketing from FEA—University of São Paulo and an M.Phil. in Marketing from London Business School.

He has a degree in Civil Engineering from POLI—University of São Paulo and in Management from FEA—University of São Paulo.

He teaches and research on several aspects of marketing and strategy: Corporate Strategy, Marketing Strategy, Marketing Management, Consumer Behavior, Communication Management, Sales Management, Influencers, Packaging, Marketing Channels, Pricing, Services Marketing, Relationship Marketing, Luxury Marketing, and Digital Marketing.

He has written articles, authored another six books, consulted, taught, and given seminars and interviews on these various subjects over the last thirty-six years.

He can be contacted at mahemzo@usp.br and at Linkedin: https://www.linkedin.com/in/miguelangelohemzo/.

List of Figures

Fig. 1.1 Jakob Kugger, by Albrecht Dürer (*Source* https://commons.
wikimedia.org/wiki/File:Albrecht_D%C3%BCrer_080.jpg) 8

Fig. 1.2 The legend of Narcissus, that fell in love with his own
reflection (*Source* https://pt.wikipedia.org/wiki/Caravaggio#/
media/Ficheiro:Narcissus-Caravaggio_(1594-96)_edited.jpg) 13

List of Tables

Table 2.1	Worldwide luxury market evolution (in € billion)	23
Table 6.1	Segments and descriptive variables	86

History and Concept of Luxury

1.1 Introduction

Chapter Objectives
In this chapter, it is discussed how luxury evolved and how the concept of luxury changed over time, up to the one we know today. This chapter is mainly based on an article by M. A. Hemzo and L. F. Hemzo (2018).

1.2 A Brief History of Luxury

Try asking a few friends what Luxury is, and you will get many different answers. This can be a problem for someone starting to study a phenomenon, as it is necessary to define and set boundaries to the object of study, if you want to understand it.

According to Brun and Castelli (2013), "most authors agree that luxury doesn't actually refer to a specific category of products but rather indicates a conceptual and symbolic dimension, which is strongly identified with the cultural values of the society of a particular historical period". Luxury is complex concept, broader than a product category.

The concept of luxury is rich and has evolved over the last millennia, becoming complex and multivariable, reflecting the evolution of human society. Luxury has acquired different meanings for different societies over time, that have accumulated and influenced its current concept, making it hard to define without a wide historical, social, anthropological, economical, philosophical, political, and theological perspectives, as previous studies that proposed different definitions have shown (Berry, 1994; Brun & Castelli, 2013; Castarède, 2006, 2008, 2014; Christodoulides et al., 2009; Cristini et al., 2016; Csaba, 2008; De Barnier et al., 2012; Dubois & Laurent, 1994; Heine, 2012; Lahtinen, 2014; Lipovetsky & Roux, 2003; Strehlau, 2008; etc.).

The concept of luxury has existed for many millennia and has been evolving over time. To fully understand today's concept of luxury, first we must review its history, from its conception in the Stone Age, to today's society (Berry, 1994; Castarède, 2006, 2008, 2014; Lipovetsky & Roux, 2003). This evolution can be summarized in four eras, that could be called the Four Waves of luxury, in the sense that, like waves, one doesn't extinguish the previous, but add to it. Of course, many remarkable moments have happened over such a period of time in human history, so these four eras propose a schematic time view of the aspects most related to luxury.

1.2.1 The Era of Magic

During the Stone Age, humankind was nomad (Berry, 1994), living from the animals they could hunt and fruits and roots they could find ripe enough for consumption. It was a hard life, fighting nature and beasts, as food was uncertain and people depended on nature, the weather, luck, apart from skill and strength. They had to learn to read signs of the cycles of the nature that could tell them about sources of nourishment and help them survive, like the best periods of the year to find food, climatic changes and trends that could be associated to herds' migrations, and so on. This intense interdependence with the environment resulted in a mystic association of magical powers to elements of nature, with these elements, such as the sun, the moon, the mountains, the sky, the animals, etc., became the first deities. The whole nature was believed to have magical powers that could provide survival of the community.

The first form of luxury (Lipovetsky & Roux, 2003) is the abundance of food, attributed to the goodness of these gods of nature, still an ethic of luxury without the concept of wealth or splendor. These humans saw some of their members, the *shamans*, as special beings that could communicate with the gods and ask for their blessings. With their help, they offered their best goods (Berry, 1994; Castarède, 2006, 2008, 2014) as gifts in rituals performed by this spiritual leader and his helpers in a consecrated place, in exchange for a better life in the future, renewing a cycle of protection and survival. These sacrifices were offered in the name of the collective (Mauss & Hubert, 1899; Silva et al., 2004), usually during a great party expressing happiness at the turning points of the nature cycles, accompanied by special music, ornaments, body paintings, and the distribution of all goods available to all members, in the belief that they were concluding a cycle and the deities would provide them with more in the future. This gift exchange implies (Mauss & Hubert, 1899) that the deity received this generosity and it would be dishonorable not to reciprocate with an alliance with the people and other benefits.

1.2 A Brief History of Luxury

The gifts, as being the best ones, more precious goods the group had, assumed magical power and virtues to attract the favors of the gods.

Today we have a strong although somewhat unconscious influence of these associations of luxury with magic powers. Gifts offered in special places and rituals for its submission are associated with this power to generate happy returns. People feel a magical power in the product when consuming luxury. Luxury consumers declare a special feeling when consuming luxury products (Kapferer, 1998).

Today we live in an era of desacralization (Lipovetsky & Roux, 2003) where the sacred has been substituted by the secular, and the mythical *shaman* has been substituted by the luxury brand artistic creator. Dion and Arnould (2011) discuss how luxury consumers unconsciously perceive magical powers of the artistic creator of a luxury brand, someone able to turn common objects into valuable works of art. They cite Bruce Kapferer (1998, 5) that magic "deals with the forces of intentionality and its transmutations that are at the heart of the creation by human beings of their social... worlds" and complement that one can "see the artistic director as a kind of magical being who not only passes on his/her revelation but also 'transmutes' (rewrites) codes of beauty and fashion and creates a distinctive imaginary world". One could add that the charisma and the magic of the brand and its creator is brought to consumers by their modern-day helpers, the salespeople, performing in special places, the flagships, the brand stores, acting as "luxury sacred temples" (Moore et al., 2010) where, through rituals of purchase and consumption it will be transferred its magical powers to the final users.

This implies that the stores have to be designed in order to evoke associations with a temple, by the design of the *servicescape* (Wirtz et al., 2020), or, in luxury, what we call the luxury *panorama* (a concept discussed in Chapter 11), making use of spacious layout and refined decor, scents, music, lightning and colors, purposeful training processes that create rituals for the experience of the brand, and appropriate dress and behavior of the salespeople. The strategic management of the whole experience is fundamental for the success of the brand. In this era of desacralization of the sacred (Belk et al., 1989), consumption is being conducted as a ritual, like a rite of beauty for cosmetics, spas, plastic surgery, physical training, etc., or rites of passage, like pregnancy, birth, birthday, society debut, marriage, mourning, and many others. The product has to be special, creating an aura of rarity and craftsmanship. The magic of a brand is an important attribute and was ranked third (Kapferer, 1998) as an attraction factor of the luxury brands. Special care should be devoted to the packaging design (Chind & Sahachaisaeree, 2012; McIntyre, 2011), that should be able to anticipate the special powers of the product inside, apart from providing protection and ease of transportation—not forgetting sustainability. Rare raw materials, specialized craftsmanship and differentiated design should be employed.

The first three composing dimensions of the concept of luxury, resulting from this era are rarity (as the gift has to be something rare), craftsmanship (The gift has to customized to the importance and tastes of the gods) and symbolic content (there is an implicit exchange contract between the *shaman*, representing the people, and the god).

1.2.2 The Era of Power

It is estimated that humankind learned to domesticate animals (Brisbin & Risch, 1997) around 11,000 BC and plants (Shelach, 2000) around 8000 BC. Initially in areas close to rivers, where water was abundant, like the Tigris and Euphrates River system, with their tributaries, in Mesopotamia, in Western Asia, as well as the Nile in Egypt, Africa and the Yangtze and the Huang He (or Yellow River) in China, agricultural techniques spread all over the world, leading to great changes in human society. Humans became sedentary to be able to explore the local land and raise animals with increased crop and herd productivity, which made it easier to provide for their existence (Berry, 1994; Castarède, 2006, 2008, 2014; Chan et al., 2014; Han et al., 2010; Lipovetsky & Roux, 2003), with less dependence on hazard hunting and collecting, and the eventual favors of nature.

The increase in production resulted is abundance and excess supply, that could be exchanged for other goods and generate wealth. Abundant food means better health, with people living longer and resulting in population growth. The different crafts in a sedentary society allows specialization, with people becoming traders, artisans, or soldiers, resulting in a stratified society with a hierarchy of social classes with different levels of power, wealth, and social status. The ability to have specialized soldiers makes theses societies more powerful, as they can conquer more land, slaves, and wealth from weaker neighbors.

The search for symbols of social position changes important social practices like dressing, possessions, dwelling, burial sites (Berry, 1994; Lipovetsky & Roux, 2003), etc., that reflect this new social hierarchy. For the more powerful citizens, luxury goods are essential social markers. The kings associate their power with the gods, and present themselves as god-kings, either as having divine origins or divine rights given by the gods. Together with the priests, they are the link with the deities, responsible for peace and prosperity. They are almighty and with the right of life and death over their people.

In religion, as humans become more powerful, one observes a process of fusion between ancient gods that were nature beings and the god-kings, in an anthropo-zoomorphic metamorphosis (Rozwadowski, 2008), where they assume more physical and (positive and negative) moral human characteristics. This fusion means that now the god-king can also be the receiver of the gifts and bringer of good things to his people. His living place and his burial places are sacred places that have to receive luxury features to symbolize this power. Arts of civilization as pottery, metallurgy, weaving, painting, music, dance, gastronomy, poetry, etc., evolve to provide luxury to these places.

Luxury is no longer only dissipated as a sign of hope of receiving it back from the gods in the future as it was in the previous era, but its accumulation now also becomes a sign of power (of the gods and the god-king). Now as a god, he has to provide for his people, so he will have to use his power and wealth for the collective good, creating public buildings like temples, monuments, statues, forums, arenas, circuses, markets, and promoting great sumptuous festivities that mark the great cycles of life and nature, and the conquests of this society. Eventually others in the court also assume this new role by association, and to express their high social status, the noble class also offers public festivities, lives in luxurious palaces, and throws ostentatious and wasteful banquets. The fragmentation of the society results in fragmentation of luxury (Berry, 1994), that assumes many arts and forms in different social circles. We have a division of the luxury in sacred and profane, public and private, in religion and in the higher classes and court.

The access to luxury for new social groups creates a negative reaction (Berry, 1994) for different reasons. At the political level, a struggle for power tried to justify the denial of access on moral grounds. Greek and Roman thinkers like Plato, Aristotle, and Cicero proposed that ostentatious and superfluous luxury was a nonnatural corruption of the virtues of the simple life, offering false pleasures that weaken the farmer, deviates the artisan from his vocation and causes the cowardice of the soldier. These were noble activities that were being corrupted by the avarice of the trader, that was more interested in monetary gains, offering the excesses of luxury for a profit. The merchants were presented as people that lived by selling the same goods for higher prices, exploring the desires of the people, and using the passions of luxury for personal gain. In his "Republic", Plato (1937) assigns the tasks of storekeeper and salesman to the unhealthy: "In well-ordered states they are commonly those who are the weakest in bodily strength, and therefore of little use for any other purpose …". Aristotle ordered economic activities (Baker, 1952) into a hierarchy of worthiness. Agriculture and handicrafts are termed natural and productive, while exchange in all its forms is less desirable. He denounces retail trade as unnatural and base, explaining that it is "justly censured, because the gain which results is not naturally made [from plants and animals] but is made at the expense of other men". Cicero says (Haney, 1949) that merchants "are to be accounted vulgar; for they can make no profit except by a certain amount of falsehood …".

This derogatory view (Steiner, 1976) of the tradesman spread its roots through the ages and eventually contaminated advertising, marketing and business in general, resulting among other things in a prejudice against luxury, and in the ancient clash of the old wealth vs the nouveau riche—the gentle noble threatened by the uneducated arrivist. One reaction was the creation of sumptuary laws, defining where and who were allowed or not to have access to luxury products, irrespective of their purchasing power, but associated to specific social classes. Luxury (Wilkins, 2008), "throughout history (in the ancient Greek times, in the Roman era, in the medieval period, and in the Renaissance up until the seventeenth century) has been limited by the guardians of an orderly society, where luxury was perceived as a danger to be limited to a public place". As an example, in 1327, under Edward III of England (Freudenberger, 1963), a law was enacted to control "the outrageous and excessive apparel of divers people against their estate and degree" and these laws would only disappear in the eighteenth century "by the increasing individualism and economic freedom of the time".

As a similar strategy of power control, the catholic church (Berry, 1994) condemned luxury for stimulating mundane pleasures and its association with the sinful and erotic woman. In the fifth century, Augustine of Hippo (Berry, 1994) appointed luxury as an excessive stimulator of passions, associated it to luxuria, sin, and sex (he also defended virginity and celibate). According to him, the consumption of luxury by women resulted in more temptations and should be avoided. People should relinquish luxury in order to save their soul.

Over this period, we observe a slow evolution of rights (Freeman, 2011), from the natural rights and the codes of Hammurabi to the Greek and Roman laws, that stablished rules that could depend on social status and other factors, to the first guarantees of human rights, where everyone has the same rights, simply for being a human being, as in the Magna Carta, signed by King John on 15 June 1215. But this trend would only consolidate with the American and French revolutions in the eighteenth century. The Magna Carta acknowledged the divine origin of the power of the king, but not his absolute powers of life and death. The power should be exerted in the benefit of the people within some restrictions.

The heritage of this second era to today's luxury derives from this association and fusion of divine and secular power. Luxury becomes a status symbol of high hierarchical position and religious, social, or military power, as still is today. Luxury arts as pottery, metallurgy, weaving, painting, music, dance, gastronomy, poetry, and others develop to represent symbols of status. The role of provider of good things (public buildings, festivities, etc.) is shared between the gods and the god-king, creating the concept denominated by Balzac (1836) as "*noblesse oblige*", a French expression meaning that "nobility has its obligations", so today we have this strong social belief that those socially well positioned should contribute to charity, social causes, public works, and the general well-being of society. Luxury as an art creator (Kapferer & Bastien, 2009) has to be a trend setter, offering what will become mainstream art in the future, sponsoring new talents, new styles, and new forms of art expression. According to these authors, "… the function of luxury is the aestheticization of society, the overtaking of the material by the spiritual, elevation through beauty and art" … "the accumulation of material wealth should encourage and offer elevation through the intangibles – here the arts – to all".

There are also relationships with art as result of the previous era—the creative designer has magic powers and the brand can exert this magic in "temples of art", as museums, galleries, biennales, and expositions sponsored by the brand. Research by Jelinek (2018) has shown that "integrating art consistently and authentically within the whole value chain system, leads to a higher brand equity". This stream of art is complex and difficult (Chailan, 2014) and is an interesting positioning strategy for luxury brands as more exclusive, making the consumer feel special and unique. This author identifies from the practices of the major global brands in the luxury industry four main types of collaboration between a luxury brand and art: Business Collaboration, Patronage, Foundations, and Artistic Mentoring. Another influence of this era is the prejudice against luxury, that is still strong today, and will only be countered in the next age, when the growth in power and wealth of the merchant class will lead to a new view on their social and economic contribution to society.

1.2 A Brief History of Luxury

Sumptuary laws were common during this age as a means to control access to status symbols only to those worthy. Today they are no longer restricted and are used by luxury brands as signs of wealth and power.

This era contributed with two new dimensions of luxury: status (as a symbol of position in society) and high perceived value (with the concept of money, luxury was associated with expensive and valuable goods).

1.2.3 The Era of Success

With the end of the middle age and the emergence of the economic policy of mercantilism (Berry, 1994; Lipovetsky & Roux, 2003; Ormaechea & Sanchez, 2013), the bourgeoisie becomes so rich and powerful with the new trade markets that they become bankers and partners of the royalty and the Church, With the intimacy, came the desire to have the same luxury they witnessed in the palaces of the religious and state powers they now rival in wealth. A good example was Jakob Kugger, "*the rich*" (1459–1525) (Strieder, 1931), German banker, industrialist, and trader, painted by Albrecht Dürer (1519) in the period when he was negotiating a loan to Charles I of Spain for his imperial election that proclaimed him Charles V of Germany.

He was active in the trade of spices with the Portuguese Crown and its colonies, he was the first non-Portuguese to invest in Brazil, in 1503, through his representative Fernando de Noronha (just three years after the official discovery by Cabral), and his fortune was estimated in today's currency in 400 billion euros (Fig. 1.1).

The end of feudalism and the beginning of the Renaissance (Berry, 1994) was characterized by the reduction of the power of the feudal lords, the increase of power of the royalty as they gather powerful mercenary armies with new military technologies (like the more efficient long bows), and we witness many battles for regional and European supremacy, that means high expenses to be financed. Apart from private financing, which incurred high interest rates and debts, inflated by the scarcity of gold and silver in Europe, mostly under control of the bankers, we have a new policy of state intervention in the economy, the Mercantilism (Blaug, 1997). Based on the idea of fostering positive balance of trade, the State wants to generate wealth by conquering colonies where cheap raw materials could be obtained and used in the production of goods by the protected and subsidized local industries, in order to substitute importation and increase exportation, with positive balance of trade. Under this policy, this period witnesses an explosive growth of wealth of those dealing with banking, imports of raw material or precious goods from the colonies and exports of manufactured goods, and imports-substitute goods supported by state incentives in protected markets.

The most remarkable example is the birth of the luxury industry in France (Berry, 1994; Burke, 1992), when Louis XIV found the national treasure depleted by war campaigns and expenses of his predecessor and, seduced by the luxury he saw in Spain at the court of his father-in-law, Philip IV, funded by the Spanish

Fig. 1.1 Jakob Kugger, by Albrecht Dürer (*Source* https://commons.wikimedia.org/wiki/File:Albrecht_D%C3%BCrer_080.jpg)

colonies, he developed a policy with his Minister of Finances Jean-Baptiste Colbert, that would turn France into the main producer of luxury in the world. Among others, he banned the Dutch tapestry and created La Administration Générale du Mobilier National et des Manufactures Nationales de Tapis et Tapisseries—Manufacture des Gobelins in 1650, he banned imports of glass, crystal, and mirrors from Venice and created La Manufacture Royale de Glaces de Miroirs, later Saint-Gobain in 1665, and he banned Chinese porcelain and created La Faïence de Rouen in 1673. In this same year, he prohibited Italian opera and plays and instituted the monopoly of La Comédie Française. As a way of reducing the power of the medieval lords and the nobility, he ordered them to move to the court, away from their base of power, and created new rules of behavior in the court, the arts of the court: etiquette at the table, ballet, opera, fencing, equitation, as new forms of status symbols. The increase in the production and offer of luxury goods and the increase in the demand for luxury goods through the wealth generated from banking, industry, and trade resulted in a new market for luxury goods, the bourgeoisie, eventually ending the exclusivity of access to luxury for royalty and church, and the sumptuary laws. This wider access can also be seen as a further step into individualism, which will become the norm in the next era.

Luxury now also becomes associated to success in acquiring wealth and success in society, of being able to rise to higher social levels through personal efforts and skills. This new market, apart from consuming the existing luxury, also created demand for new forms. They still used the existing symbols of power and wealth, like great castles and palaces, armies of servers, ostentatious banquets and parties,

1.2 A Brief History of Luxury

and patronage of arts as a way of expressing their power and prestige. But they also started the declericalization of arts, which used to represent only divinities and kings (Lipovetsky & Roux, 2003) and now portraits the newcomers, as for instance in the famous pictures "Portrait of Merchant", by Jan Gossaert or "A Merchant of the German Steelyard: Hans of Antwerp" by Hans Holbein the Young, where the sitters are depicted in expensive clothes but in more informal poses in their workplace, with instruments of their trade, as documents, quill pens, and coins. A quest to achieve immortality through the arts created a strong demand for paintings, statues, and other forms of representation, and a new form of literature was created, the autobiography.

In this way, a new form of distinction as a luxury status symbol in this period is the personal association with arts, through the expression of individual good taste and culture, the chasing of esthetic and erudite pleasures, as expressions of one's value. This individual desire of distinction leads to a new form of patronage, not public as before, but now in a private way. This new and strong demand for luxury items for private pleasures creates a dynamic market for artworks, antiquities, production of manuscripts, translation and copy of Greek, Latin, and Oriental texts, the emergence of archeology, and the creation of private collections and libraries that would eventually become the museums.

This new-acquired status of the bourgeoisie brings new debates to religious and economic thinkers of the time about the concept of the individual and its rights, challenging the existing powers and rights of the church and the state.

Martin Luther, originally an Augustinian monk, was a key player in the Protestant Reformation (Berry, 1994), rejecting many teachings and practices of the Catholic Church, when he published his 95 theses in 1517, criticizing the sales of indulgences and the interference of the church in the state, contesting the authority of the Pope, defending the bible as the only true source of the words of God (Plass, 1944), and restoring the ancient concept of universal priesthood, where all baptized Christians can be in direct contact with God, without the need of the church's priests (Luther, 1958). The defense of more power for the people (and the resulting valorization of the individual) and the exhortation for all to become literate to be able to read the bible contributed to the diffusion of these ideas and to advance many changes in the social structure of power.

In the economic field, many thinkers are discussing the old restrictions of power concentrated in the hands of church and state, proposing moral and economic reasons to have it shared with the new powerful class, the merchants and bankers. The old reasoning proposed that luxury was dangerous to the society and should only be used under control of the sumptuary laws and conducted in a limited form in public places as benefits from the church and state to the people.

Nicholas Barbon (1640–1698) criticized (Berry, 1994) the mercantilism and the state as centralizer and wealth accumulator, the idea that luxury was superfluous and harmful to the nation and defended free market. He proposed that the will of the people should drive the market, influencing later thinkers such as Keynes and Schumpeter. In his view, trade caters to the legitimate and just needs of the body, the mind, and the soul, pleasure, and well-being in life, because these needs are noble and distinguish men from the basic needs of the beasts. The needs of the soul are infinite and can generate infinite markets, in particular for luxury and fashion, stimulating the economy. This brings a new dimension to the concept of luxury, that luxury can be all good things in life that satisfies superior needs.

Bernard de Mandeville (1670–1733) acknowledged (Berry, 1994) that luxury had some shortcomings, but these were human flaws that existed independently of luxury, but, on the other hand, luxury had many compensatory virtues, providing personal and social well-being, economic growth, as the quest for pleasure and happiness was a high need of the human being, making people more active and prosperous, and contributing to the wealth of the nation.

Influenced (Berry, 1994) by the pioneering ideas of the father of liberalism (a moral philosophy of liberty and equality), John Locke (1632–1704), in the following eighteenth century the movement of the Enlightenment (1715–1789) proposed the use of reason, analysis, and individualism in place of the authoritarianism and intolerance of the church and the state, the expansion of civil rights, and in particular, reinforced the defense of luxury as beneficial to people and society.

David Hume (1711–1776) proposed (Berry, 1994) that only excess of luxury was pernicious and corruptive for society, but the search for physical and mental pleasures, with refinement, is desired in a civilized society that cares for the well-being of its members and can be a driving force more important to social development than just common political goodwill.

Adam Smith (1723–1790) also defended luxury as positive to the well-being, as long as the excesses were avoided. The invisible hand of the market guarantees that luxury answers to a demand derived from collective will, resulting in more specialization, productivity, and the development of art and sciences, generating growth, wealth, and well-being.

All these ideas contributed to counter the ancient prejudice against luxury, making it a legitimate trade, as long as it did not conduct to excesses.

As an opposing ideology (Steiner, 1976), at the end of nineteenth century, "*hearkening back to Aristotelian roots, basic Marxist doctrine has been a major contributor to the hostile image of marketing*". They go back to Greek times to criticize traders and producers when they see "value as emanating almost entirely from the creation of form utility. He does grudgingly concede that transportation and storage are productive economic activities, not because the creation of place and time utility is valuable, per se, but on the grounds that shipping and warehousing are a continuation of the process of production". The social function of the trader is no longer recognized. "In a characteristic explanation of the source of value, Marx tells us: '*Already in the minute when the commodity is finished, before it leaves the hands of its first vendor, it must be worth as much as the final purchaser, i.e., the consumer, pays for it in the end*'". This should lead to a generalized prejudice (Berry, 1994) against luxury in communist governments, with restrictions, taxations, and even prohibition.

The consolidation of the concept of individual rights continues and two significant moments are the American independence revolution (1776) and the French revolution (1789), another step to the next era of individualism.

1.2 A Brief History of Luxury

As luxury becomes more individual (Lipovetsky & Roux, 2003), sumptuary laws are gradually extinguished and fashion becomes less rigid and hierarchic, and the old apparel that involved and dissimulated the body, reflecting the hierarchic social immobility, is abandoned by new ways of expressing subjective personal tastes and preferences. The costumes are tighter, molded to the body and its shapes, more ephemeral, elaborated, colorful, detailed, mundane, ludic, capricious, and directed to human pleasures, adding a new dimension of merriment, taste, exuberance, and dissipation.

Fashion creators are recognized and valued as bearers of the creative magic of luxury and its esthetic pleasures, no longer anonymous producers, but authors that sign their creations and influencers of new trends. The occupation becomes well remunerated and socially recognized, and those able to create unique pieces, in opposition to the serial craftwork, are able to have their own "*maisons*", commercial houses that originated the great luxury brands. From the nineteenth century on we have the birth of many luxury brands, among others: Christofle (1830), Jaeger-LeCoultre (1833), Hermès and Tiffany (1837), Fabergé (1842), Cartier (1847), Patek Philippe (1951), Goyard (1853), Louis Vuitton (1854), Burberry (1856), Panerai and Chopard (1860), Lalique (1885), Lanvin (1889), Ritz (1898), etc.

The luxury fashion industry kept growing and in the twentieth century it became a relevant economic sector, especially in France, where (Lipovetsky & Roux, 2003), in 1925, "haute couture" represented 15% of the country's total exports, mainly to other countries of Europe and the United States, and Chanel produced about 28 thousand pieces, employing four thousand people.

The popularization of luxury created a new concept, the semi-luxury, or false luxury (Lipovetsky & Roux, 2003), with the industrialization of craftsmanship, creating standardized, degraded copies to new middle classes that aspired to luxury, with lower prices, more quantity and more accessible. This serial handicraft offered *bric-à-brac* jewelry, curios, statues, rugs, furniture, etc., selling in a new format of luxury temples, the department stores, like the pioneer "Le Bon Marché" (1838), in Paris, and the Liberty store (1875), in London. They introduced low prices, fixed prices, return guarantee, free access, wide line of products, and advertising. A false democratization that made luxury much more popular, although distorting the original concept.

The two World Wars had a significant impact on society and luxury. The threat of dictatorships, the suffering of the wars, the increasing role of women in the workforce, and the valorization of democracy, equality, and the individual led to a rejection of the most visible signs of status and power and, in the words of Balzac, "*the luxury of simplicity*", the esthetics of discretion, offered democratically with the support of the technological knowledge and industrial capacity obtained with the war effort.

In summary, over this period, it can be observed that mercantilism brought new wealth and status to the bourgeoisie that had its social value recognized, and its access to luxury morally and economically justified. This changed luxury to a more private, personal, subjective experience, where esthetic and erudite pleasure and taste became relevant, catering to the higher needs of the human being, and that was positive for society, as long as there are no excesses. Luxury is no longer exclusive to those with power in church and state but is also associated to personal success through work and skills. The view that luxury is bad for society is gradually dismissed.

Creative artists that can offer personalized luxury solutions gain status and economic power in this new market, originating the *maisons* and the luxury brands.

The dissemination of the concept of the individual increase demand for the democratization of luxury and industrialization answers with a *"false luxury"*, industrialized craftsmanship offered in the new temples of luxury consumption, the department stores.

Three new dimensions can be identified from the characteristics of this era: complexity of acquisition (as personal taste, education, preferences, etc., also influenced the perception of luxury), aesthetic content (great pleasure derived from the beauty of luxury goods) and lifestyle (how luxury was integrated in the way one lived and consumed).

1.2.4 The Era of Individualism

The concept of the individual and his rights (Berry, 1994; Castilho, 2006; Lipovetsky & Roux, 2003) evolved over the last eras and in the after-war period, society reached a new stage where the process of deinstitutionalization of the church and the state led to deep changes in the concepts of family, religion, sexuality, fashion, politics, etc. Without the guiding principles of the old authorities, people began to think about how to find happiness and solve social problems by themselves. A quest for social justice, reduction of poverty and unemployment, and the reduction of state intervention and taxes, resulted in more social conscience, coupled with an individualist drive that borders narcissism, where the influence of even the closer equals is not relevant, free from any conventions (Fig. 1.2).

This constitutes what Lipovetsky calls the era of Hypermodernity, where we have an exacerbation (and not a contestation) of the values created in modernity, elevated in an exponential form. A liberal society, characterized by movement, fluidity, and flexibility, by the culture of the excess, the intense and the urgent, the demand for undefined progress without defined destiny, a demand for the right to instant happiness, prestige, beauty, and luxury, to take pleasure in being different, original, privileged, ready to lead his life according to his own interests, enjoy experiences, and the most intimate emotions. Luxury (Truong et al., 2009) is not just to express social class, but becomes a way to strengthen self-image, admire oneself, see oneself as unique, and self-reward this singleness.

This leads to a wide diversification of life models, with different references. Luxury becomes diversified and directed to the masses, a mass phenomenon and a democratic right. Individualism values products that help one to detach from the crowds, hedonism increases demand for products that offer immediate pleasure, and narcissism looks for products that improve physical appearance, eternal youth,

1.2 A Brief History of Luxury

Fig. 1.2 The legend of Narcissus, that fell in love with his own reflection (*Source* https://pt.wikipedia.org/wiki/Caravaggio#/media/Ficheiro:Narcissus-Caravaggio_(1594-96)_edited.jpg)

and health. Now the worst thing that could happen to someone is to become old and ugly. The concept of luxury is now defined subjectively by each consumer.

This new mindset is answered by the new luxury (Danziger, 2005, 2007; Silverstein & Fiske, 2003; Silverstein et al., 2008; Truong et al., 2009), a much different kind of luxury, when compared to the old luxury of the previous eras. The products in demand in the new luxury are the esthetic surgery clinics, the spas, the health clinics, sports and leisure activities that reinforce the cult of the perfect body, and retirement homes where old people can remain (or, at least, feel) young. Experiences become more important than goods, luxury has to offer pleasure, voluptuousness, and a feast of senses and emotions. It doesn't have to be expensive or exclusive, but it could be small rewards for oneself, a self-caress, a small mindless madness. One can use an experience to play an aspirational role, a ludic game, or to pretend to be rich for a few moments. This led to a relevant growth in the hospitality industry, with the travel industry (Kotler et al., 2017) becoming the world's largest industry. Before COVID-19, international travel has receipts of over $1.33 trillion and over 1.25 billion travelers, and experts believe that in a short time this market will resume these numbers. Gastronomic experiences, personalized travel packages, spiritual retreats, all can be new destinations. The pleasure of consumption is also a luxury, and the department stores are joined by the luxury shopping centers and the outlets as new temples of luxury.

The recent preoccupation with sustainability in luxury (Cherapanukorn & Focken, 2014; Joy et al., 2012; Kapferer & Michaut, 2015; Kapferer & Michaut-Denizeau, 2017; Winston, 2016) led to a greater conscience on the origins and suppliers of the raw materials, sources and conditions of labor, and possible environmental impacts.

For luxury companies, this new market presents a new scale of numbers of customers and income. Luxury companies used to be small familiar businesses working in market niches with resources to conquer bigger markets, and a new business model had to be created. Business entrepreneurs initiated a process of fusions and acquisitions of individual brands that resulted in three global conglomerates (LVMH, Richmond, and Kering) that own more than 200 of the most prestigious brands. As there were not enough managers trained in luxury in the market, they brought experienced executives from the retail sector and trained them in details of this new consumer. An investment portfolio approach was adopted, with managers responsible for short- and long-term profitability, growth financed through public offer of company shares in the stock exchange, brand extensions were directed to these new subjective desires of consumers, oriented by marketing research. The main stylist has freedom of creation but has to achieve financial goals, product lines have smaller life cycles, are launched to a global network of stores, and supported by strong mediatic campaigns. Most expensive products are not usually profitable but provide prestige to new luxury products, like perfumes, cosmetics, and apparel accessories. Product lines are wider to cover a fragmented market with many segments. A new concern is the combat of counterfeits.

In summary, the increasing conscience of individual rights and the after-war democratization processes in many countries led to a new demand for luxury goods, denominated *"the new luxury"*, based on the concepts of democratization, experiences, individuality, lifestyle, brand purpose, and social responsibility. The managerial strategic answer of the sector was to develop great conglomerates of global companies offering a wide array of more affordable products and services to a much wider public with an ever-increasing profit over the last three decades.

In a nutshell, luxury today is a complex market with an offer that draws on the characteristics of these four eras to combine the promise of magic, power, success, and individual expression.

The main new dimension of luxury that this last era contributed was narcissism, resulting from the increasing individualism and will to express one's personality.

1.3 The Concept of Luxury

The concept of luxury is wide, subjective, and complex, because of its rich story of evolution over several millennia. From the literature it can be identified four eras of the luxury history—magic, power, success, and individualism—that represent the four eras of development. Over these eras, one can identify nine dimensions that compose the construct of luxury.

1.3 The Concept of Luxury

Luxury began as a relationship of spiritual and material exchanges of nomad communities with their deities, offering in the name of the collective what they had most precious. Even today, luxury products are believed to be selected from the best and have magic powers to bring the best things. The brand experience should be performed in a magic luxury panorama. Its sale should be conducted in a special location, the luxury temple, purchased in a ritual that restores these powers, conducted by the salesman as a representative of the magical creator of the brand, protected by a special packaging, and consumed in a specific ritual. The first three dimensions resulting from this era are rarity, craftsmanship, and symbolic content.

As societies become sedentary, they increase their production and become rich, powerful, and populous, being able to trade and conquer other lands and wealth. Power creates social hierarchy and status symbols. The most powerful are identified with the gods and assume some of their rights and obligations, and luxury becomes the symbol of power and a way to bring well-being to the public through the patronage of public buildings, arts, culture, and leisure. Prejudice against luxury and sumptuary laws are created as ways to keep luxury under restricted control and practiced mostly publicly. This era contributed with two new dimensions of luxury: status and high perceived value.

The ascension of the mercantilist bourgeoisie through banking and trading brings a new protagonist to the consumption of luxury. Initially to emulate the power symbols of the state and the church, they also want to express their personal success. This transformed luxury into a more private, personal, and subjective experience, where esthetic and erudite pleasure and taste are also relevant. The moral justification that luxury satisfies the higher needs of the human being and contributes to the economic and social well-being of society, as long as there are no excesses, reduces the prejudice. Three new dimensions can be identified from the characteristics of this era: complexity of acquisition, aesthetic content, and lifestyle.

As the concept of individual and his rights consolidate, individualism, in parallel to narcissism and hedonism, results in a new concept of luxury, the new luxury, connected to the new values of luxury, associated to the concepts of democratization, experiences, individuality, lifestyle, brand purpose, and social responsibility. The luxury industry adapts to this new world by creating through mergers and acquisitions of great conglomerates of global companies, bringing concepts from retail and finance, and offering a wide array of more affordable products and services to a much wider public, supported by strong distribution and promotion, with an ever-increasing profit. The main new dimension of luxury that this last era contributed was narcissism.

Over time, it is observed how luxury evolved by the influence of the evolution of societies, incorporating nine dimensions: rarity, craftsmanship and symbolic content, status and high perceived value, complexity of acquisition, aesthetic content and lifestyle, and narcissism.

Today's concept of luxury is a complex blend of these nine dimensions of luxury, in different degrees for different fragmented segments of the luxury market.

Each segment aspires to a different composition of these dimensions in their luxury goods and services, which means that marketing managers in the market have to know deeply how their segments behave in order to develop the most fitting offer for each of these segments. This has allowed the big luxury conglomerates to have a brand portfolio with dozens of brands, each one positioned to a different public, or persona, without cannibalization.

1.4 Evolution of Consumption of Luxury

Luxury is a social construct and the way it is perceived depends on the penetration of consumption in the environment of this consumers. A recent study by IPSOS (Crampton, 2021) in different Asian markets identified five stages in the process of spreading the access to consumption of luxury, characterized by the degree of access different social levels have access to this market. These five stages are:

Subjugation—countries characterized by authoritarian rule, wide poverty, and deprivation, where only a small political elite has access to luxury, up to the highest levels of consumption. The rest of the population has little or no concept of luxury and no expectation of ever accessing even the most entry-level, accessible products.

Start of money—In countries that are presenting economic growth, the masses can buy white luxury goods and the social elite starts buying higher luxury goods, still very oriented to brand popularity.

Show off—countries where the masses start acquiring products of luxury as symbols of wealth and display their economic status.

Fit in—countries where luxury has been accepted on a large scale and the consumption is fueled by the need to conform.

Way of life—those countries where consumers are locked into luxury habits and buyers are confident and discerning.

Some of the countries studied had parts of their population in different social levels that were in different stages of this evolution.

1.5 Summary

> The concept of luxury evolved over four eras (of Magic, Power, Success, and Individualism), the Four Waves of Luxury, that contributed with nine attributes to the concept of luxury: Rarity, Artisanal, Symbolic Content, High Price and Value, Status, Complexity of Acquisition, Aesthetic Content, Lifestyle, and Hedonism.
>
> Luxury developed into a complex concept over millennia and any study or strategy should consider this broad view and not just partial views that equate luxury to superfluous, wasteful, or sinful. It has important

economic and social contribution to the society, but the network of associated concepts it developed over time has to be respected, in order to satisfy consumers' desire for luxury.

Today's market is fragmented into several segments that value in different ways these four constructs, which led to luxury companies to develop strategies of offering for different segments, different compositions of the nine attributes in their luxury products and services.

Recently COVID-19 had a strong impact on the market, but the real chances are still difficult to spot. A first analysis suggests that there will mostly be impacts related to a more intensive use of the digital, on consumer behavior in relation to the fear of the virus, and on business processes to deal with this new situation.

Bibliography

Baker, E. (Ed.). (1952). *The politics of Aristotle* (p. 28). Clarendon Press.
Balzac, H. (1836). Le Lys dans la Vallée.
Belk, R. W., Wallendorf, M., & Sherry, J. F., Jr. (1989). The sacred and the profane in consumer behavior: Theodicy on the odyssey. *Journal of Consumer Research, 16*, 1–38.
Berry, C. J. (1994). *The idea of luxury: A conceptual and historical investigation*. Cambridge University Press.
Blaug, M. (1997). *Economic theory in retrospect*. Cambridge University Press.
Brisbin, I. L., & Risch, T. S. (1997). Primitive dogs, their ecology and behavior: Unique opportunities to study the early development of the human-canine bond. *Journal of the American Veterinary Medical Association, 210*(8), 1122–1126.
Brun, A., & Castelli, C. (2013). The nature of luxury: A consumer perspective. *International Journal of Retail and Distribution Management, 41*, 823–847.
Burke, P. (1992). *The fabrication of Louis XIV*. Yale University Press.
Castarède, J. (2006). Apresentação Seminários sobre o Luxo ESPM, São Paulo, 21/03/2006.
Castarède, J. (2008). Luxe et civilisations, Éd Eyrolles.
Castarède, J. (2014). Le Luxe. Que sais-je? PUF, 8 ed.
Castilho, K. (2006). A produção do luxo na mídia. In K. Castilho & N. Villaça (orgs.), *O Novo Luxo*. Editora Anhembi Morumbi
Chailan, C. (2014). Marketing exclusivity through the arts. Actes du congrès de l'Association Française du Marketing
Chan, W. W. Y., Chester, K. M. T., Chu, A. W. C., & Zhang, Z. (2014). Behavioral determinants that drive luxury goods consumption: A study within the tourist context. *Research Journal of Textile and Apparel, 18*(2), 84–95.
Cherapanukorn, V., & Focken, K. (2014). Corporate social responsibility (CSR) and sustainability in Asian luxury hotels: Policies, practices and standards. *Asian Social Science, 10*(8), 198.
Chind, K., & Sahachaisaeree, N. (2012). Purchasers' perception on packaging formal design: A comparative case study on luxury goods merchandizing. *Procedia—Social and Behavioral Sciences, 42*, 436–442.
Christodoulides, G., Michaelidou, N., & Li, C. (2009). Measuring perceived brand luxury: An evaluation of the BLI scale. *Journal of Brand Management, 16*, 395.
Crampton, T. (2021). *Evolution of Asia's Luxury Obsession*. https://www.thomascrampton.com/china/luxury-asia-ipsos/. Accessed 31 Mar 2021.

Cristini, H., Kauppinen-Räisänen, H., Barthod-Prothade, M., & Woodside, A. (2016). Toward a general theory of luxury: Advancing from workbench definitions and theoretical transformations. *Journal of Business Research, 70*, 101–107.
Csaba, F. F. (2008). *Redefining luxury: A review essay* (Working paper). Copenhagen Business School.
D'Arpizio, C. (2013). Bain & Co. Luxury goods worldwide market study.
D'Arpizio, C. (2014). Bain & Co. Luxury goods worldwide market study.
D'Arpizio, C. (2015). Bain & Co. Luxury goods worldwide market study.
D'Arpizio, C. (2016). Bain & Co. Luxury goods worldwide market study.
D'Arpizio, C. (2017). Bain & Co. Luxury goods worldwide market study.
D'Arpizio, C. (2018). Bain & Co. Luxury goods worldwide market study.
D'Arpizio, C. (2019). Bain & Co. Luxury goods worldwide market study.
D'Arpizio, C. (2020). Bain & Co. Luxury goods worldwide market study.
Danziger, P. G. (2005). *Let them eat cake: Marketing luxury to the masses—As well as the classes*. Dearborn.
Danziger, P. G. (2007, May). New luxury. Global Cosmetic Industry; 175, 5.
De Barnier, V., Falcy, S., & Valette-Florence, P. (2012). Do consumers perceive three levels of luxury? A comparison of accessible, intermediate and inaccessible luxury brands. *Journal of Brand Management, 19*(7), 623–636.
Dion, D., & Arnould, E. (2011). Retail luxury strategy: Assembling charisma through art and magic. *Journal of Retailing, 87*(4), 502–520.
Dubois, B., & Duquesne, P. (1993). The market for luxury goods: Income versus culture. *European Journal of Marketing, 27*(1), 35–44.
Dubois, B., & Laurent, G. (1994). Attitudes towards the concept of luxury: An exploratory analysis. *AP—Asia Pacific Advances in Consumer Research, 1*, 273–278
Dubois, B., & Laurent, G. (1995). Luxury possessions and practices: An empirical scale. *European Advances in Consumer Research, 2*, 69–77.
Freeman, M. (2011). *Human rights: An interdisciplinary approach* (2nd ed.). Wiley.
Freudenberger, H. (1963). Fashion, sumptuary laws, and business. *Business History Review, 37*, 37–48.
Grilec, A., Vukusic, D., & Dujic, D. (2020). Communication strategies of luxury brands during COVID-19 crisis. In *Economic and Social Development: Book of Proceedings* (pp. 281–290).
Han, Y. J., Nunes, J. C., & Drèze, X. (2010). Signaling status with luxury goods: The role of brand prominence. *Journal of Marketing, 74*(4), 15–30.
Haney, L. H. (1949). *History of economic thought* (4th ed.). Macmillan Co.
Heine, K. (2012). The concept of luxury brands. *Luxury Brand Management, 1*(2), 193–208.
Hemzo, M. A., & Hemzo, L. F. (2018). A general theory of luxury: How magic, power, success and the individualism shaped today's luxury. In *SEMEAD—Seminários em Administração* (Vol. 21). EAD/FEA/USP.
Jelinek, J. S. (2018). Art as strategic branding tool for luxury fashion brands. *Journal of Product & Brand Management, 27*(3), 294–307.
Joy, A., Sherry, J. F., Jr., Venkatesh, A., Wang, J., & Chan, R. (2012). Fast fashion, sustainability, and the ethical appeal of luxury brands. *Fashion Theory, 16*(3), 273–295.
Kapferer, B. (1998). *The feast of the sorcerer: Practices of consciousness and power*. University of Chicago Press.
Kapferer, J. N. (1998). Why are we seduced by luxury brands? *Journal of Brand Management, 6*(1), 44–49.
Kapferer, J. N., & Bastien, V. (2009). *The luxury strategy: Breaking the rules of marketing to build luxury brands*. Kogan Page.
Kapferer, J. N., & Michaut, A. (2015). Luxury and sustainability: A common future? The match depends on how consumers define luxury. *Luxury Research Journal, 1*(1), 3–17.
Kapferer, J. N., & Michaut-Denizeau, A. (2017). Is luxury compatible with sustainability? Luxury consumers' viewpoint. In J. N. Kapferer, J. Kernstock, T. O. Brexendorf, & S. M. Powell (Eds.), *Advances in luxury brand management* (pp. 123–156). Palgrave Macmillan.

Bibliography

Kapferer, J. N. (2012a). Abundant rarity: The key to luxury growth. *Business Horizons, 55,* 453–462.

Kapferer, J. N. (2012b). *The new strategic brand management: Advanced Insights & Strategic Thinking* (5th ed.). Kogan Page.

Kotler, P., Bowen, J. T., Makens, J. C., & Baloglu, S. (2017). *Marketing for hospitality and tourism.* Prentice Hall.

Lahtinen, S. (2014). *Meanings for luxury fashion brands among young women in Finland and China* [Master's Thesis, University of Tampere].

Lipovetsky, G., & Roux, E. (2003). *Le luxe éternel.* Gallimard.

Lovelock, C., Wirtz, J., & Hemzo, M. A. (2012). Marketing de Serviços. 7ª ed. Pearson.

Luther, M. (1958). Concerning the ministry (1523). In C. Bergendoff (Ed. and Trans.), *Luther's works* (40:18 ff.). Fortress Press.

Mauss, M., & Hubert, H. (1899). Essai sur la nature et la fonction du sacrifice. Année sociologique, n. 2.

McIntyre, M. P. (2011, June 15–17). The gendered bottle: Meaning-making in luxury packaging. In *Current issues in European cultural studies* (pp. 343–353). Linköping University Electronic Press.

Moore, C., Doherty, A. M., & Doyle, S. (2010). Flagship stores as a market entry method: Perspectives from luxury fashion retailing. *European Journal of Marketing, 44*(1/2), 139–161.

Ormaechea, S. L., & Sanchez, J. S. (2013). Los atributos definitorios de uma marca de lujo para los consumidores. *Intangible Capital, 9*(3), 903–930.

Plass, E. M. (1944). What Luther Says, 3 vols. CPH, 1959, 88, no. 269; M. Reu, Luther and the Scriptures (p. 23). Wartburg Press.

Plato. (1937). The Republic. In B. Jowett (Trans.), *The works of Plato* (p. 64). Tudor Publishing Co.

Puaschunder, J. M. (2020, September 27). *Value at COVID-19: Digitalized healthcare, luxury consumption and global education.* Luxury Consumption and Global Education.

Rozwadowski, A. (2008). Centering historical-archaeological discourse: The prehistory of central Asian/south Siberian shamanism (pp. 105–117). Left Coast Press, Inc.

Sarwari, D., Huq, S., & Minar, T. A. (2020). COVID-19: The way luxury hotels deal with the pandemic. Available at SSRN 3690758.

Shelach, G. (2000). The earliest Neolithic cultures of Northeast China: Recent discoveries and new perspectives on the beginning of agriculture. *Journal of World Prehistory, 14*(4), 363–413.

Silva, C. L., Cerchiaro, I. B., & Mascetti, I. (2004). Consumo como Espiritualidade e Consumo do Luxo: O que o consumidor tem a dizer. XXIX ENANPAD – Encontro da Associação Nacional de Pós-Graduação e Pesquisa em Administração. São Paulo, set.

Silverstein, M. J., & Fiske, N. (2003). Luxury for the masses. *Harvard Business Review, 81*(4), 48–57.

Silverstein, M. J., Fiske, N., & Butman, J. (2008). *Trading up: Why consumers want new luxury goods—And how companies create them.* Penguin.

Steiner, R. L. (1976, July). The Prejudice against Marketing. *Journal of Marketing, 40* (3), 2–9

Strehlau, S. (2008). *Marketing do luxo.* Cengage Learning.

Strieder, J. (1931). *Jacob Fugger the rich: Merchant and banker of Augsburg, 1459–1525.* Adelphi Co.

Truong, Y., McColl, R., & Kitchen, P. J. (2009). New luxury brand positioning and the emergence of masstige brands. *Journal of Brand Management, 16*(5), 375–382.

Wilkins, J. (2008). Athenaeus, the navigator. *Journal of Hellenic Studies, 128,* 132–52.

Winston, A. (2016). Luxury brands can no longer ignore sustainability. *Harvard Business Review, 8*(2), 1–3.

Wirtz, J., Hemzo, M. A., Lovelock, C. (2020). *Marketing de serviços: pessoas, tecnologia e estratégia* (8th Edn.). São Paulo.

The Luxury Market

2.1 Introduction

Chapter Objectives
In this chapter, we discuss the evolution of the luxury market, witnessing the resilience it has shown over the last decades, the main players in this market, and the main impacts of the COVID-19 in its performance.

2.2 Pré-COVID-19

2.2.1 Market Numbers

The human being has always differentiated himself (Lipovetsky & Roux, 2003) by his creativity and the ability to dream, design, and produce objects that go beyond the functional needs, but that also appeal to the beautiful and inspirational. For a long time, this artisan worked in small workshops producing a few pieces that were valued for those with distinct tastes, but still occupying a low status position in relation to other workers. But he only became really valued and recognized in the nineteenth century, with a new status that allowed him to be accepted into a higher social class.

As this occupation becomes well remunerated and socially recognized, as those able to create unique pieces, in opposition to the serial craftwork, they started creating to have their own "maisons", commercial houses that originated the great luxury brands. From the nineteenth century on we have the birth of many luxury brands, among others: Christofle (1830), Jaeger-LeCoultre (1833), Hermès and Tiffany (1837), Fabergé (1842), Cartier (1847), Patek Philippe (1951), Goyard

(1853), Louis Vuitton (1854), Burberry (1856), Panerai and Chopard (1860), Lalique (1885), Lanvin (1889), Ritz (1898), etc.

As seen in the previous chapter, in the decade of the 1980s behavioral changes in society created a new potential for luxury, that many traditional family-based luxury companies found hard to attend, incurring cost, revenue, and debt problems, that drove them to the brink of bankruptcy. At the same time, visionary entrepreneurs like Bernard Jean Étienne Arnault, François Pinault, and Johann Peter Rupert realized the great future potential of the market and started acquiring these companies and building the brand conglomerates we have today.

The main reference on luxury market data are the reports developed by the Consulting company Bain & Co., in partnership with Fondazione Altagamma, the Italian association of luxury brands. These reports encompass both luxury goods and experiences, and it comprises nine segments, led by luxury cars, luxury hospitality and personal luxury goods (Apparel, Beauty, Leather goods, Watches, Shoes, Jewelry), which together account for more than 80% of the total market. The other smaller segments are fine wines and spirits, fine food and dining, fine art, design furniture, private jet, private yatches, and cruises.

In Table 2.1 a compilation of data from the BAIN Report Global Luxury editions from 2011 to 2021 and forecasts for 2022 and 2023 is presented. Before 2009, only information on the personal goods segment was available. It is a period of expansion and democratization of the market, with constant growth only affected by special moments over this period, as the September 11 attack, the SARS epidemy and the European cambial crisis. In these moments the growth was reduced, but quite quickly the segment resumed the previous trend. Contrary to popular belief, the luxury market is not immune to crisis, but has shown great resilience to recover quickly.

From 2010 to 2019 the growth has been continuous, with oscillations resulting from global events, but averaging 9% per year, a better performance than the global economy, or the stock exchange, for instance.

It is important to highlight that these reports changed some criteria over the years, as data about private yatches were first included in 2011, fine arts were only presented from 2013 on, and cruises only in the period 2009–2016, what can cause some impact on the temporal analysis.

The general consensus in the industry in 2018 was that this trend would continue for a long period, the global personal luxury goods market was estimated to grow 3–5% per year through 2025.

The event of COVID-19 was a watershed in the market, but the most recent reports are showing a V-shaped recovery, with 2021 returning to 2018 levels, and an estimated growth of 10% over the next years. Its impact is discussed in more detail in topic '1.2.1'.

2.2 Pré-COVID-19

Table 2.1 Worldwide luxury market evolution (in € billion)

Year	Personal goods	Cars	Hospitality	Fine wines and spirits	Fine food and dining	Fine art	Design furniture	Private jets	Private yatches	Cruises	Total	Annual variation (%)	Obs.
1995	70												
1996	76											8.6	
1997	84											10.5	
1998	88											4.8	
1999	98											11.4	
2000	116											18.4	
2001	122											5.2	September 11, terrorist attack to USA
2002	120											−1.6	SARS
2003	128											6.7	$/€ cambial crisis
2004	139											8.6	
2005	147											5.8	
2006	150											2.0	
2007	161											7.3	
2008	159											−1.2	Subprime and financial crisis
2009	147	210	91	35	30		16		8		537		
2010	167	245	93	40	33		17		6		601	11.9	

(continued)

Table 2.1 (continued)

Year	Personal goods	Cars	Hospitality	Fine wines and spirits	Fine food and dining	Fine art	Design furniture	Private jets	Private yatches	Cruises	Total	Annual variation (%)	Obs.
2011	186	280	107	45	35		18	16	7		694	15.5	Japan earthquake
2012	207	299	127	51	38		28	16	7		773	11.4	
2013	212	319	138	55	39	31	28	17	7	1	847	9.6	Socioeconomic turbulence
2014	219	351	150	58	40	34	29	18	7	1	907	7.1	Chinese stock market turmoil
2015	245	405	176	63	45	36	32	19	7	2	1030	13.5	
2016	244	438	183	66	46	39	33	18	7	2	1076	4.5	Terrorist attacks in Europe
2017	254	489	191	70	49	39	35	23		2	1152	7.1	
2018	262	495	190	71	50	41	41	21		2	1173	1.8	
2019	281	550	206	76	53	34	42	24		2	1268	8.1	COVID-19
2020	217	503	85	68	45	23	38	22		1	1002	−21.0	COVID-19
2021	288	551	79	77	49	27	45	22		1	1139	13.6	Back to 2018
2022	330										1253	10.0	Estimated
2023	370										1378	10.0	Estimated

Sources BAIN REPORT Global Luxury 2011–2021

2.2.2 Players

The market is composed of many players, some of them great conglomerates, other minor ones, and independent companies. Some of them are presented. The data are mainly from Wikipedia (https://en.wikipedia.org/) and the companies' sites. The objective is not a comprehensive description of all companies, but a general overview of the main players in the luxury market, remembering that the given numbers are estimates based on different official and unofficial sources.

Conglomerates
A present characteristic of the luxury market is the predominance of great conglomerates.

LVMH Moët Hennessy Louis Vuitton SE (LVMH), a French group founded in 1987 (http://www.lvmh.com/) by Bernard Jean Étienne Arnault is the biggest group. It was initially created by the fusion of Moët et Chandon and Hennessy, and next, the Louis Vuitton company. The main holding company is Christian Dior. Today it has more than 120 thousand employees, with revenue above €42.6 billion, and a portfolio of more than seventy luxury brands, spread across six segments:

Wines and spirits (Ao Yun, Ardbeg, Armand de Brignac, Belvedere, Bodega Numanthia, Cape Mentelle, Chandon, Château Cheval Blanc, Château d'Yquem, Cloudy Bay, Dom Pérignon, Glenmorangie, Hennessy, Krug, Mercier, Moët & Chandon, Newton Vineyard, Ruinart, Terrazas de los Andes, Veuve Clicquot, Volcan de mi tierra, Whistlepig, Woodinville, Wenjun, etc.).

Fashion and leather goods (Berluti, Céline, Charles & Keith, Christian Dior, Deus Ex Machina, Emilio Pucci, Fendi, Fenty, Givenchy, Kenzo, Loewe, Loro Piana, Louis Vuitton, Marc Jacobs, Moynat, Nicholas Kirkwood, Patou, Rimowa, Stella McCartney, etc.).

Perfumes and cosmetics (Acqua di Parma, Benefit Cosmetics, Fresh, Givenchy Parfums, Guerlain, Kendo, Bite Beauty, Fenty Beauty by Rihanna, Marc Jacobs Beauty, KVD Vegan Beauty, OleHenriksen, Kenzo Parfums, Maison Francis Kurkdjian, Make Up For Ever, Parfums Christian Dior, Perfumes Loewe, etc.).

Watches and jewelry (Bulgari, Chaumet, FRED, Hublot, TAG Heuer, Tiffany & Co., Zenith, etc.).

Selective retailing (DFS, La Grande Epicerie, La Samaritaine, Le Bon Marché, Sephora, Starboard Cruise Services, etc.).

Other activities (Belmond Hotels, Caffè-Pasticceria Cova, Cheval Blanc Hotels, Royal Van Lent Shipyard, Princess Yachts, Les Echos (financial paper), Pinarello (bicycles), etc.).

The second greatest group is the French-based Kering (http://kering.com/). It was originally founded as Pinault S.A. in 1963 by François Pinault, and became the retail conglomerate Pinault-Printemps-Redoute (PPR) in 1994. The group increased their focus on luxury, selling non-related business as Printemps, a retail chain, and changed their name to Kering in 2013.

Today it has more than 80 thousand employees, revenue above €15.9 billion, and a portfolio of more than twenty luxury brands. Gucci, Saint Laurent, and

Bottega Veneta are the main brands and generate 84% of the group's revenue. Gucci alone is responsible for more than 50% of the total revenue.

The main brands in their portfolio are: Alexander McQueen, Altuzarra, Balenciaga, Bottega Veneta, Boucheron, Brioni, Christopher Kane, Cobra, Dodo, Electric (surfware), Girard-Perregaux, Gucci, JeanRichard, McQ, Pomellato, Qeelin, Sergio Rossi, Sowind Haute Horlogerie, Tomas Maier, Ulysse Nardin, Volcom (surfware), Yves Saint Laurent, etc.

The third greatest group is Richemont (http://richemont.com/), the Swiss-based company, founded in 1988 by South African Johann Rupert.

Today it has more than 35 thousand employees, with a revenue above €14.2 billion, and a portfolio of more than twenty luxury brands.

It is divided into three operating divisions:

Jewellery Maisons (Cartier, Van Cleef & Arpels, Buccellati, Giampiero Bodino, etc.).

Specialist Watchmakers (A. Lange & Söhne, Baume & Mercier, IWC Schaffhausen, Jaeger-LeCoultre, Officine Panerai, Piaget, Roger Dubuis, Vacheron Constantin, and the joint venture with the Ralph Lauren Watch & Jewelry Co.).

Other Businesses (Azzedine Alaïa, Chloé, Dunhill, Lancel, Montblanc, Peter Millar, Purdey, YOOX NET-A-PORTER, etc.).

Luxury cars also have automotive conglomerates. The main ones are:

Daimler AG, previously named Daimler-Benz and DaimlerChrysler, commonly known and referred to as Mercedes-Benz, is a German-based corporation headquartered in Stuttgart. It is one of the world's leading car and truck manufacturers.

Today they have almost 300 thousand employees, with a revenue above €172.7 billion, and a portfolio of many luxury brands, among them Mercedes-Benz, AMG, Maybach, Smart, etc.

The group's subsidiary Mercedes-Benz AG sells around 2 million cars with the Mercedes-Bens brand a year, has 150 thousand employees, and revenue of around €100 billion.

Bayerische Motoren Werke AG, or simply BMW, is a German car and motorcycle manufacturer based in Munich. They follow a pure premium brand strategy, developing, manufacturing, and marketing their products under the brands BMW, MINI, and Rolls-Royce.

The BMW brand sells around 2 million cars yearly, has around 133 thousand employees, and revenue of around €80 billion.

The MINI car is a British brand, manufactured in the Netherlands. They sell around 350 thousand cars yearly, have around 2.0 thousand employees, and revenue of around €6 billion.

Rolls-Royce Motor Cars Limited is a British luxury automobile maker subsidiary based in Goodwood. They sell around 4 thousand cars yearly, have around 1.3 thousand employees, and revenue of around €0.95 billion.

Volkswagen AG, is a German motor vehicle manufacturer headquartered in Wolfsburg, that operates both in the mass and the luxury car markets and owned partially by the Porsche and Piëch family. They sell luxury passenger cars under the Audi, Bentley, Bugatti, Lamborghini, and Porsche brands, and popular passenger cars under the SEAT, Škoda, and Volkswagen brands.

The Audi AG subsidiary originated from Auto Union, a fusion of Horch, Audiwerke, DKW, and Wanderer, and is a German car manufacturer based in Ingolstadt. They sell around 1.8 million cars yearly, have around 97 thousand employees, and revenue of around €55 billion.

Dr.-Ing. h.c. F. Porsche AG, or Porsche AG, is a German high-performance car manufacturer subsidiary based in Stuttgart. They sell around 240 thousand cars yearly, have around 24.4 thousand employees, and revenue of around €21.5 billion.

Bentley Motors Limited is a subsidiary of English origin, situated in Crewe. They sell around 9 thousand cars yearly, have around 3.6 thousand employees, and revenue of around €1.4 billion.

Automobili Lamborghini S.p.A. is an Italian subsidiary based in Sant'Agata Bolognese. They sell around 5 thousand cars yearly, have around 1.5 thousand employees, and revenue of around €0.58 billion.

Bugatti Automobiles S.A.S. is a subsidiary of French origin, head office in Molsheim, specialized in high-performance luxury cars. They sell around 80 cars yearly, have around 300 employees, and revenue of around €70 million.

On aggregate, the five VW luxury brands sell around 2,054,080 cars yearly, employ around 126,800 skilled people, and generate revenue of around €78.5 billion.

Stellantis N.V. is an automotive manufacturer headquartered in Amsterdam, formed by the 2021 merger of Italian-American company Fiat Chrysler Automobiles and French company Groupe PSA. The portfolio of automotive brands of the group is composed by the luxury brands: Abarth, Alfa Romeo, and Maserati. Other brands of the group are Chrysler, Citroën, Dodge, DS Automobiles, Fiat, Fiat Professional, Jeep, Lancia, Mopar, Opel, Peugeot, Ram Trucks, and Vauxhall Motors.

Abarth & C. S.p.A. is an Italian racing and road car maker subsidiary headquartered in Turin. The estimated number of units sold yearly is somewhat above 35 thousand cars, they have around 35 employees and revenue estimated to be around €22 million.

Alfa Romeo Automobiles S.p.A. is an Italian premium car manufacturer subsidiary located in Turin. They sell around 150 thousand cars yearly, have around 900 employees, and revenue of around €100 million.

Maserati S.p.A. is an Italian luxury vehicle manufacturer subsidiary established in Modena. They sell around 30 thousand cars yearly, have around 1.1 thousand employees, and revenue of around €1.6 billion.

Minor Players

Another luxury conglomerate is the relatively smaller Prada S.p.A (http://www.prada.com/), an Italy-based company founded in 1913 as Fratelli Prada by Mario Prada. The company had their peak in the 1990s, but due to debts had to sell some of their brands, such as Fendi, Gucci, Helmut Lang, Amy Fairclough, Ghee, and Jil Sander.

Today Prada has more than 12 thousand employees, revenue above €3.9 billion, and a portfolio of five luxury brands: Church'sCar Shoe, Luna Rossa, Miu Miu, Pasticceria Marchesi, and Prada.

Coach IP Holdings LLC, Coach New York or simply Coach is an American luxury design house specialized in handbags, luggage, accessories, and ready-to-wear, headquartered in New York City. Founded in 1941 by the Cahn family, Lillian Cahn, and Miles Cahn, today is a subsidiary of Tapestry, Inc., that also owns Kate Spade New York.

They have an estimated revenue of around €5 billion and about 1 thousand stores worldwide.

Tata Motors Limited is an Indian automotive manufacturing company headquartered in Mumbai, and is part of Tata Group, an Indian conglomerate also headquartered in Mumbai. They produce passenger cars, trucks, vans, coaches, buses, sports cars, construction equipment, and military vehicles. They are the owners of the English Jaguar and Land Rover luxury brands, the Korean Daewoo, and the Indian Tato popular brands.

Jaguar Land Rover Automotive PLC is the holding company of Jaguar Land Rover Limited, a British automotive company subsidiary based in Whitley, where the two brands are produced in a unified operation unit. They sell around 450 thousand Land Rovers and 174 thousand Jaguars yearly, have around 40 thousand employees, and a combined revenue of around €27 billion.

Independents

Although mergers and acquisitions are increasingly common in this market, there are still many independent luxury companies, with more modest revenues. Some of them are as follows:

Burberry (http://www.burberry.com/) is an England-based company, founded in 1856 by Thomas Burberry, the inventor of gabardine. They are active in the markets of ready-to-wear items including trench coats, leather goods, footwear, fashion accessories, eyewear, fragrances, sunglasses, and cosmetics, all under the brand Burberry.

Burberry was an independent family-controlled company until 1955, when the majority control was bought by Great Universal Stores (GUS). In 2001 they entered the stock market with a successful IPO and in 2005 GPO divested his investments.

Today they have more than 9.9 thousand employees and revenue above €2.6 billion.

Chanel (http://chanel.com/) is a French-based company created in 1909 as a millinery shop and in 1910 as a fashion house, by Coco Chanel. She had strong sense of style and innovation and became popular by introducing simpler designs that those currently in fashion, still influenced by trends from the previous century.

After her death in 1971, Jacques Wertheimer, a previous partner that assumed the control of the company after her exile after the World War II, bought the controlling interest of the House of Chanel. In 1974, Alain Wertheimer, son of Jacques Wertheimer, assumed control of Chanel S.A.

The company is still controlled by the family Wertheimer. The company is currently directed by owners Alain Wertheimer and Gérard Wertheimer, grandsons of Pierre Wertheimer. Jacques Wertheimer and Pierre Wertheimer are also owners.

They operate in the markets of women's high fashion and ready-to-wear clothes, luxury goods, accessories, perfume, cologne, makeup, skincare, fine Jewelry, watches, wine, and stores.

Today they have more than 20 thousand employees and revenue above €10.9 billion.

Aston Martin Lagonda Global Holdings PLC (https://www.astonmartin.com) is a British independent manufacturer of luxury sports cars and grand tourers, based in Gaydon. In 2013, Aston Martin agreed to a technical partnership with Daimler AG to supply Mercedes-AMG engines and electrical systems. In 2018 they had their IPO. In 2020 Canadian investor Lawrence Stroll, leading a consortium that paid £182 million for a 25% stake in the company, became the major stock holder. The company invested in brand extension, in real estate building, with a 66-storey luxury condominium tower called Aston Martin Residences in Miami, Florida, with global property developer G&G Business Developments in 2016, and in a design and brand studio in Shanghai in 2018.

They sell around 5 thousand cars a year, have around 3 thousand employees, and revenue of around €0.61 billion.

Cantieri Azimut (https://it.azimutyachts.com/) is an Italian yacht-manufacturing company based in Viareggio, owned by the Italian investor Paolo Vitelli, that produces boats from 10 to 37 meters. They also own Benetti, another luxury ship building company, that produces boats from 37 to 70 meters.

They sell around 3 hundred boats a year, have around 2.5 thousand employees, and revenue of around €0.6 billion.

Breitling SA (https://www.breitling.com) is a Swiss luxury watchmaker based in Grenchen, founded in 1884 by Léon Breitling in Saint-Imier and currently privately owned by CVC Capital Partners. They have the product lines Navitimer, Chronomat, Emergency, Emergency II, and Breitling for Bentley.

They sell around 150 thousand watches a year, have around 4.5 hundred employees, and revenue of around €0.36 billion.

Calvin Klein Inc. (https://www.calvinklein.com/) is an American fashion house founded in 1968 by designer Calvin Klein and his childhood friend, Barry K. Schwartz, headquartered in Midtown Manhattan, New York City. Today they are owned by the American clothing company PVH Corp., formerly known as the Phillips-Van Heusen Corporation, who also own the brands Van Heusen, Tommy Hilfiger, IZOD, Arrow, Warner's, Olga, True & Co., and Geoffrey Beene.

They have around 11.5 thousand employees and revenue of around €3.6 billion.

Dolce & Gabbana (https://www.dolcegabbana.com/en/) is an Italian luxury fashion house founded in 1985 by Italian designers Domenico Dolce and Stefano Gabbana and based in Milan, and are also the owners of the brand Dolce&Gabbana (spelled without spaces, unlike the name of the company).

They have around 3.1 thousand employees and revenue of about €1.29 billion.

Giorgio Armani S.p.A. (https://www.armani.com/countries/index) is an Italian luxury fashion house founded in 1975 by Italian designer Giorgio Armani, based in Milan. They operate in a wide range of the luxury market, in haute couture, ready-to-wear, leather goods, shoes, watches, jewelry, accessories, eyewear, cosmetics, hotels, and home interiors.

They have about 4.3 thousand employees and revenue of around €5.90 billion.

The House of Fabergé (https://www.faberge.com) was a Russian jewelry firm founded in 1842 Gustav Fabergé, but was nationalized by the Bolsheviks in 1918. In 1924 his grandsons Alexander and Eugène Fabergé opened Fabergé & Cie in Paris, with the brand FABERGÉ, PARIS and they closed down in 2001.

The reunification of the Fabergé brand was announced in 2007 and the Fabergé family, with Tatiana Fabergé and Sarah Fabergé, both great-granddaughters of Peter Carl Fabergé, as founding members of the Fabergé Heritage Council, a division of Fabergé Limited.

In 2013, Fabergé Limited was sold to the gem mining company Gemfields for 142 million new shares in Gemfields plc, worth $90 million.

Salvatore Ferragamo S.p.A. (https://www.ferragamo.com) is an Italian luxury goods company, mainly shoes, founded in 1927, with headquarters in Florence. Currently the majority owners are still the Ferragamo family: Salvatore's five children, 23 grandchildren, and other relatives.

They employ about 4 thousand people, have over 654 mono-brand stores, and revenue of around €0.96 billion.

Ferrari S.p.A. (https://www.ferrari.com) is an Italian luxury sports car manufacturer, founded by Enzo Ferrari in 1939, currently based in Maranello, Italy.

After an IPO in 2015, the ownership today is split between Exor N.V. (22.91%), Piero Ferrari (10.00%), and the public (67.09%).

They have about thirty Ferrari boutiques worldwide, employ about 4.2 thousand people, produces about 10.1 thousand cars yearly, and revenue of around €3.77 billion.

Goyard (https://goyard.com) is a French trunk and leather goods maker, established in 1853 by François Goyard and headquartered in Paris.

In 1998, Jean-Michel Signoles bought Goyard and turned the privately owned company into an internationally renowned brand.

They own about 10 boutiques worldwide, and are present in about other 10 retails spaces around the world, employ about 2.3 hundred people, and have revenue of around €38 million.

Hackett Limited (https://www.hackett.com) is a British multichannel luxury retailer of clothing for men and boys, with a broad range of apparel and accessories. It was founded in 1983 in London, by Jeremy Hackett and Ashley Lloyd-Jennings, from a stall on London's Portobello Road, selling high-quality used clothes.

In 2015, Hackett (as part of the Pepe Jeans Group) was bought by Lebanese firm M1 Group and by LVMH subsidiary L Capital Asia. Today they have 1.6

hundred stores globally, employ about 2.8 hundred people, and have revenue of around €1.65 hundred million.

Hermès International S.A. (https://www.hermes.com) is a French luxury goods manufacturer founded in 1837 by Thierry Hermès, specialized in leather goods, lifestyle accessories, home furnishings, perfumery, jewelry, watches, and ready-to-wear items. His son Charles-Émile moved the original shop to today's address. His grandchildren Adolphe and Émile-Maurice introduced the zipper with exclusive rights in France and brought his three sons-in-law (Robert Dumas, Jean-René Guerrand, and Francis Puech) as business partners. Robert Dumas-Hermès (he incorporated the family name) assumed in 1951, and his son Jean-Louis Dumas became Chairman in 1978, and the company went public in the French stock exchange in 1993. He resigned in 2005, and today a sixth-generation member of the Hermès-Dumas family, Axel Dumas, son of Olivier Dumas, Jean-Louis's brother, is the Executive Chairman. The Hermès family, as partners of Émile Hermès SARL, collectively own 65.1% of the capital.

Today they have around 3 hundred stores globally, about 14.3 thousand employees, and revenue of around €6.88 billion.

Hugo Boss AG (https://www.hugoboss.com) is a German luxury fashion house, founded in 1924 by Hugo Boss, and headquartered in Metzingen. Initially supplying the Nazi government with uniforms, after his death, in 1948, they focused on men's suits, went public in 1988, and added perfumes and women's and children's clothes collections.

Today they have around 1.1 thousand stores globally, about 14.7 thousand employees, and revenue of around €2.73 billion.

Lalique (https://www.lalique.com) is a French glassmaker, founded in 1888 by glassmaker and jeweler René Lalique, that produces glass art, decorative art, and luxury goods. He was succeeded by his son Marc Lalique. After his death in 1977 Marie-Claude Lalique took control of the company, sold the company to Pochet in 1994, which sold it in 2008 to a partnership of Art & Fragrance and Financière Saint-Germain and, in 2010, Art & Fragrance, headquartered in Zurich, became full owners.

Today they have around 1.1 thousand stores globally, about 7.2 hundred employees, and revenue of around €132 million.

Lanvin (https://www.lanvin.com) is a French high fashion house, founded by Jeanne Lanvin in 1889. Today it is controlled by the Shanghai-based conglomerate Fosun International.

Today they have about 3.2 hundred employees and revenue of around €62 million.

Lotus Cars Limited (https://www.lotuscars.com) is a British automotive company, founded in 1948 by Colin Chapman, headquartered in Hethel, Norfolk, that manufactures luxury sports cars and racing cars, famous for their performance in Formula One, with 7 Constructors' Championships and 6 Drivers' Championships. The company is currently owned by Chinese multinational Geely (51%)—that also owns Volvo—and Etika Automotive (49%).

They sell about 1.6 thousand cars a year, employ about 1.4 thousand people, and have revenue of around €13.2 million.

Christian Louboutin Ltd. (http://christianlouboutin.com) is a French company, founded in 1991 by the French-Egyptian fashion designer Christian Louboutin, and his partners Henri Seydoux, Bruno Chamberlain, and Faheema Moosa, that produces luxury goods as shoes, purses, wallets, cosmetics, and fragrances, currently located in Paris and still privately owned by them. His trademark is the high-end stiletto footwear with shiny, red-lacquered soles.

Today they produce about 600 thousand pairs of shoes a year, have about 4.2 hundred employees, and revenue of around €250 million.

Luxottica Group S.p.A. (http://www.luxottica.com) is an Italian eyewear conglomerate and the world's largest company in the eyewear industry, supplier for many of the main luxury brands, founded by Leonardo Del Vecchio in 1961, in Agordo north of Belluno, Veneto, which is home to most of the Italian eyewear industry. Today the group is based in Milan. The company entered the stock exchange in 1990, in 2018 they merged with the French Essilor, becoming EssilorLuxottica SA. Today Del Vecchio is still the principal share owner and Executive Chairman of Luxottica. Luxottica has about 80 thousand employees, and revenue of around €9.49 billion, and EssilorLuxottica in total has about 140 thousand employees and revenue of around €14.4 billion.

McLaren Automotive (http://www.mclarenautomotive.com) is a British automotive manufacturer, producer of luxury super cars, founded as McLaren Cars by Bruce McLaren, a Formula One pilot since 1958, in 1965 in Woking. Today it is a subsidiary of the McLaren Group.

They produce about 4.8 thousand cars a year, have about 3.7 thousand employees, and revenue of around €1.75 billion.

Moschino S.p.A. (http://www.moschino.com) is an Italian luxury fashion house, founded in 1983 by Franco Moschino in Milan, producer of leather accessories, shoes, luggage, and fragrances.

The brand has been part of the Aeffe fashion group and SINV Holding S.p.A. since 1999.

They have about 150 boutiques worldwide, employ around 120 people, and have revenue of around €23 million.

Ralph Lauren Corporation (http://ralphlauren.com) is an American fashion company producing products ranging from the mid-range to the luxury segments, founded by Ralph Lauren in 1967, producing, marketing, and distributing products in four categories: apparel, home, accessories, and fragrances. They are presently a publicly traded holding company, headquartered in New York City and Ralph Lauren is the Executive Chairman and CCO.

They have about 500 directly operated stores, employ about 18.2 thousand people, and have revenue of around €6.18 billion.

Tod's S.p.A. (http://www.todsgroup.com), or Tod's Group, is an Italian company producer of luxury shoes and other leather goods, founded in 1920 by Filippo Della Valle. His grandson Diego Della Valle, the elder son of Dorino Della Valle, expanded the original workshop and turned it into a factory and is currently Chairman of the company. The company traded in the stock exchange and the Della Valle Family owns a share of 50.3%.

They have about 220 stores worldwide, employ 3.1 thousand people, and have revenue of €0.99 billion.

Ermenegildo Zegna Group (http://www.zegna.com) is an Italian luxury fashion house, founded in 1910 by Ermenegildo Zegna, with his brothers Edoardo and Mario, in Trivero, Biella Province of the Piedmont region. He concentrated on using high-quality fabrics, first sourcing from all over the world, and then verticalizing the company with own wool mills. In 1942, his sons Aldo and Angelo entered the company, and assumed the company in the mid-1960s, expanded to ready-made suits and later to made-to-measure service. During the 1990s, the third generation of the family entered the business, with Angelo's son, Ermenegildo "Gildo" Zegna, becoming CEO in 1997 and his cousin Paolo, the Chairman, is still active today. Anna Zegna is President of Fondazione Zegna, and Angelo remains in the company as the Honorary Chairman.

Today the Ermenegildo Zegna Group, privately owned by the Zegna Family, is the largest menswear brand in the world by revenue, operating about 480 stores, employs 6.5 thousand people and has revenue of €1.16 billion.

Zimmerli AG (http://www.zimmerli.com) is a Swiss manufacturer of luxurious underwear, renowned for its use of natural fibers and special production techniques, founded in 1871 by Johann Jakob Zimmerli in Aarburg. Its products are worn all over the world by kings, politicians, and celebrities, e.g., Clint Eastwood and Arnold Schwarzenegger.

The company faced financial difficulties on several occasions during its nearly 150-year history. In 1997, Walter Borner, a textile engineer, bought the company and assumed the role of CEO, and managed the turnaround by repositioning the Zimmerli brand, focusing on high quality and emphasizing "Made in Switzerland", and stopping license production for third parties with low rentability, improving the results. In 2007 the company was sold to the German von Nordeck Holding GmbH & Co.

They sell through 15 mono-brand stores and ecommerce, employ 75 people, and have revenue of €22 million.

2.3 Post-COVID-19

The luxury market is an interesting and attractive global market that has consistently grown at positive rates (D'Arpizio, 2013, 2014, 2015, 2016, 2017, 2018, 2019, 2020) over the last years, till 2020, when it fell sharply, due to the COVID-19 epidemy. In the beginning, the magnitude of the pandemic was not fully known, and the first estimates of the researchers were that the market would recover in a few months, but today this is expected to happen in a slower rhythm in 2021, intensifying only over 2022 and 2023.

2.3.1 Financial Impacts

The luxury industry has been heavily impacted by the COVID-19 crisis in 2020. The overall luxury market, encompassing both luxury goods and experiences, shrank by 23% at current exchange rates, to approximately €1 trillion globally, back to its 2015 levels. It is estimated that the market will only reach the previous peak of €1.2 trillion by 2023.

The market of personal luxury goods reacted in different ways over the regional markets of the world.

Mainland China has been the only region globally to end the year on a positive note, growing by 45% at current exchange rates to reach €44 billion, due to redirecting the consumer power to the local market. The share of purchases made online nearly doubled from 12% in 2019 to 23% in 2020. Scenarios for China in 2021 are varied, and Bain forecasts growth ranges from between +10 and 12% to between +17 and 19%, depending on macroeconomic conditions, the evolution of COVID-19, and the speed of return to travel globally, as well as the resilience and confidence of local customers (D'Arpizio, 2020).

Europe was severely affected by the collapse in global tourism. Local consumption remains, but regional consumption fell by 36% at current exchange rates to €57 billion.

The Americas were less affected, but they were also impacted, with this market falling by 27% at current exchange rates to €62 billion. In the United States, department stores started moving away from city centers.

In Asia, Japan had mixed performance, where the strong brands, perceived as timeless and as long-term investments were more resilient. This market shrunk by 24% at current exchange rates to €18 billion in 2020. The rest of Asia was heavily impacted, with Hong Kong and Macau among the worst affected. The region contracted by 35% at current exchange rates to reach €27 billion.

In the Middle East the impact was dampened by the adoption of shorter periods of lockdown and the reversion of the previous expenditures abroad to the local market, although with differences among these countries.

Australia was heavily impacted by the spread of wildfires, in conjunction with the reduction of foreign tourists, creating difficulties for the local hospitality sector, falling more than 50%.

With the resumption of global travel (particularly of tourism out of China) in 2021, luxury sales in the Middle East, Japan, and Europe are leaving this turbulent period and gradually driving the market growth and returning to pre-pandemic levels.

2.3.2 Digitalization Impacts

The need of social isolation, followed by selective and full lockdowns, had a strong impact on distribution channels, as many physical businesses were prohibited to operate, or limited to restrict periods of opening. In particular for essential consumption, as food and medicine, consumers rapidly overcame previous fears and restrictions to online purchase, as that remained for many the only option available, increasing the presence of online in all aspects of consumer's life. Online brings some advantages as speed and convenience that make it attractive. This had a positive impact on the demand of the digital services companies, with sharp increase in sales of software and hardware to support businesses more appropriate for these moments of isolation, such as delivery and communications. Some experts estimate that this sector advanced five years in one.

In the luxury market, online sales reached €49 billion in 2020, compared to €33 billion in 2019. Online purchase share went from 12% in 2019 to 23% in 2020, practically doubling. The online channel is expected to become the leading channel for luxury purchases by 2025, leveraging the omnichannel transformation trend.

Online and mono-brand stores were important distribution channels for the recovery observed in 2021. After a 50% increase from 2019 to 2020, online channels continued to grow by 27% from 2020 to 2021 to reach an estimated €62 billion in market value this year, introducing and consolidating digital experiences.

On the other hand, this dramatic increase came at the expense of the bricks-and-mortar channel. Bain consultants expect the total number of stores operated directly by luxury brands in 2020 to remain stable, and a possible trend of decline in store networks in 2021.

Brands will need to adjust their customer experience, focusing more on the planning of the best delivery of their experience, with the use of research and new techniques as those from Consumer Experience (CX) and Design Thinking. The design of the place or interface where the experience happens will become even more important for consumer satisfaction, as well as the selection of the right people to interact with the consumer, and their continuous training. The delivery of the experience can also benefit from concepts from User Experience (UX). Big data analytical skills will also become more relevant, as the volume of consumer data increases every year.

After-service will increase in importance, both in creating processes to retain satisfied clients, and reducing rates of consumer defection (churn), and by creating channels for complaints and insatisfaction, processes for obtaining quick solutions to failures and complaints, and structure to review and reengineer inefficient processes that cause experience delivery failures, bottlenecks, and other sources of insatisfaction.

Bain experts expect wholesale distribution to be affected by emerging trends such as perimeter contraction, polarized performance, and entry of new players. Luxury brands will look to increase their control on their channel. The retail channel will increase its participation, and in few years will surpass the wholesale channel.

2.3.3 Behavioral Impacts

This epidemy also had a behavioral impact on luxury consumption, that is still premature to evaluate properly, as it is a process in progress, but some trends have been observed, that could be discussed in two aspects: isolation and social questions.

A new and uncertain moment, with a lethal impact, resulted in fear and a new conscience of safety. Apart from government restrictions, people are afraid to expose themselves in agglomerations, or even leave home except for basic activities, such as buying food or medicine. They also fear to contaminate close relations, particularly older ones (Sarwari et al., 2020). This resulted in preferring to only have contact with small groups or close ones, and only with all safety precautions. For a small but interesting niche, this created a market for providers, in particular those in experiential luxury, of out-of-home experiences in a "bubble", that is, some opportunities to enjoy some of the "old" experiences in a protected environment, with rigid protocols, plenty of information to reduce the fear and induce confidence, for small groups (family members or close ones) extremely protected from any external threat, like traveling in private jets and staying in isolated resorts with no contact at all with anyone else, not even employees, or just a few selected ones. There is also some preference for shorter distances, privileging local tourism (Puaschunder, 2020; Sarwari et al., 2020).

Many countries closed their frontiers to foreigners originating from more contaminated countries. Hotels, restaurants, and other hospitality businesses that focused on tourists had to close due to lockdowns, or at least operate under limited conditions, as strict sanitary precautions and reduced capacity due to the need to maintain social distance in closed environments. These factors resulted in restrictions to travel and tourism that have marked an acceleration of a rebalancing of where luxury purchases are made, as these tourists remained at home, and had to buy in their home markets. Bain estimates that the current share of purchases made locally reached 80–85% in 2020 and expects it to represent between 65 and 70% even when foreign purchases regain relevance in the future, especially initially in China and the broader Asian region.

Mainland China is a special case, as it is the only region globally to end the year with positive numbers, growing by 45% at current exchange rates to reach €44 billion. Local consumption increased across all channels, categories, generations, and price points.

Concern about social questions, as sustainability and environmental issues, diversity, and inclusion have increased among luxury consumers in 2020. Younger generations, who are projected to be responsible for 180% of the growth in the market from 2019 to 2025, are increasingly asking companies to develop actions that help in tackling social and racial injustice. These consumers want their consumed brands to align their actions with their vision and desire for purpose.

The suffering people are witnessing also created a pressure on the consumers to demand that companies show humanitarian feelings, recognizing company donations for research, hospital equipment production or donation, support for volunteer work, actions to prevent unemployment, etc. (Grilec et al., 2020).

In a longer term, some research suggests that these behavior changes may not be permanent, but just create a repressed demand that, as soon as things get back to near-normal conditions, there will be a "revenge of consumption", as observed before in other similar events over history, as in the fourteenth century, when after the great plague there was an extraordinary increase in luxury consumption, the end of the Middle Ages and the Renaissance, characterized by survivors' joie de vivre and self-determination, the beginning of fashion, or with the Belle Epoque after the First World War, or the explosion of consumption after the Second World War (Puaschunder, 2020).

A recent phenomenon is the second-hand luxury market, that grew by 65% between 2017 and 2021, with increased demand and a growing offer, while the firsthand items presented only 12% growth.

Second-hand luxury products are attractive because they are cheaper, giving access to good-quality products at accessible prices, are sustainable, give a second life to existing products, it is exciting to hunt bargains, and allow consumers to find options not available as new.

Bain estimates that this market soared to reach €33 billion in 2021, driven by this increasing attention,

2.3.4 Category Consumption Impacts

In the global market, all personal luxury goods categories have seen decline in 2020. Shoes losses were partially compensated by demand in sneakers, but still fell by 12% to €19 billion while jewelry saw sustained demand in Asia and benefited from online sales. That category remains polarized with high jewelry and iconic entry priced items leading the recovery.

Watches and apparel declined by 30%. For watches, COVID-19 intensified the already critical secular consumption pattern shifts of the category. Formal wear demand had a sharp decline and apparel companies had increasing competition from social media savvy brands that were already experienced in direct-to-consumer channels.

Across product categories, entry-price items increased their share, reaching more than 50% of volumes sold in 2020. In this accessible luxury sector, apart from refined pricing strategies, brands had to face new entrants from emerging brands with relevant purpose and business models more attuned to the customer of today.

Looking at the luxury market as a whole, Bain expects that experience-based goods (which they define as design furniture, fine wines and spirits, fine dining, hotels, and exclusive vacations) are expected to recover faster than personal goods (leather accessories, apparel, watch and jewelry, perfumes, and cosmetics) as people are returning to parties and events. In 2021, due to the increase in informality, personal luxury goods sales, in particular shoes, accessories, and jewelry, increased in 32%, returning to pre-2019 levels. Big occasion, dressing, luxury cars, hospitality, fine wine, and spirits, overall, a shift from intangible experiences expending to tangible products is observed.

2.3.5 Managerial Decisions Impacts

The COVID-19 epidemy brought a scenario that is different from anything companies—in all sectors—have faced in the last one hundred years. The uncertainty levels increased dramatically and companies are having to quickly learn how to deal with many novel situations that they still don't have enough information to understand properly.

In this pandemic scenario of uncertainty, managers are having to make vital decisions based on few or no similar experiences in their past experience. This means that companies will have to intensify their information collecting and processing, with more updated research, more intense use of databases and big data, benchmarking and collaborating with competitors, and swiftness in spreading this information in the right format to the right decision-makers. They will also have to be quickly updated on new governmental laws and restrictions that may change quickly with strong impact on the company operation (Sarwari et al., 2020).

The volume of data provided by digital channels also drove companies toward the intensification of their use, incorporating in some cases Big data technologies in a faster rhythm (Puaschunder, 2020).

Companies will also have to intensify the use and analysis of metrics derived from these data to better monitor performance and anticipate losses in clients, satisfaction, and revenues (Sarwari et al., 2020).

The speed of digitalization over this period has been significantly higher, as other distribution channels were blocked and for many companies it was the only remaining option. Those not prepared had to learn quickly in order to survive, making quick decisions that might not be the best, due to lack of time for proper analysis, while those that had digital channels, in many cases as a secondary channel, suddenly saw a great increase in its participation, and could leverage previous learning (Puaschunder, 2020).

One challenge in this scenario is to understand how to keep the physical experience quality that clients were used to, to the new digital environment and its limitations as there are no tactile, aromatic, or gustative senses to use in the construction of the experience (Puaschunder, 2020). They have to leverage the already acquired abilities related to experience design and delivery, and satisfaction management, adding the advantages of speed and convenience brought by the digital.

Another challenge is to integrate and modify logistic processes originally developed for physical channels, to the new digital channels (Puaschunder, 2020). This implies changing the main fluxes of logistics: information, documents, product characteristics, communication, etc. This will probably result is many changes in processes, training, and all interfaces with clients, as well as the technology. Also, the physical selling points will have to adapt layouts to guarantee minimum distances and protection equipment for both clients and employees, information communications on new proceedings, all without affecting the experience itself (Sarwari et al., 2020).

An additional challenge will be to adapt client communication to the new digital channels, and also include informational content on protocols and health procedures that guarantee safety to clients (Grilec et al., 2020; Puaschunder, 2020; Sarwari et al., 2020).

2.3.6 Managerial Opportunities and Dilemmas

Luxury consumers are not all equal, and will behave in different ways, some may be able to cope better with this difficult period than others. Managers need to make a realistic analysis of the competitive environment to establish the best marketing strategies for the coming years. The sector of luxury has been impacted by a decline of 20%, while many others faced rates above 50%, and some simply were forced to close and lose all revenues, so in general it can be considered that there are still some opportunities to be explored, with suitable strategies, based on the remaining market potential and the most solid information available. The luxury segment could be seen as relatively small, as less than 1% of the population has consumption access to it, but still is a market forecasted to reach globally €1 trillion, so should be full of potential to be explored.

In terms of effect of the impact, one can identify three different segments (Hemzo, 2015):

The Unaffected are those who have managed to maintain their purchasing power, are not concerned and do not intend to change their consumption behavior. The company should strengthen its performance with them, show that their products remain essential to their lifestyle, and continue to offer superior service, and intensify efforts to retain its VIPs. Nothing should affect their shopping experience. It may even be time to launch a new product, or acquire a brand of a competitor, that can become a success in this segment. But as this is the most attractive segment, companies should be prepared to face tough competition for them.

The little affected are those who are in a stable situation, but are concerned, and intend to consume more selectively and less ostentatiously. They have become more demanding and had to postpone large purchases, but keep buying many others. Companies should promote their quality, identity, and differentials, and make clearer the benefits of their brand, to keep this segment loyal.

The most affected are those who are in a situation of uncertainty, due to the loss of a high management position, or crisis in their companies, and have become more dependent on their savings, investments, and assets. They are being more selective in their consumption, considering downgrading to other luxury brands, repair what they own instead of buying a new one, postponing expenses, especially with jewelry, travel, culture, and leisure. Companies should invest in advisory communication, and guides on how to buy less, but better. Helping the customer make these choices, make their services more accessible, and offer hedonic benefits.

These changes bring new opportunities that demand new strategies to better profit from them. The first reaction to be avoided by companies is to generically cut back on their marketing efforts to reduce costs. Marketing plays a fundamental role in strengthening a brand, and any reduction should only be made with criteria, discretion, care, and creativity, preferring the scalpel and surgical action, rather than the use of the axe in the cuts. Research actions should be kept as priorities, which help to better understand how the consumer behaves, how best to satisfy him, and how to design communication actions, which increase the value of the brand, brand equity, reinforce identity, and emotional ties with the client.

Some trends were already present, but were intensified by the pandemic (Girod, 2018), and companies should increase their efforts to adapt to them. Changes in the competitive environment bring new challenges and intensify existing ones, as it is now discussed.

Existing clients are loyal and responsible for most of the revenues of the company, but they tend to become older and eventually will have to be replaced by new ones. Millennials are becoming more important and should be part of the strategy of any company, but they have new habits, lifestyles, and preferences that may conflict with the existing ones, so the company has to attract them, but without alienating older ones, particularly their VIPs.

Social responsibility means better working conditions for internal and third-part employees so companies have to be more attentive to working ethics inside and outside the company, and sustainability, facing issues such as the use of fur, chemical products, resources from endangered species, environmental pollution resulting from production activity, etc.

As these consumers value more luxury brands with similar values to theirs, authenticity and transparency have become very important, as negative reactions to incorrect pronouncements or actions can lead to boycott and drop in sales. The company is expected to act according to its true values and be responsive to any reaction. On the other hand, mystique is an important component of the brand identity, in order to create an idealistic or romantic image, to be explored through storytelling in all communication, which may sometimes mean not disclosing too much details.

Another challenge will be to find a balance between communication geared to strengthening brand equity and communication with the direct objective of leading to store visit and product purchase. Working on the stories related to the brand heritage is very important in luxury, but also is the direct effort to close sales.

Consumers look for novelties, and innovation is always welcome, even demanded by the consumers, but they also value the brand tradition of having an atemporal lifestyle, the consistency and expertise that flows through all the history of the brand, so companies have to be careful to innovate, but always remain true to their origins and roots. Usually, luxury brands offer universal values that rarely become obsolete, but the way they are perceived by consumers and incorporated in their lifestyles may differ over time. This has a direct impact on the way the brand communicates with their consumers.

Attracting new consumers can mean having to offer entry products with lower prices for not so demanding consumers, still learning the codes of luxury, and more oriented to brand prestige. Designing and producing these products involve changes in processes, different raw materials, human skills, suppliers, cost structures, and communication and distribution channels, demanding different managerial skills that may not be easy to obtain. On the other hand, these products may alienate frequent consumers, accustomed to higher product and service standards and more exclusivity. Companies have to be careful not to lose present consumers in order to acquire new ones.

In terms of internal structure, companies have to become less hierarchical and quicker to respond to fast changes in the competitive environment, but always careful not to affect the stability of consolidated corporate learning.

The new digital channels bring many new challenges. Logistics processes have to be adapted, data generated has to be processed and used in order to improve decisions, but without forgetting the advantages of the analogue channels to offer better experiences and services. A combination of the two worlds, the phygital model, aims to combine the personal touch and richer experience of the physical with the advantages of speed, wider offer, and convenience of the digital. The same applies to promotional events, like promotional shows to release new collections, initially very exclusive, only frequented by the best clients and influencers, that became more accessible through digital channels that allow greater reach and new possibilities, as real-time broadcasting with brand-costumer interaction and immediate purchases.

Flexible managerial processes have to be adopted in order to react quicker to changes identified by the huge volume of data now available, and the forced reclusion with the wide implementation of home office that changed perceptions about remote work and their advantages, as save of productive time lost in commuting and the practicality of working without leaving home, although the personal contact with peers and superior may feel lacking.

New factors that became important after the surge of COVID-19 also have to be considered. Due to the fear of contamination, people are much more aware of sanitary conditions of the places they may frequent, and companies have to adapt to serve just small groups, under strict protocols of protection, both for consumers and service people.

Fear and legal restrictions have reduced longer travels, meaning that those depending on foreign consumers will be heavily impacted, and will have to learn to redirect their efforts to attract regional and local consumers, still willing to travel shorter distances.

It's time for managers to step up the effort to retain existing customers and better evaluate the productivity of marketing resources, in terms of profitability and value generation, taking advantage of the moment to reduce waste and products of low attractiveness and already obsolete by the action of competitors, directing resources to novelties that best meet their target audience, perform actions that reinforce their institutional brand, and in training and qualification of its professionals, leaving the company better prepared for the future, when a recovery of the economic scenario occurs, which should surely come with some patience.

2.4 Summary

> The luxury market is full of potential and was growing consistently before the event of COVID-19, apart from specific moments of global crisis that were eventually surpassed.
> Today the pandemic affected almost the whole world—except China—with losses from 20% up, the experts consider this market resilient and capable of resuming previous levels in about two years.
> The main challenges faced today have been somewhat intensified by this need of quick recovery, and the increasing digitalization, which has to incorporated without losing the personal touch of the physical stores, the increasing importance of the millennium, with different values that have to be understood and adapted by the luxury companies, the need to have people and structures more flexible and agile to respond quickly to these changes, and the fear to leave isolation due to the risks of contamination, that could only be minimized by strict sanitary protocols.

Bibliography

D'Arpizio, C. (2011). Bain & Co. Luxury goods worldwide market study.
D'Arpizio, C. (2012). Bain & Co. Luxury goods worldwide market study.
D'Arpizio, C. (2013). Bain & Co. Luxury goods worldwide market study.
D'Arpizio, C. (2014). Bain & Co. Luxury goods worldwide market study.
D'Arpizio, C. (2015). Bain & Co. Luxury goods worldwide market study.
D'Arpizio, C. (2016). Bain & Co. Luxury goods worldwide market study.
D'Arpizio, C. (2017). Bain & Co. Luxury goods worldwide market study.
D'Arpizio, C. (2018). Bain & Co. Luxury goods worldwide market study.
D'Arpizio, C. (2019). Bain & Co. Luxury goods worldwide market study.
D'Arpizio, C. (2020). Bain & Co. Luxury goods worldwide market study.
D'Arpizio, C. (2021). Bain & Co. Luxury goods worldwide market study.
Girod, S. J. G. (2018). *Luxury brands need to reconcile seven dilemmas and chart new territory.* Reinventing Luxury Strategy Conversations. IMD.
Grilec, A., Vukusic, D., & Dujic, D. (2020). Communication strategies of luxury brands during COVID-19 Crisis. In *Economic and Social Development: Book of Proceedings* (pp. 281–290).
Hemzo, M. A. (2015). Marketing para ambientes conturbados. *LUXUS Magazine*.

Bibliography

Lipovetsky, G., & Roux, E. (2003). *Le luxe éternel*. Gallimard.
Puaschunder, J. M. (2020, September 27). *Value at COVID-19: Digitalized healthcare, luxury consumption and global education*. Luxury Consumption and Global Education.
Sarwari, D., Huq, S., & Minar, T. A. (2020). *COVID-19: The way luxury hotels deal with the pandemic*. Available at SSRN 3690758.

Luxury Market and the Service-Dominant Logic Paradigm

3.1 Introduction

Chapter Objectives
In this chapter we discuss the service-dominant logic, a change of paradigm that helps understand how luxury products are more profitable, thanks to the use of distinctive competences, skills, and knowledge of their personal.

3.2 The Evolution of Marketing and Service-Dominant Logic Paradigm

Making money through commerce is an idea as old as money itself. But the best way to do it has evolved dramatically over time.

We live in an era of a paradigm shift. A new way of thinking business has developed since the beginning of this century, substituting a traditional view that has been popular since the Industrial Revolution.

Initially, traders would search for artisans that could supply good-quality products and make them available to costumers close and far from this source. This could range from bringing vegetables from the countryside to the main cities, to offering rare products from distant lands. The price would vary accordingly.

With the industrial revolution, a new standard of product and production was stablished.

Previously, artisanal products were hand-made by people and the final quality could depend on the humor and inspiration of the artisan at the moment. It was produced in limited quantities, and the resulting product could be perceived as of different value depending on the unit and the user. The price corresponding to this value was agreed between seller and buyer for each transaction.

Industrial products, on the other hand, were mass-produced, with a very similar and reasonable quality, with a more similar perceived value, and price would vary only according to transport costs and the ability of the seller to promote its qualities. In general, they were attractive and innovative, and demand was ample.

In this period, marketing was mainly concerned with product mix decisions, as defining the right attributes, and guaranteeing that production was enough to answer demand, of distribution decisions, as selling competent distributors that could make the products available in his regions.

Price mix decisions were simple and based on production costs, with an added margin.

Promotion mix decisions were left mostly to the distributors.

In summary, in this initial period of marketing management, the main mix decisions were centered around the two Ps—Product and Place.

After the Second World War the technology increased its speed of development, and innovation become more accessible, resulting in many players entering markets with new offers in the same product category, resulting in more diversity of options and characteristics. This increases competition and becomes more important for companies to explain these differences to their customers in order to conquer market share. This increases the managerial focus on promotion decisions, in order to explain differentials, create awareness, favorable attitudes, desire, and increase purchase decisions.

Different options offer different value proposals and are associated to different levels of market price, making price strategy more complex, as costs, demand, and competition had to be balanced.

These new two aspects of the competitive market led to a more complex marketing management process, that was systematized by McCarthy in the 1960s (Khan, 2014) as the four Ps—Product, Place, Promotion and Price—known as the Marketing Mix.

From the 1960s on, the concepts, theories, and learnings about strategy became more important to companies, due to the increasing complexity of the competitive market, and three new concepts were incorporated at the strategical level of marketing management: Segmentation, Target, and Positioning.

It became apparent that markets had fragmented, and personal characteristics of consumers were leading to different kinds of demand for distinct products that were being made more and more available. Companies realized that it was necessary to develop specific marketing plans for each different profile in the market. To identify this profile, it was necessary to divide, or segment the market, into parts that were homogeneous inside the group and heterogenous among the other groups, and select those more attractive, according to each company's interest. This profile, or description of the selected segment, is now referred to as the **Persona**.

The need to express differentials was known for some time, and the concept of USP—Unique Selling Proposition—became used by many companies, the idea of identifying the main differential of a product, and stressing this aspect in the communication, in order to increase the probability of being preferred over a competitor, something unique that would justify their choice over other options.

This concept was expanded in the 1980s (Ries & Trout, 2001) as **Positioning**, the occupation in the customer's brain of a position that associates positive characteristics, benefits, and experiences related to a certain brand, in order to present this brand as the natural solution to a need, without the need to go through all the usual process of selecting alternatives, gathering information, and developing and applying criteria for selecting the best option.

These two decisions—Persona and Positioning—added a new superior strategic layer to the marketing mix: defining them properly would highly improve and streamline the further mix decisions.

Marketing has always in some way been concerned with creating superior value propositions to lead to transactions that would result in obtaining value (usually in the form of money) for the company.

But the competitive scenario in the last decades of the last century was showing that the current paradigm was not being enough to generate value above the average of the market, as production productivity and the spread of the technology was resulting in an ample offer, but of similar products, as they resulted from similar raw goods and productive processes. And consumers were becoming more demanding as they got used to frequent innovation and improved quality. It was more and more difficult to find ways to differentiate oneself from the competition, when a new paradigm was proposed (Vargo & Lusch, 2004).

This new paradigm proposes that the problem with the old one was that it was conceptually based on creating value by transforming raw materials into processed material, through technologies and equipments that were in use by many competitors, resulting in more competition and lower levels of differentiation.

The new paradigm proposes that higher value can be proposed by applying special competences in a participative process with consumers, to use the intangible superior knowledge of people in the company and the inputs of consumers over a determined period of time to offer the service of building together a fitting solution to the consumer's problem, and generate a flux of revenues resulting from satisfactory experiences that lead to repetition of purchases and creating bonds of fidelity and loyalty. This has significant implications to luxury businesses, that are more similar to the new paradigm, offering differentiation through special people's knowledge and competences, the artisans and creators.

The old paradigm was focused on a single transaction, while the new one focuses on retaining the costumers over time, generating several satisfactory transactions over their lives.

The old paradigm was based on the value of possessing a physical good that was owned and could be stored for use at any time, while in the new paradigm, the value is based on a "psychological ownership", the memories of good experiences that resulted in satisfaction mainly derived from services, and the positive attitudes related to the expectation that they could be accessed and repeated in the future, whenever the need arises.

This new paradigm changes the focus of the decisions related to the 4 Ps, and adds new decisions that now become more relevant. Now creating a good relationship over all contact points with the client is fundamental, and that involves having the right person with knowledge and skills to interact with the consumer and deliver the experience, define the best processes to direct this process, design the environment where these contacts happen, called the Panorama, and to manage the resulting satisfaction from these encounters, in order to guarantee that they have been successful.

The new paradigm proposes that there are several (some say infinite) potential opportunities to embed services in the company offer to increase the proposed value. But this change demands a new way to make the marketing decisions, creating **Products** as services, **Price** as Value Propositions based on benefits, **Places** that create omnichannel distribution structures and experiences, in the possible location (and digital presence), and **Promotion** that through interaction and coproduction helps understanding the more subtle and intangible aspects of the services and how they satisfy Personas' needs. This implies a new interpretation of the traditional 4 Ps. They become more ample and complex in order to really deliver great memorable experiences, and add four new Ps: People, Process, Panorama, and Productivity (Wirtz et al., 2016, 2020), reflecting new decisions that become part of the realm of marketing.

In relation to these new four Ps, some questions have to be highlighted. **People** are responsible for conducting the delivery of the experience, interaction with the customer, and applying their differentiated skills in coproducing the best solutions to presented needs and generating satisfaction. As the marketing manager is responsible for the satisfaction of the costumer, he also has to have the authority to select and direct those people that will be delivering the service experience that will result (or not) in satisfaction. With the technical support of the HR team, Marketing has to define the profile of candidates to be recruited, both hard and soft skills, train them continuously, in order to have them always prepared and updated to fully apply their knowledge and competences, and to properly motivate and energize the team.

Processes guarantee that the service experience will be delivered at the same level of quality, independent of the point of interface between customer and employee, assuring a minimum desired level of satisfaction. This implies mapping the processes that deliver the experience, analyze how they work, in order to prevent delays and failures, correct the identified deficient processes, and stablish control parameters to guarantee uniform performance. The main challenge will be to stablish processes that are standardized enough to guarantee that costumers will get the same level of experience in all contact points, but still leaving room for the frontline personnel to use their creativity and knowledge to improve the experience as necessary.

The **Panorama** manages the sensorial, psychological, and social inputs that affect the emotional state of service delivery experience. Designing the Panorama is fundamental for creating the most appropriate emotional state for each successful experience. The sensorial inputs are those that operate through our five senses, the distribution of the space and the visual communication design, while the psychological and social inputs are those exchanged among people (client, personnel, third parties) present in the environment.

Productivity manages and measures the use and results of the resources applied to creating and developing experiences and the resulting degree of satisfaction that it generates. It integrates the concepts of resources and productivity with quality, experience, satisfaction, recovery of failures, fidelization (strengthening the intention to return) and loyalty (generating advocates and positive word-of-mouth) building, and the main related metrics.

All these eight decision groups have to be managed aligned to the two strategic decisions—Persona, that shows the needs and decisions the customer present, and Positioning, that defines the identity and the differentials of the service.

All these decisions will be discussed in length in the next chapters.

3.3 Luxury Services

What distinguishes luxury products from luxury services? This discussion is mainly based on Wirtz et al. (2020). It is already recognized that marketing management of traditional goods is distinct from the management of luxury goods (Kapferer & Bastien, 2009). But there are few studies on luxury services, with some studies mainly of hotels, dining, and healthcare, although discussing particular characteristics, and not differences.

We can highlight the main distinctive characteristics of the luxury services. Services in general differ from goods in relation to ownership. While goods belong to an owner, services are available for a limited time, usually charged by a time period (hour, day, opening hours, etc.). This makes it more difficult to identify its value.

Luxury services differ from luxury physical goods over these four questions.

Non-ownership, they are experiences enjoyed over a certain period of time, with definite moments for beginning and for ending, but that they are so rich, so exciting, so pleasurable, that leave great memories and the will to repeat them.

Psychological possession, as these memories have value, and hold a special and valuable experience in the consumers' life. This value can be extended by physical souvenirs that bring back memories and helps relive these precious moments.

Lower conspicuous consumption is another interesting characteristic, as experiences and intangible, so they can't be visually appealing as a big logo in a t-shirt, or the iconic look of a luxury car. This means that it is also more challenging to promote and present the value of the luxury service, as even if you can get other clients to endorse and talk about their experiences, there is no guarantee that it will be repeated exactly with a different client.

Finally, there is **lower risk of counterfeiting**, as physical luxury goods can be reproduced, at least partially, with cheaper materials and labor, but luxury services are much more dependable on the *savoir-faire*, personal skills, acquired over time and much harder to assimilate and imitate, some of the passed down from generation to generation.

It is also relevant that luxury services differ from luxury goods by the more general characteristics of services.

Intangibility means that they have few or no physical materiality, so they cannot be touched to be appreciated. Can't be stored to be used later, has no property to be transferred.

Heterogeneity is related to the question that services and normally provided by people, and the resulting service varies according to the skill of each personnel, physical and mental conditions, level of energy, motivation, etc. While a machine can be switched on and immediately start to produce at optimal level, people vary their productivity over time.

Inseparability represents the fact that services are delivered by a process, a sequence of activities with a final result, and partial sequences will not have the same value as the whole process.

Perishability is associated to the limited availability of the service over time. The access to the service is usually controlled by a time period, with stablished start and finish, resulting that it is usually charged by the hour, and if you want to enjoy it longer, you have to pay proportionally more for it. When the time period is over, the access is blocked.

These characteristics bring more complexity to the management of luxury services, and to provide extraordinary exclusive hedonic luxury experiences, more marketing decisions have to be made, in comparing to luxury goods.

The new decisions add new dimensions to the marketing mix, that could be described as the new "service" Ps:

People have to be managed in order to have the best necessary skills in the business.

Processes need to be designed to guarantee a minimum level of heterogeneity in the experiences.

Panorama is very important to create the right emotional state that promotes the degree of confidence and rapport between client and employee.

Productivity, especially satisfaction metrics, are fundamental to ensure fidelization and loyalty of the most important clients.

3.4 Summary

> In this chapter, the new paradigm of services is presented, how marketing changed from the conquest to the retention paradigm, resulting in the services-dominant logic, and how this affected marketing decisions and the marketing mix and the 10 Ps. A new approach is necessary to answer to the new complexities that managing services bring.
> The text is based mainly on Vargo and Lusch articles, and the book on marketing services of which I am co-author (Wirtz et al., 2020).

Bibliography

Kapferer, J. N., & Bastien, V. (2009). *The luxury strategy—Break the rules of marketing to build luxury brands*. Kogan Page.

Khan, M. T. (2014). The concept of 'marketing mix' and its elements (a conceptual review paper). *International Journal of Information, Business and Management, 6*(2), 95.

Ries, A. l., & Trout, J. (2001). *Positioning: The battle for your mind*. McGraw Hill.

Vargo, S. L., & Lusch, R. F. (2001). Evolving to a new dominant logic for marketing. *Journal of marketing, 68*(1), 1–17.

Wirtz, J., Hemzo, M. A., & Lovelock, C. (2020). *Marketing de serviços: pessoas, tecnologia e estratégia* (8th ed.).

Wirtz, J., Holmqvist, J., & Fritze, M. P. (2020). Luxury services. *Journal of Service Management, 31*, 665–691.

Wirtz, J., & Lovelock, C. (2016). *Services marketing: People, technology*. World Scientific Publishing Company.

How to Position a Luxury Product

4.1 Introduction

Chapter Objectives
In this chapter, the concept of positioning is discussed. It is argued that, unlike fast-moving consumer goods, positioning strategies in luxury marketing are largely based on creating an identity of uniqueness, innovation balanced with tradition, and the use of story-telling and focused communication with their target. I combine ideas from marketing services and Kapferer and Bastien (2009) and some other authors on marketing for luxury.

4.2 How to Convince Clients that Your Brand Has a Valuable Differentiation

The need to express differentials was known for some time, and the concept of USP—Unique Selling Proposition—became used by many companies, the idea of identifying the main differential of a product, and stressing this aspect in the communication, in order to increase the probability of being preferred over a competitor, something unique that would justify their choice over other options.

This concept was expanded in the 1980s (Ries & Trout, 2001) as mentioned before, as **Positioning**, the occupation in the customer's brain of a position that associate positive characteristics, benefits, and experiences related to a certain brand, in order to present this brand as the natural solution to a need, without the need to go through all the usual process of selecting alternatives, gathering information, and developing and applying criteria for selecting the best option.

From a problem solution perspective, consumption decisions are based on a perceived need, that in order to find a good solution, people gather information, from several sources, on characteristics of available products and services in market that could be potential ways of attending those needs. He analyzes this information based on subjective criteria, like what he thinks the solution can better fill his need. This way of thinking is learned over time from previous experiences and what he hears and is persuaded to be true. Based on this analysis, he chooses the one that in his opinion is the most valuable.

Learning is stored in the brain, probably in a hierarchical way, in a tree-like structure, where associated ideas are stored together, and activating one also activates another. For instance, car brands are closer, so when you think of one you tend to remember others. When you think of a particular brand, you also think of associated characteristics that you learn about this brand. For instance, thinking the brand Audi may bring associations like rallies, German technology, high performance, etc. In this way, the brain has stored its learning in a structured way that makes it easy to retrieve this learning when necessary.

The aim of positioning is to create a strong image in the mind of the consumer, which supports their purchasing decisions, through associations with attributes and benefits. Memory has limited capacity and a brand must be among the most remembered, with strong and positive associations, so that it influences the consumer to be your customer.

Memory also tends to weaken over time when not used, so it is important that the learning process be repeated over time, in order that that memory remains prominent.

After the company has segmented the market and selected its target markets, it must define (Churchill & Peter, 2017) how it will position itself, in terms of differentials, advantages, and benefits it will offer.

Positioning (Kotler & Armstrong, 2016) is the action of projecting the offer and image of the company so that it occupies a differentiated place in the mind of the target audience.

Positioning associations are constructed through communication tools, sending persuasive and credible messages to consumers, in order to create and maintain this strong image.

As memory is limited, your brand has to be stronger than most of the competitors', in order to be recalled.

Ries and Trout (2001) define positioning as a battle for a space in the mind of the consumer.

In summary, memory (Solomon et al., 2017) organizes the information into a limited number of areas, which are localized by similarity. That is, what we learn is stored in a network of associations, which link, for example, tags and their attributes to each other. Memory holds only the most significant information, so if a brand does not occupy one of these positions, associated with a benefit or differential, it tends to be forgotten.

Managers work with the various marketing tools to create a strong brand image, so that it is easily remembered when a need associated with it is aroused.

The result of positioning (Kotler & Armstrong, 2016) is the successful creation of a customer-focused value proposition, that is, there is a compelling reason for

4.2 How to Convince Clients that Your Brand Has a Valuable Differentiation

the target market to prefer to be given supply—for a relatively higher price, it is receiving better quality, greater practicality, greater security, etc.

The strategy for positioning communication basically works with two contents in the messages: points of similarity and points of difference. To create positioning, communication actions must show what are the similarities and differences between your offer, and that of your competitors.

The points of similarity help the consumer understand which category the brand belongs to, and the least one should expect from it, while the points of difference show what the brand has the best, compared to its competitors.

By selecting a target market, the company is also choosing the competitors it will compete with. It is important for her to show her clients that she belongs to that market, so that she is considered among the alternatives in her consumer decision-making process.

The competitive reference structure (Kotler & Armstrong, 2016) defines the competing brands of a brand, and therefore those that must be analyzed for the definition of competitive strategies. Competitors in a category are the products with which the brand competes and which act as close substitutes, from the consumers' perspective, and it should also be considered future competitors, including new technologies. Competitors may be from the same sector, i.e., manufacturers of similar products, or from the same market, i.e., manufacturers of other products, but acting as substitutes for the brand.

For example, if a tourist in a foreign city is considering whether to spend his money on a meal at a restaurant, or to use this money to go to a musical show, these two options can both be considered as competitors in the leisure market, and this fact should be considered in the positioning strategy.

The evaluation of the competitor can be done through a system of assignment of gradings and weights to the main attributes related to success in the market, such as quality, practicality, availability, technical assistance, support of the sales team, maintenance, warranty, etc.

It is necessary to conduct research with your target to identify these gradings and weights, that may be different in other segments, and have this information incorporated into your positioning strategy. The research will help identify the particular parity points (Kotler & Armstrong, 2016), which are associations of attributes and benefits that are shared with other brands, that are relevant to your target.

Points of parity can be further distinguished as parity of category and parity of competition.

Category parity points are attributes or benefits those consumers consider essential within a particular category of products or services. These are the mandatory minimum items that everyone in the category should have, and consumers will only consider a brand if it also owns them.

For instance, if your brand is related to clothes, it must be perceived as part of the clothes category.

Competition parity points are associations that seek to nullify brand elements that are perceived as weaknesses, either by denying that they exist, or by denying competitors' assertion that they exist. You must communicate that your brand doesn't have the usual weaknesses that one could expect from this product category.

The second type of content of any positioning message should be the points of difference.

Points of difference are the attributes or benefits that consumers strongly and positively associate with a brand, and that they believe cannot be achieved or surpassed by other brands.

Three criteria (Kotler & Armstrong, 2016) are required for a brand association to create a really relevant point of difference:

- Be desirable for the consumer—the point must be personally relevant to the consumer, and have credibility in this statement, through concrete evidence in a persuasive message.
- Be deliverable by the company—the company must possess the internal resources necessary for delivery of the point of difference, and must be able to take the effort of creating and assuming the necessary associations
- Be differentiated from the competition—the association must lead to an authentic and credible offer the target perceive as superior over competitors.

The strategy of positioning a brand should take into account two points, the parity and the difference points, because both are important in the consumer's decision.

First consumers evaluate competing brands based on the parity points, whether the brand can belong to the desired category, offering attributes that meet their basic expectations. Then, when evaluating the brand against the competitors, the consumer will look at the points of difference, to identify which option best meets their needs and offer better perceived value.

Value is a subjective and dynamic expression of the total utility of that brand. It can be increased through credible and persuasive communication. Depending on what has already been learned over the past and may change with future learning, it is necessary for the management to closely monitor consumer's behavior to best attend to his needs.

In positioning, benefits are used to show the value that the brand represents, while attributes are used as benefit support references.

For example, the benefit of a car being fast is supported by attributes such as a V12 engine, and 500 horsepower.

One way to communicate brand positioning is through the brand mantra (Kotler & Armstrong, 2016):

> ... *a short sentence, composed of three to five words, which irrefutably captures the essence or spirit of its positioning ... is an articulation of the heart and soul of the brand, closely related to other branding concepts such as "brand essence" and "main brand promise".*

For instance, BMW uses "ultimate driving experience", summarizing the brand promise and positioning in three words.

Other examples are Apple's "think different", Nike's "just do it", Harley Davison's "All for Freedom. Freedom for All", De Beers' "Diamonds are forever", etc.

The brand mantra is usually developed aimed both at the brand's employees and external partners, and the target, seeking to communicate simply the values of the brand, and how this public should guide their behavior in the relationship with the customer.

The brand mantra (Kotler & Armstrong, 2016) must meet three criteria:

- Communicate—must define the category of the brand's business and establish the limits of the brand
- Simplify—should be short, incisive and vivid in its meaning, allowing easy memorization
- Inspire—must be personally meaningful and relevant, reinforcing values.

4.3 Positioning Communication Strategies

Having defined the communication strategy, management should start communication with its brand mantra, and positioning communication with the consumer, so that he understands in which category the product competes and what its parity points are, and what its points of difference in relation to its competitors.

The internal public should be the first target of the communication, as they must be prepared to act accordingly when contacting the consumer, otherwise a difference in the way they may behave in different situations may compromise the perception of the desired positioning.

The product category communication (Kotler & Armstrong, 2016) directed to the external public must:

- Advertise the benefits of the category—in general the benefits of the brand are used to advertise its category, such as durability, practicality, taste, etc.
- Compare to exemplary products—show that the brand can be considered as part of a set of other well-known brands
- Rely on a name that describes the product—concise names that list positive brand benefits and attributes are often used for facilitating understanding and memorization.

The message of communication should also consider strategic alternatives of differentiation (Kotler & Armstrong, 2016):

- Employee-based—differentiation through well-trained personnel who deliver superior quality care
- Channel-based—differentiation through better coverage, expertise, and performance of distribution channels
- Image-based—differentiation by creating images with strong associations with social and psychological needs of consumers
- Service-based—differentiation through more competent and faster complementary services that offer greater reliability, flexibility, and innovation.

The company should also monitor its consumers and evaluate the receptivity and timeliness of its positioning. Market, competitor, and competitive developments can make positioning obsolete, leading to the need for repositioning, when new benefits and attributes more relevant in the market are communicated.

4.4 Other Elements of the Marketing Mix also Position the Brand

Most of the marketing decisions contain some form of information that the consumer use in his evaluation.

Price can signal an association with quality, exclusivity, and craftsmanship.

The reputation of the location, in particular if in a shopping or a street associated to the category, can increase the perceived value.

The material, format, and colors of the packaging have specific associations that should be selected in order to create a homogeneous perception.

Standardized processes can lead to a better perception of professionalism and care for the consumer.

Physical appearance and educated manners of all those involved in contact with the client can contribute to create a better perception of quality, professionalism and expertise.

The overall ambience is fundamental to create, as discussed before, the perception of the "temple of luxury".

4.5 Some Differences When Positioning Luxury Products

Although all strategies discussed above that been tested successfully in the consumer market, it is important to stress that the particular characteristics of the attributes of luxury may demand some adaptations.

In luxury, one of the main characteristics is uniqueness. There should be nothing equal, so there should be nothing that could be compared to it. Even if there are other luxury products in the category, each offers a distinctive benefit, has a different identity, and is geared toward different consumer segments.

The brand has strong roots that made her what she is today, a story that she shares with no other brand, a feeling of timelessness, of authenticity, can't be reproduced without living the whole journey the brand went through. It is the pinnacle of the journey; the others were left in the middle of the way. It is independent, true only to her values and roots. Doesn't look at others to make her choices and trace her route.

In this sense, the communication is not comparative, but a valorization of this journey, and the storytelling is the best strategy, telling how the brand built its character and identity, how her creator stablished a strong culture that perpetuated these values, and how they are reflected in her products.

4.6 Positioning in the Luxury Cars Segment

Each luxury segment will have a set of relevant attributes that brands recognize as relevant for their consumers, and develop their positioning accordingly.

Take the luxury car market, for instance. Research has shown their consumers perceive the brands in terms of design (sports × elegant) and characteristics of use (comfortable × performance).

In the mind of the consumer, there are two dimensions that can be represented by a two-dimension space, one for design and the other for use. This results in four quadrants, with the following combinations:

- Comfortable, sports design cars—brands associated with luxury cars with sports design, but also very comfortable, but sacrificing a bit of the performance, like Mercedes and Jaguar.
- Performance, sports design cars—brands associated with luxury cars with sports design, with high performance but sacrificing a bit of the comfort, like Porche and Lamborghini.
- Comfortable, elegant design cars—brands associated with luxury cars with elegant design, very comfortable, but sacrificing a bit of the performance, like Rolls-Royce and Bentley.
- Performance, elegant design cars—brands associated with luxury cars with elegant design, of high performance, but sacrificing a bit of the performance, like Aston Martin and BMW.

In cases like the pairs of brands above, the brand may resource to a third dimension to further differentiate itself from competitors.

For instance, Mercedes uses the brand mantra "The Best or Nothing", focusing on excellence, while Jaguar uses "The Art of Performance", highlighting skills and craftsmanship.

In another example, Rolls-Royce uses "Trusted to Deliver Excellence", meaning reliability and uniqueness, while Bentley uses "Be Extraordinary", focusing on how their consumers will feel in an experience with the car.

4.7 Summary

In this chapter the concept and strategies of positioning a brand are presented. Positioning is a process to imbed in the mind of the consumer a desirable image, so that he creates a positive association between needs and the brand as a solution to this brand.

As the mind has limited memory, it is necessary to occupy a space in it with different actions related to the marketing mix, that allow the brand to remain a strong remembrance, to be activated at the right moment.

Unlike traditional products, luxury products have to be presented and remembered as unique, not comparable to other brands.

Bibliography

Churchill, G. A., & Peter, J. P. (2017). *Marketing*. Saraiva Educação.
Kapferer, J. N., & Bastien, V. (2009). *The luxury strategy—Break the rules of marketing to build luxury brands*. Kogan Page.
Kotler, P., & Amstrong, G. (2016). *Principles of marketing* (16th ed.). Pearson.
Lovelock, C., Wirtz, J., & Hemzo, M. A. (2011). *Marketing de serviços: pessoas, tecnologia e estratégia*.
Ries, A. l., & Trout, J. (2001). *Positioning: The battle for your mind*. McGraw Hill.
Solomon, M. R. et al. (2017). *Consumer behavior: Buying, having, and being*. Pearson.
Wirtz, J., & Lovelock, C. (2016). *Services marketing: People, technology*. World Scientific Publishing Company.

Luxury Consumer Behavior

5.1 Introduction

Chapter Objectives

This chapter presents an overview of the main concepts related to theories about individual, behavioral, social, and anthropological factors related to luxury consumption behavior, and how they can be used to segment and best describe different profiles of luxury consumers supported mainly by research from BCG and Altagamma, and academic articles on luxury and luxury consumption behavior.

Consumption behavior is influenced by several factors, which can be grouped into four major groups: personal factors, psychological factors, social factors, and cultural factors. Influenced by these factors, a consumption decision develops from a five-step process: problem recognition, search for information, evaluation of alternatives, purchase decision, and post-purchase behavior.

Consumers' preferences for luxury brands are based on the satisfaction of their social goals. These social goals always coexist and perform as compensation for each other. The dissatisfaction of one social goal would promote their expectation of the satisfaction of another social goal (Zhang et al., 2019).

Buying luxury brands serve various consumer needs and motives such as a desire to portray a specific social class position, communicate a desired public self-image and provide self-concept reinforcement, a visible proof that the consumer can afford higher-priced products (Nia & Lynne Zaichkowsky, 2000; Zhang et al., 2019). Luxury services, on the

> other hand, are less conspicuous (Wirtz et al., 2020), but can fulfill the other needs above.

5.2 Consumer Behavior

According to Solomon (2017), consumer behavior:

> ... is the study of how individuals, groups and organizations select, buy, use and discard goods, services, ideas or experiences to meet their needs and desires.

Therefore, it is the study of the consumption behavior of several groups, with specific characteristics in their consumption actions. Individuals consume for their own benefit, while groups take into account the interests of their members, and organizations, and their profitability goals.

The consumption process is not limited to the act of consumption itself, but begins at the moment when a need is awoken that requires a consumption solution, and extends to the post-purchase stage, with the use, the disposal after consumption, and the evaluation if the satisfaction of the need actually occurred.

It is important for the marketing manager (Kotler & Amstrong, 2016) to know at each of these steps what are the main influencing factors of consumer behavior in action at that moment. These factors can be grouped into four major groups: personal factors, psychological factors, social factors, and cultural factors.

5.2.1 Personal Factors Influencing Consumer Behavior

The personal characteristics of the consumer have significant influence on their consumer behavior.

Age (Solomon, 2017) has a determining factor on consumption, as the person goes through different age groups. Initially the child consumes what the family determines, but as it grows, it begins to participate and influence the choices. When contacting other children, it suffers influences and his preferences are shaped. These steps compose the life cycle, as one becomes adolescent, adult, father, widow, etc., and passes (Kotler & Amstrong, 2016) through episodes or crucial transitions of life—marriage, birth of children, diseases, transfers, divorces, changes in employment and city, retirement and widowhood, leading to the emergence of different consumption needs.

Usually, the single direct their consumption to products in smaller quantities, the newlywed invests in his home, parents with newborn swarms, food, and pediatricians, with the growth of children arise educational expenses with adult children there are time and resources for new activities, and with widowing, turns to individual consumption.

However, this traditional family model is no longer so common, and variations and changes can occur in this sequence, with the new marriage of divorced and widowed, and non-traditional family formats.

Professional occupation (Kotler & Amstrong, 2016) also influences consumption behavior, especially in the B2B market. Formal professions may require more formal clothing, and vice versa. Higher-status professions often demand higher spending on clothing and accessories.

The economic pattern is also an economic factor in consumption. Disposable income limits the value to be directed to consumption, as well as financial stability, which provides greater security for consumer decisions, and attitudes and values in relation to spending and savings.

Personality (Kotler & Amstrong, 2016; Solomon, 2017), another influencing factor of consumption, is:

> ... a set of distinct psychological traits, which lead to relatively coherent and continuous reactions to the stimuli of the environment.

Among the main personality traits, we have self-confidence, degree of dominance, autonomy, submission, sociability, defensive posture, and adaptability.

It is also possible to build the personality of a brand, so that it acquires the desired traits, through positioning strategies. In this case, the consumer tends to prefer brands that have personality characteristics similar to his own.

A lifestyle (Kotler & Amstrong, 2016; Solomon, 2017) is:

> ... a standard of living of a person expressed by activities, interests and opinions; represents the person "in its entirety" interacting with their environment.

There is a strong association between lifestyle and consumption, and the consumer seeks coherence between their lifestyle and the characteristics of their consumer product.

5.2.2 Psychological Factors Influencing Consumption Behavior

The four main psychological factors (Kotler & Amstrong, 2016; Solomon, 2017) that influence consumption behavior are motivation, perception, learning, and memory.

Theories of Motivation

Motivation originates in needs. The need (Kotler & Amstrong, 2016) is resulted from a state of tension where we miss something, which can be physiological, such as hunger, sea or discomfort, or psychological, with recognition, esteem, or integration.

This state of tension generates a reason for us to move, acting in the search for the satisfaction of this need.

The three main theories of motivation (Kotler & Amstrong, 2016) are those of Freud, Maslow, and Herzberg.

For Sigmund Freud (Kotler & Amstrong, 2016; Solomon, 2017), the individual's behavior is partly unconscious, which makes it difficult to understand their motivations. The actions and motivations are due to the interaction between three elements of the psyche: id, superego, and ego. The id represents the wild and animal component of the human being, which seeks the survival of the species, through the stimulation for sexual reproduction, and individual survival, through competitiveness in relation to other people. The superego represents the restrictions and social rules that allow coexistence in the group and cooperation with others. The ego is the element that evaluates the demands and desires of the other two elements and decides which one will meet, within your pursuit of satisfaction.

For the manager, it is important to understand how different products can stimulate these components and be chosen as the appropriate decision for the satisfaction of the need.

The theory of Abraham Maslow (Healy, 2016; Kotler & Amstrong, 2016; Solomon, 2017) proposes that the motivations present a certain order, in a hierarchical structure by the degree of urgency.

The first need is to meet physiological needs, such as seeding and hunger. Satisfied with the first, the person leaves for the satisfaction of the second, and so on.

The second need is safety, physical and psychological. She seeks shelter and distance from threats.

These first two are called basic or prophylactic needs. In most modern societies, they are relatively well served. Therefore, they are the closest to the most present, and that are most of interest to marketers, since they can offer products and services as satisfaction to them.

The third need is social, to belong to a social group and be accepted by it.

The fourth need is for esteem, to have people around who like it.

These two are called psychological needs.

The fifth and final is the need for self-realization, to feel that you have your life, you play a fundamental role in your society and for yourself.

Frederick Herzberg's theory (Kotler & Amstrong, 2016) presents two groups of factors, the dissatisfactor factors (factors that cause dissatisfaction) and satisfactor factors (factors that cause satisfaction). The absence of dissatisfactor factors is not enough to motivate a purchase, it is necessary for the presence of satisfactor factor. The dissatisfactor factors are practically mandatory, but not enough for motivation. What really leads to the decision of closing of the sale are the appropriate satisfactor factors.

Perception Theories

Perception (Kotler & Amstrong, 2016) is:

> ... *the process by which someone selects, organizes and interprets the information received to create a meaningful image of the world.*

In this process, the five senses receive stimuli from the world around, which are selected by the importance we identify in them, filtering the unnecessary ones. These stimuli are organized and interpreted within a logic that we learn throughout our lives and that are personal and subjective.

People can (Kotler & Amstrong, 2016; Solomon, 2017) have different perceptions of the same object due to three processes: selective attention, selective distortion, and selective retention.

The attention is (Kotler & Amstrong, 2016) the allocation of the processing capacity that we dedicate to a certain stimulus. We are exposed to thousands of stimuli a day, which mostly do not relevant to our needs. Most of them are filtered by selective attention, within three criteria:

- Relationship with a current need—we tend to select the stimuli related to topics that we are currently interested in.
- Expectation or predictability of the stimulus—the context generates a certain expectation, and we tend to select the stimuli we were already hoping to find in that context.
- Stimulus intensity—the higher the intensity, in relation to normal, the greater the chance of selecting the stimulus.

Selective distortion is the tendency we have to interpret stimuli based on our previous knowledge.

Selective retention is the tendency to more easily recall information that confirms our opinions and preferences.

Learning Theories

As we receive and interpret stimuli, we take information that is a learning tool.

Learning (Kotler & Amstrong, 2016) consists of changes in a person's behavior resulting from experiences.

The main learning theories (Solomon, 2017) are divided into two groups: behavioral and cognitive.

In behavioral or behaviorist theories, it is understood that learning occurs through processes of stimulation and response, that is, that the application of a given stimulus conditions a certain response. For example, the horse that receives a lump of sugar each time it performs an action correctly, but receives nothing when it does not do the desired action, learns to associate the reward with the correct attitude, which it learns in order to receive the reward.

In this theory, the marketing professional seeks to associate the rewards desired by the consumer with his product and brand, so that when seeking the satisfaction of a need, he directly seeks the specific product.

In cognitive theories, it is proposed that each person, based on his repertory and life history, is able to receive stimuli, interpret them logically in his brain, in a personal way, and reach conclusions that reinforce or alter his behavior.

The first group is also called stimulus–response theories or the black box theory, since it assumes that each stimulus is associated with a given response, and that internally it is not necessary to know the mental mechanisms of the person, since he will always react in the same way.

In the second group, it is assumed that cognitive processes in your brain interpret the stimulus, in a varied way according to the individual, and each individual gives the answer that he considers most appropriate.

In this second theory, the marketing professional presents arguments that are mentally processed and may or may not be accepted by the consumer, based on their past experiences and knowledge already acquired.

Theories of Memory

Memory (Solomon, 2017) is a mental mechanism of learning storage. It is composed of three elements: sensory memory, short-term memory, and long-term memory.

Sensory memory is associated with the five senses, storing information that stimulates sensitive areas of stimulus capture at a given moment, such as the skin surface, in the case of touch, or air vibrations, in the case of hearing. They receive the stimulus and transmit it, erasing it practically afterward. Neurological transmission resulting from the stimulus, that when it attracts attention, is forwarded to the short-term memory, where it will be stored for a few moments (in the order of minutes) and will be discarded if it is not interpreted as relevant. If it is relevant, it will be directed to long-term memory, where it may remain available for a long period of time. Thus, the relevant information and experiences accumulated throughout life are stored in this long-term memory.

The most accepted in memory information storage model is associative network memory, composed of nodes that represent information, and connections that connect information that have themes in common with each other. Thus, when a node is activated, the nearby information also generates the retrieval of associated information. For example, when talking about a car brand, memory can recover close associations related to different attributes of car, such as performance, power, economy, comfort, practicality, etc. The marketing professional should seek to create and strengthen positive associations between their brand and the desired attributes.

Retrieval of memory information depends on the time and time it was stored, associations with other information, and the degree of repetition of the memory storage process.

The Psychology of Luxury Consumption

The psychology of luxury consumption (Dubois et al., 2021).

> ... is governed by a set of tensions between what luxury means to the self and the external forces that define luxury consumption. These tensions shape consumer behavior, from the level of desire for luxury products and services, to the types of signals viewed as luxury and acquired and displayed as such, and to post-consumption consequences of consuming luxury.

Psychological factors, that are subjective, interact with external factors, that also depend on the story of the life of each individual and their society, driving the consumption behavior, so it is also important to study this interaction.

5.2.3 Social Factors Influencing Consumer Behavior

Social factors are associated with the social groups that the consumer attends, and their interactions with them. (Kotler & Amstrong, 2016) are reference groups, family, social roles, and status.

Reference groups (Kotler & Amstrong, 2016; Solomon, 2017) are those that directly or indirectly influence a consumer's attitudes, opinions, and behaviors.

The groups with which one interacts continuously and informally are from primary groups such as family, friends, neighbors, and co-workers.

Secondary groups are more formal and have less interaction, such as religious groups, professionals, class associations, etc.

People (Kotler & Amstrong, 2016; Solomon, 2017) are influenced by their reference groups by observing new behaviors and lifestyles and identifying with attitudes and behaviors of groups they admire and imitate.

People can also be influenced by groups they don't belong to. It may be the aspirational groups to which she would like to belong, and the dissociative groups, which she rejects and does not wish to be associated with.

Within the groups, we usually find (Kotler & Amstrong, 2016) opinion leaders, people who are recognized as knowledgeable of products and services and who have their opinions followed and valued. Their profile is usually that of highly confident, socially active people and frequent users of the category they give an opinion about.

By participating in a group, the person begins to play in him (Solomon, 2017) a certain social role, that is, a sequence of attitudes and behaviors that the group establishes as appropriate for its members and that he hopes to be followed.

The behavior and fulfillment of social roles gives the member a position, or social status, and represents their importance within that society. To indicate this position (Solomon, 2017), the member can use status symbols, and among the main ones, we find the house, the car, decorative objects, and clothing.

The family (Kotler & Amstrong, 2016; Solomon, 2017) is the primary reference group with the greatest influence on the consumer, and the most important consumer group in society.

We can distinguish two basic types of family: the orientation family, consisting of parents and siblings, where he learns the values of life in relation to factors such as religion, politics, and economy, and the family of procreation, composed of the spouse and children.

The consumption decision in the family, traditionally in the hands of the husband, has passed increasingly to the wife, and more recently, has also increased the participation of children. Children as young as five years old already know the brands and ask for those of their preference, and have an increasing budget that comes from allowances and gifts from relatives.

Practices and validations (Schrage et al., 2012) of luxury, under fluctuating social conditions over time, result in different usages, as was discussed in relation to the evolution of luxury. From a symbol of status and power, today it became more subtle, a form of social differentiation through taste (Bourdieu et al., 1987), expressing refinement and affluence, as a result of increasing social mobility. The democratization of luxury in the fourth wave breaks the association of luxury consumption and a specific social class, the highest ones. Today everyone has the right to access luxury, and luxury is for all, and not only the "virtuous".

5.2.4 Cultural Factors Influencing Consumption Behavior

Culture (Solomon, 2017) is the set of knowledge and practices of a group that have been learned and accumulated over time, in a given environment, and that are determinants for the survival and evolution of this group. It represents acceptable behaviors for the group to continue to exist.

Culture (Kotler & Amstrong, 2016) is the main determinant of a person's desires and behavior through their values.

Values (Solomon, 2017) are rules about what is worth more or less in a person's life, within a given culture. Establishes what is right or not for related actions (Kotler & Amstrong, 2016) achievement and success, disposition, efficiency, practicality, progress, material comfort, materialism and spiritualism, individualism, freedom, well-being, humanitarianism, youth, etc.

Values are important to the manager, because consumer decisions are made consistently with the values practiced by a particular culture, and therefore the promise of value, the benefits, and practices of the brand should not go against them.

Cultures (Kotler & Amstrong, 2016) are composed of subcultures, more specific groups within a culture. Among the many subcultures, we have nationalities, religions, ethnic groups, and regional groups.

Virtually all societies (Kotler & Amstrong, 2016) present social stratification and social classes (Solomon, 2017), relatively homogeneous and lasting divisions, organized hierarchically, where their members tend to present similar values, interests, and behaviors.

Each class has specific preferences for products and brands, by means of communication, and have differences in language and vocabulary.

Different criteria of social classification are possible. In Brazil the criterion of classification by social class has recently been updated, and now is based on the possession of key products, the degree of literacy, and access to basic public services. Each item corresponds to a number of points, which summed up correspond to seven extracts. Other countries use different criteria of classification, like income or culture and class behavior characteristics.

Culture influences luxury consumption through different norms, reference groups, and self-concepts (Gurzki & Woisetschläger, 2017). Different cultures have varied cultural values and norms (Hofstede, 1980) that influence the way people define and consume luxury (Dubois & Laurent, 1994).

Across markets, income and cultural affiliation seem to be positively related to luxury consumption (Dubois & Duquesne, 1993). While some characteristics of status consumption such as the brand are stable across cultures, their impact differs across countries (Shukla, 2010).

Understanding how these cultural differences influence consumer behavior is important because the perceived value of luxury goods is co-created by the consumer (Tynan et al., 2010).

5.3 Consumer Decision-Making Processes

A consumption decision (Kotler & Amstrong, 2016) is not an isolated act, but the result of a process, or sequence of activities, that can develop over a considerable period of time.

This process is described through the five-stage model of consumption decision.

Problem recognition, information search, alternatives evaluation, purchase decision, and post-purchase decision.

Based on this model, we can observe that the purchase starts well before the purchase itself, and continues even after the purchase has been made.

It should also be noted that when the search and analysis of information is more complex, this process is more time consuming, while for simple consumer decisions, such as non-durable consumer goods, for example, it can be fast.

It should also be remembered that as the purchase decision repeats, the experience gained in previous decisions is stored in memory, which can cause the following decisions to be made faster.

5.3.1 Problem Recognition

The purchasing process (Kotler & Amstrong, 2016) begins when a need, aroused by internal or external stimuli, is identified, motivating actions to satisfy it. That is, if the need is not awakened, there is no motivation for the beginning of the purchase process.

Through research, the marketing professional must know what are the stimuli that arouse needs for their products, so that they can direct their offer to them.

5.3.2 Information Search

Consumers (Kotler & Amstrong, 2016) tend to seek a limited amount of information, allowing them to evaluate their alternatives without wasting excess energy.

Generally (Solomon, 2017) information is sought until the perceived risk in the purchase is reduced to an acceptable level.

The information is obtained from internal sources (memory, which stores learning from previous experiences) and external sources.

The four main external sources of information used by decision-makers are:

- Personal—family, friends, neighbors, acquaintances. Usually, these closer personal people have good credibility and are often consulted in decisions.
- Commercials—advertising, websites, sellers, representatives, packaging, showcases. People consider these sources of less credibility, since they know that they are paid by the brand and presented seeking to positively influence it in the purchase. But they are used in the decision, because consumers assume that regulatory communication bodies do not allow exaggeration in their information.
- Public—mass media (reporters, journalists, interviewed experts), consumer classification organizations.
- Experiential—handling, examination, use of the product. They often have a strong effect on product evaluations because they are considered independent.

The search process starts from the main known brands, and as the information is obtained, a part can be discarded from the process of choice, if it does not meet the desired prerequisites of the product, resulting in a set of candidates for consumption, which become alternatives to be evaluated in the next step.

It is important that the manager, through surveys, identifies how their target audience seeks this information, so that they can provide it at the appropriate time. And you should also know the information that is used to select the alternatives, so that your product is among them.

5.3.3 Alternatives Evaluation

The information collected (Kotler & Amstrong, 2016; Solomon, 2017) is used to develop consumer beliefs and attitudes.

Belief (Kotler & Amstrong, 2016) is the descriptive thinking that someone keeps about something. That is, it is what she came to believe about this object, based on the information analyzed.

Attitudes (Kotler & Amstrong, 2016) are evaluations, feelings, and predispositions of action lasting, favorable or not, in relation to some object or idea.

From what the consumer believes and has developed appreciation, he will evaluate the amount he can receive from each alternative.

The value expectation model (Kotler & Amstrong, 2016) proposes that the perceived value used in the evaluation of a product is evaluated in the value of the positive and negative beliefs of a brand, weighted by the importance attributed to them.

5.3.4 Purchase Decision

The purchase decision (Kotler & Amstrong, 2016) evaluates five basic elements of the sale: the brand, the point of sale, the quantity to be purchased, the time the purchase will be made, and the form of payment.

Several choice models have been identified as being used by the consumer, which can be divided into two groups, compensatory and non-compensatory models.

In compensatory models, a low perceived value attribute can be compensated by another high value one, for example, an automobile that does not have high performance but is economical.

In non-compensatory models, there is a minimum perceived cut-off value, and if any of them are not reached, the alternative is excluded. For example, when buying a computer, it can be established that the RAM must be at least 8 Mb, and any model with lower RAM will be discarded.

The final decision will then fall to the product that has the best total perceived value.

5.3.5 Post-Purchase Behavior

After the acquisition of the best evaluated alternative (Kotler & Amstrong, 2016), the consumer moves on to its use, evaluating their satisfaction with their decision, and eventually discarding the product.

The use creates the consumption experience, which will be evaluated, and determines the moment of replacement. The marketing professional should check the period it takes for the product to be consumed, in order to evaluate how to offer its replacement.

Satisfaction with the decision will be a function of the comparison that the consumer will make between their expectations and the effective performance of consumption. If this assessment is positive, there is a greater possibility of the purchase being repeated and customer loyalty.

Disposal (Solomon, 2017) can be done by reselling in a secondary used market or shipping for recycling of raw materials. The marketing professional should evaluate the weights of the different destinations, consider the competition of the used market for their new products, and must develop and maintain the necessary structure for the recycling of the total discarded volume carried out.

5.3.6 Decision-Making in Luxury

According to the different industry and market characteristics, luxury brand managers must understand customer behavior including experience, satisfaction, and decision-making behaviors for consumption to achieve sustainable growth (Park & Ahn, 2021).

With a wide array of services (Siahtiri et al., 2022) directing their luxury and status appeal, consumers must make choices in an increasingly contested marketspace (Wirtz et al., 2020).

For luxury services (Siahtiri et al., 2022), consideration set size is an important brand performance measure that has important implications for marketers as it determines a brand's market performance. The consideration set size is moderated by the service brand's status. The effect of self-identification on consideration set size is mediated by the positive anticipated emotions consumers expect to experience when using the service.

Four factors of influence (Husic & Cicic, 2009; Uzgoren & Guney, 2012) in decision-making in the consumption of luxury products include luxury brands, patron status, fashions, and experiences, being the brand and status symbol factors with higher influence rate.

5.4 Summary

We saw in this chapter that consumption behavior is influenced by several factors, which can be gathered into four major groups: personal factors, psychological factors, social factors, and cultural factors. Influenced by these factors, a consumption decision develops from a five-step process: problem recognition, search for information, evaluation of alternatives, purchase decision, and post-purchase behavior.

Luxury consumption decision-making is a complex process that depends on these four factors, and their study is fundamental to provide insights for the manager.

Bibliography

Bourdieu, P. et al. (1987). *Distinction. A social critique of the judgement of taste*. Harvard University Press.

Dubois, B., & Duquesne, P. (1993). The market for luxury goods: Income versus culture. *European Journal of marketing, 27*, 35–44.

Dubois, B., & Laurent, G. (1994). Attitudes towards the concept of luxury: An exploratory analysis. *ACR Asia-Pacific Advances*.

Dubois, D., Jung, S. J., & Ordabayeva, N. (2021). The psychology of luxury consumption. *Current Opinion in Psychology, 39*, 82–87.

Gurzki, H., & Woisetschläger, D. M. (2017). Mapping the luxury research landscape: A bibliometric citation analysis. *Journal of Business Research, 77*, 147–166.

Healy, K. (2016). A theory of human motivation by Abraham H. Maslow (1942). *The British Journal of Psychiatry, 208*(4), 313–313.

Hofstede, G. (1980). Motivation, leadership, and organization: Do American theories apply abroad? *Organizational Dynamics, 9*(1), 42–63.

Bibliography

Husic, M., & Cicic, M. (2009). Luxury consumption factors. *Journal of Fashion Marketing and Management: An International Journal, 13*, 231–245.

Kotler, P., & Amstrong, G. (2016). *Principles of marketing* (16th Edn.). Pearson.

Nia, A., Lynne Zaichkowsky, J. (2000). Do counterfeits devalue the ownership of luxury brands? *Journal of Product & Brand Management, 9*(7), 485–497.

Park, J., & Ahn, J. (2021). Editorial introduction: Luxury services focusing on marketing and management. *Journal of Retailing and Consumer Services, 58*, 102257.

Schrage, D., et al. (2012). The domestication of luxury in social theory. *Social Change Review, 10*(2), 177–193.

Shukla, P. (2010). Status consumption in cross-national context: Socio-psychological, brand and situational antecedents. *International Marketing Review, 27*, 108–219.

Siahtiri, V., O'cass, A., & Nabi, N. (2022). Unlocking consumer consideration set size formation for luxury services: A study of self-identification, brand status and anticipated emotions. *International Journal of Consumer Studies, 46*, 2488–2502.

Solomon, M. R. (2017). *Consumer behavior: Buying, having, and being*. Pearson.

Tynan, C., Mckechnie, S., & Chhuon, C. (2010). Co-creating value for luxury brands. *Journal of Business Research, 63*(11), 1156–1163.

Uzgoren, E., & Guney, T. (2012). The snop effect in the consumption of luxury goods. *Procedia-Social and Behavioral Sciences, 62*, 628–637.

Wirtz, J., Holmqvist, J., & Fritze, M. P. (2020). Luxury services. *Journal of Service Management, 31*, 665–691.

Zhang, W., et al. (2019). Consumers' implicit motivation of purchasing luxury brands: An EEG study. *Psychology Research and Behavior Management, 12*, 913.

Defining the Persona: Segmentation and Targeting

6.1 Introduction

Chapter Objectives
In this chapter the importance of segmenting consumers is highlighted, using the appropriate strategies and methodologies for segmenting markets, evaluating attractiveness, and selecting the best targets.

This selected target will constitute the Persona, a concept that presents a detailed profile of a typical member of this segment.

In conclusion, we discuss luxury consumers segments identified in the literature and present the results of a metastudy that identified the twelve global luxury segments (Ostentators, Imitators, Exclusivists, Oriented to quality, Experientials, Cradle of gold, Luxury tourists, Oriented to technology, Luxury democrats, Social Wearer, Little Prince and Fashionistas), based on a metanalysis of over 25 different articles on luxury consumers segmentation.

6.2 Targeting, Evaluating, and Selecting

One of the company's main strategic decisions involves choosing the target markets where the company intends to operate. To do this, it must develop a market segmentation.

In summary, identifying different subgroups, put together by similar characteristics. From the total number of segments, those that do not meet certain criteria should be dismissed. The segment should have needs that are within the company's objectives and values. The activation shouldn't demand more resources than what the company has available or could access in case of need. Their sales should present the desired profitability and growth potential. After screening the potential candidates, the remaining shall or not be selected, according to their attractiveness and available competences.

6.3 Why Target Segments and Not Attend the Whole Market

In the discussion in the previous chapter on consumer, we saw how different people are and their choices are subjective, depending on their characteristics, their environment, and their life history. Acting in the market with a unique product, without taking into account this diversity of needs and desires, can lead to offering sub-optimal products that do not truly satisfy any given consumer.

To avoid this problem, after we have known the markets that strategic planning has indicated as priorities, we have identified subgroups of consumers that have similar characteristics.

These subgroups are called market segments, and being homogeneous, we have greater success if we create specific marketing plans for each of them, which has been called target market marketing.

Market Segmentation (Semenik & Bamossy, 1995) is:

> ... the process of taking the total heterogeneous market (diverse) and its division into smaller segments or subgroups that are more homogeneous (similar) in the physical and behavioral characteristics related to the purchase of the company's products or services.

For effective target market marketing (Kotler & Amstrong, 2016), marketing managers need to:

- Identify and profile distinct customer segments that differ between groups in their needs and preferences
- Select one or more segments of interest for company entry
- Identify for each segment the main benefits that differentiate the company's products, to define market positioning.

This process of segment definition, selection of target markets and establishment of positioning are the main strategic marketing activities, and that will serve as the basis for the decisions of the marketing compound.

6.4 How to Segment Consumer Markets

The construction of the segments (Churchill & Peter, 2017; Kotler & Amstrong, 2016) is based on the variables where the segments have the greatest diversity.

These variables most common in marketing studies can be grouped into five bases, or sets of segmentation variables: geographic, demographic, psychographic, behavioral, and media.

6.4.1 Geographical Segmentation

Geographic segmentation uses variables associated with the description of the Earth and its regions. The main geographical units (Churchill & Peter, 2017; Kotler & Amstrong, 2016) are nations, regions, states, cities and neighborhoods, demographic density, climate, etc.

Climate and geographic morphology have strong effects on behavior. Natural geographical barriers, such as rivers and mountains (Solomon et al., 2017), or artificial barriers such as highways and walls, can cause groups to be isolated and develop different habits. The availability of resources in each region, for example, such as coastal fishing or mountain hunting, can influence eating habits.

Tappert (2007) defines geomarketing as the …

> … *optimization of marketing and sales through the application of a geographic information system.*

According to Schlüssler (2000), geomarketing includes …

> … planning, coordination, and control of companies' customer-oriented marketing activities through a GIS. (geographic information system)

It is an approach to marketing that allows the adaptation of the marketing mix to the way the market organizes itself in space, that is, allows the analysis of variables relevant to marketing through the visualization of this data in geographic maps. The mapping allows the identification of concentration points of the analyzed variables, allowing the analysis more quickly, visually.

6.4.2 Demographic Segmentation

Demographic segmentation, one of the basest formats of segmentation, is based on the characteristics of the population (Churchill & Peter, 2017; Kotler & Amstrong, 2016) and its individuals: age, sex, income, occupation, education level, family life cycle, religion, race, ethnicity, generation, nationality, and social class.

They are variables that are easy to measure and tend to be correlated with different patterns and consumption behaviors.

Here are some of the variables (Kotler & Amstrong, 2016) used in segmented markets:

- Age and stage in the **life cycle**—desires and energy vary throughout the growth of the individual, as well as changes in their physique, changing their consumption preferences. In the clothing market, for example, we have clothes for newborns, under one son, under five, schoolchildren, teenagers, and so on.

- **Phase of life**—the phase of life defines the main concern of a person, such as living alone or with another person, going through divorce or second marriage, caring for elderly children or parents, etc., and their consumption will be focused on solutions to these concerns.
- **Sex**—men and women present different attitudes and behaviors, due to genetic traits and their socialization process. Women have a more community profile, men are more individualistic and have goals. Men like to read information about a product, women often relate to a product on a more personal level. Women control or influence most consumer decisions of goods and services.
- **Income**—Income represents the average individual or family revenue. Once the taxes have been paid, part is directed to pay fixed commitments, such as rents, and the rest is divided between consumption and savings. The value focused on consumption is also known as discretionary income, the one which will really activate the consumer economy. It should be remembered that people with the same income do not always have the same spending pattern, because they have different lifestyles.
- **Generation**—a generation is a group of people who were born at the same time, who were influenced by the time they were born, through music, politics, and events of the period, and who share important cultural, political, and economic experiences.
- **Race and culture**—different ethnic and cultural segments present different needs and desires, requiring specific actions through multicultural marketing.

Major demographic generations:
Several studies in recent decades have identified different demographic generations and their influence and consumption behaviors. The main ones (Kotler & Amstrong, 2016) are:

Generation Alpha—those born after 2010 have already been called Generation Alpha. Regarding the most recent generation, research is beginning to help understand their characteristics and differences, as for instance, they should probably tend to prefer learning through games and projects with heavy use of technology, but this is just one of several speculations that have been discussed at the moment.
Generation Z—those born between 1995 and 2010. It is the zapping generation (which means that they are multiscreen and swap among various gadgets, such as TV, Internet, streaming, mobile, games, mp3 players, etc.). They are digital natives, were born and find natural the use of technology in everyday life, being very influenced by its various forms and the digital influencers they follow frequently.
Generation Y—also known as millennials, are those born between 1979 and 1994, were raised in a period of relative wealth, have technical knowledge and are connected practically since birth on the Internet, care about social and environmental issues, with a strong sense of independence, and are selective and confident.

Generation X—born between 1964 and 1978, are considered an intermediate generation between the two that precedes and succeeds, having lived the beginning of technology in life and consumption, and the part of the recession phase of the economy, are pragmatic and individualistic. They consider themselves self-sufficient and able to deal with any situation.

Baby boomers—are born between 1946 (end of World War II) and 1964. They have high purchasing power and account for three-quarters of US wealth. Entering the 60s and 70s, they are experiencing a return to the past, being large consumers of products that prevent aging, and consumer goods in general.

6.4.3 Psychographic Segmentation

Psychographic segmentation (Kotler & Amstrong, 2016; Solomon et al., 2017) divides consumers based on psychological and personality traits, lifestyles, and values.

One of the most popular psychographic segmentation systems is VALS, from Strategic Business Insights.

VALS is a system that classifies consumers into eight groups, based on four demographic questions and thirty-five adhering questions.

The main dimensions of the VALS are the motivation of the consumer, in the horizontal axis, which can be principles, achievement, or self-expression, and, in the vertical axis, the available resources.

The eight groups are divided into two groups, those with high resources and those with low resources.

Those with high resources are:

- **Innovative**—successful, sophisticated, active, and with high self-esteem. They have refined taste and consume luxury products
- **Satisfied**—mature, satisfied, reflective, motivated by ideals, value order, knowledge and responsibility, seek durability, functionality, and value in products
- **Successful**—goal-oriented filmmakers focused on family and career, prefer prestigious products, social status symbols
- **Experimenters**—young, enthusiastic, and impulsive, seek variety and enthusiasm, seek clothes and accessories for fashion, entertainment, and socialization.

Those with scarce resources are:

- **Believers**—conservative, conventional, and traditional, prefer family products, of national manufacture, are faithful to established brands.
- **Battlers**—follow the latest fashion, enjoy fun, but are limited to available resources, consume aspirational brands

- **Doers**—practical, realistic, self-sufficient, prefer basic products, of national manufacture, that are practical and functional.
- **Survivors**—older, more resigned, face changes with concern and are trustees to their favorite brands.

This segmentation can be useful in at least two ways: for a company that is in a market, it can identify which segments often buy their products most often, and use profile information to make adjustments to their offering, and for companies that want to enter a market, observe which segments want products with the company's competencies profile, and direct their actions to them.

6.4.4 Behavioral Segmentation

Behavioral segmentation (Kotler & Amstrong, 2016; Solomon et al., 2017) divides consumers into subgroups, based on variables related to the purchasing process, such as their degree of knowledge, attitudes toward the product to be purchased, experience of use and reactions to the product.

The main behavioral segmentation variables are:

- **Needs and benefits**—for the same product, it is possible that different consumers are seeking to meet different needs, and therefore the expected benefits will be different. The toothpaste market is an example, where we can find this product offering several benefits, such as leaving white and shiny teeth, preventing cavities, avoiding bad breath, removing yellowish from the cigarette, whitening teeth, and reducing sensitivity, among others.
- **Decision roles**—it is also possible to have collegiate purchase, where different people perform different roles: initiator, influencer, decision-maker, buyer, and user. Predominantly, women play a strong decision-making role in the consumption of the family, from the husband's clothes, the feeding of the children, to the car, and the decoration of the house. Identifying decision-makers (and also other roles) in the purchasing process is critical to properly targeting marketing actions.
- **Variables related to use**—we can highlight several variables related to use that are relevant for effective market segmentation:
  - *Occasions*—occasions of purchase may be associated with activities of a given temporal moment, such as time, and which tend to be routine, or to the motivation that led to that occasion, such as special events such as travel, business, meeting with family or friends, etc. Consumption on special occasions tends to be different from that in routine situations, with different consumer choices, so the importance of your knowledge to direct marketing actions

- *Status as a user*—depending on the degree of familiarity and use of the product, markets can be segmented into non-users, potential users (prospects), new users, frequent users, and former users, each with different attitudes, values, and behaviors.
- *Degree of use*—depending on the intensity of product use, we can have segments of light users (low frequency of consumption), medium users, and heavy users (high frequency of consumption)
- *Stage of consumption disposition*—when a new brand enters the market, it is not yet known, until the marketing actions begin, when the consumer goes through the following stages below:
    Know but have not tried
    Have tried once
    Consumes occasionally
    Consumes frequently
    Consumes very often
- *Degree of loyalty*—brand loyalty makes the consumer have a different tendency to repeat their consumption again, as well as to indicate to others. We can have four groups:
    Very trustable—always buy the same brand
    Divided faithful—buys between two or three preferred brands
    Fickle—has low degree of loyalty and changes brand frequently
    Infidels—no brand loyalty, are primarily geared toward price and convenience
- *Attitudes toward the product*—the attitude is a position that the person has in relation to an aspect of a product, and that can be positive or negative, to different degrees:
    Enthusiast—defends and disseminates the product
    Positive attitude
    Indifferent attitude
    Negative attitude
    Hostile—always takes advantage of opportunities to attack and criticize the product.

As an example of segmentation by needs and benefits in the premium wine market, Kotler and Amstrong (2016) describes a survey developed by Constellation Brands, where it can be observed the variety of needs and benefits that consumers seek in the same product:

- **Enthusiasts**—12% of the market, female predominance, average annual income of about US$ 76,000, great knowledge about wines
- **Satisfied**—14% of the market, do not know much about the market, tend to buy the same brands, 50% of their consumption is white wine of zinfandel grape.

- **Experienced buyers**—15% of the market, love shopping, believe that it is not necessary to spend a lot to have a good wine, like to take advantage of promotions
- **Traditionalists**—16% of the market, predominantly women, average age of 50 years, their values are strongly traditional, like to buy brands they know or have heard of, from older wineries.
- **Self-centered**—20% of the market, higher percentage of men, average age of 35 years, consume wine as a form of expression of their identity, and pay for the product that meets this need
- **Overwhelmed**—23% of the market, find it difficult to buy wine. Being the largest segment, they can be a market opportunity for companies that can establish good communication with them, teaching and simplifying the purchasing process.

In practice, this type of research is conducted with the use of the multivariate statistical techniques of cluster analysis.

6.4.5 Media Usage Segmentation

A form of segmentation that is little used, but which can also be effective for dividing segments (Robertson et al., 1984), especially when combined with the previous ones, is based on consumer media consumption, that is, through which media or media the consumer receives his information. Each media, depending on its content and frequency, attracts different consumers, and this knowledge is important to direct marketing communication to the media that are consumed most frequently by its target market.

Theater as a media, for example, reaches only a small portion of the population, usually of higher educational and income levels, which may justify a sponsorship or a specific communication action for products focused on this profile.

A soap opera on a national TV network, on the other hand, reaches broad profiles of the population and can be indicated for mass consumer products.

6.5 Criteria to Evaluate Potential Targets

These various evaluation bases allow you to segment the market in multiple ways.

However, not all segmentation is relevant to obtain segments that really reflect the diversity of subgroups in the market.

Kotler and Amstrong (2016) and Churchill and Peters (2017) propose five criteria to assess whether a particular segmentation strategy will be useful for discriminating between the different subgroups. The segment has to be:

- **Measurable**—it is important that there exist operational ways to measure the segment characteristics, such as in the case of size, purchasing power, and characteristics of the consumer profile
- **Substantial**—the segment must have enough size and potential to justify its selection as a candidate for the company's performance. Very small segments may not be able to deliver the desired return.
- **Accessible**—it should be possible to reach and meet this segment
- **Differentiable**—segments must exhibit different behaviors and different responses from each other.
- **Actionable**—it should be possible to develop effective marketing programs to attract and serve the segments.

6.6 How to Evaluate and Select Targets

The segmentation process only divides a big market into smaller subgroups.

The next activity, now that we know the number and characteristics of each segment, is the evaluation and selection process (also known as Targeting) of each segment, so that only the best ones where the company should operate are chosen.

6.6.1 Target Market Valuation

Identifying multiple market segments doesn't imply that a company should work with all of them, as some be very interesting, and other not profitable at all. For this analysis of which ones to serve, evaluation criteria should be established. This evaluation should be based on two basic criteria, the attractiveness of the segment, and the competencies of the company.

Attractiveness means defining whether it is feasible and profitable to enter this segment, and can be evaluated in several ways, which generally involve a system of assignment of points, within a scale, depending on market size, growth rate, size and potential volume, position in the product life cycle, profitability rate, degree of risk, potential for economies of scale, among others metrics. This evaluation will result in a ranking of the attractiveness of each segment.

The company's competencies represent the knowledge of its personnel, the strategic decisions and objectives of the company's performance, and the resources it has available, or has the capacity to obtain, and its cultural and ethical values.

The segments evaluated for attractiveness should now be evaluated based on these competency criteria, and those that do not meet them are discarded.

6.6.2 Target Market Selection

The previous step resulted in a certain number of segments, which meet the company's competencies and are hierarchical by its potential.

The company has three basic strategic alternatives to make this choice:

- Total market coverage—the company chooses to meet all selected segments, adopting for each one a specific marketing strategy, with a product developed to measure and the other components of the marketing mix adjusted to its characteristics. By the volume of resources demanded, only large companies can choose this strategy
- Multi-segment expertise—the company chooses only a few of the segments, within its available resource constraints and desired minimum profitability
- Concentration in a single segment—the company chooses only that segment that, in its evaluation, is the best of all. It develops a deep knowledge of this segment and directs all its resources and competencies in its characteristics, seeking leadership in this segment and the practice of premium prices.

6.7 Luxury Segmentation

The luxury market is a relevant global market that has consistently grown over the last years at attractive rates, as seen in a previous chapter. The literature has responded to this demand by developing segmentation studies of different geographical, sectorial, cultural, and temporal luxury markets, but each of them have only explored segments existing in their own countries and in specific context. The opportunity has matured to conduct a study aggregating common segment profiles over these markets.

Luxury is a global market and the description of global segments would be an important tool for supporting marketing managers in making their strategic decisions. Segmentation is an important productivity tool for companies to tune their offer to the market, preventing waste in investments on irrelevant attributes and accumulation of stocks of unsold products, and generating more satisfaction for the consumers. This knowledge is particularly important in the luxury market, where consumers expect a very personal, customized experience.

In this session, it is identified and aggregated different segments in the luxury market already identified in the literature, based on consumer behavior variables, into metasegments of similar profiles that could base a proposition of a global segmentation of luxury consumers.

Metanalysis (Egger & Smith, 1997; Marck, 1967; Martinez, 2007) is a research technique that aims to analyze and combine many different studies related to a specific hypothesis, integrating the results of a systematic review. Metasegments were identified based on common characteristics present in each cluster described in each article.

In this case, 25 articles that conducted segmentation of luxury consumers were analyzed, identifying almost 50 segment profiles. The main characteristics of each segment were compiled, in search of common traces, based on the segmentation variable used, the variable category (demographic income, net assets, profession, age, education, product category) or socio-behavioral (status, lifestyle, motivation, attitudes, values, and semiotic repertoire), resulting in twelve metasegments, presented in Table 6.1:

This analysis shows that after a few decades of academic interest, luxury segmentation has been object of several studies in different countries, industrial sectors, cultures, and moments, resulting in a mature body of knowledge ready to be integrated in a systematic way.

Five demographic and seven socio-behavioral variables have been used in the clustering techniques of the selected studies, reflecting the complexity of these consumers.

Common segments do exist and the twelve different profiles found in the study allow the proposition of a global segmentation model of luxury consumers.

They can be used as an initial basis for marketing strategic decisions of global companies competing in the luxury market, aligning the marketing mix to specific benefits sought by each metasegment. Companies could expect to find each segment in any new market, and have specific global corporative strategies for acting in each of them, aligning their efforts and achieving higher productivity. If a segment is not found in a specific country, it could be an indication of possible dormant markets that could be nurtured and explored in the future.

6.8 Summary

The company's main strategic decisions involve the choice of target markets within the market where the company wishes to operate. Market segmentation identifies subgroups that are different from each other, but composed of members of a similar profile. From the total number of segments, those that do not meet the company's ethical and cultural objectives and values are discarded, require resources that it does not have and that do not present the desired financial profitability. Applying these restrictions, the company will decide to act in one, some, or all of the segments that meet its attractiveness and competency criteria.

Table 6.1 Segments and descriptive variables

	Metasegment	Common key characteristics	Statistical segment	Variable category	Segmentation variable	Authors
1	Ostentators	Buy by impulse; Consume where they can be seen; Want to show "I've made it"	Veblenians	Socio-behavioral	Status	Vigneron and Johnson (2004)
			Nouveau Riches	Demographic, Socio-behavioral	Income, Status	Solomon et al. (2017)
		Buy by vanity; Consume to exhibit and reinforce social position	Exhibitionists	Socio-behavioral	Motivation	Castarède (2006)
			Ego-defended achievers	Socio-behavioral	Status, Motivation	Chan et al. (2014)
		Know the five top brands, but their codes	Medialites	Demographic, Socio-behavioral	Income, Status	Geargeoura (1997)
		Prefer showy products, big logos, big watches Follow influencers, in particular the "*fashionistas*"	The Extravagant Prestige-Seekers	Socio-behavioral	Values	Wiedmann et al. (2009)
		Potential consumers of counterfeit products	Luxury as reward	Socio-behavioral	Status	Gardyn (2002)

(continued)

6.8 Summary

Table 6.1 (continued)

	Metasegment	Common key characteristics	Statistical segment	Variable category	Segmentation variable	Authors
2	Imitators	Aspire to belong to a higher group	Bandwagon followers	Socio-behavioral	Status	Vigneron and Johnson (2004)
		Influenced by superiors, celebrities, and media influencers	Intermediary luxury	Socio-behavioral	Product category	Allérès (1991)
		Buy what the references use or endorse Luxury is the key to be accepted in higher circles	Fashion victims	Socio-behavioral	Motivation	Brun and Castelli (2013)
		Consume well-known brands that are status symbols				
		Conservative, buy good value for money (duty-free, outlets, thrift shops)				
3	Exclusivists	Prefer products that others don't have	Snobs	Socio-behavioral	Status	Vigneron and Johnson (2004)
		Is concerned with being different from anyone else	conspicuous fashionistas	Socio-behavioral	Status	Chan et al. (2014)
		Like to be the first to have	Elitists	Socio-behavioral	Semiotic repertoire	Dubois et al. (2005)
		Want unique, bespoken products	Exclusivists	Socio-behavioral	Lifestyle, Values	Hemzo and Silva (2009)
		Like the experience with the creator				

(continued)

Table 6.1 (continued)

	Metasegment	Common key characteristics	Statistical segment	Variable category	Segmentation variable	Authors
4	Oriented to quality	They value superior performance Prefer higher quality products and services Want the best money can buy	Quality lovers	Socio-behavioral	Motivation	Brun and Castelli (2013)
			Perfectionists	Socio-behavioral	Status	Vigneron and Johnson (2004)
			Utilititarians	Socio-behavioral	Motivation	Castarède (2006)
			Functional luxury	Socio-behavioral	Status	Gardyn (2002)
			Rational Functionalists	Socio-behavioral	Values	Wiedmann et al. (2009)
5	Experientials	They value "the experience" Want to have pleasure in the consumption They want to "feel good" Look for self-gratification Want to have emotions Want to try new sensations Value the hedonic side of luxury Prefer luxury traveling and dining to buying	Hedonists	Socio-behavioral	Motivation	Brun and Castelli (2013)
			Shopping hedonists	Socio-behavioral	Status	Chan et al. (2014)
			Hedonists	Socio-behavioral	Status	Vigneron and Johnson (2004)
			Viventials	Socio-behavioral	Motivation	Castarède (2006)
			The Introvert Hedonists	Socio-behavioral	Values	Wiedmann et al. (2009)
			Indulgence luxury	Socio-behavioral	Status	Gardyn (2002)

(continued)

6.8 Summary

Table 6.1 (continued)

	Metasegment	Common key characteristics	Statistical segment	Variable category	Segmentation variable	Authors
6	Cradle of gold	Have an extensive luxury culture	Extreme affluents	Socio-behavioral	Motivation	Danziger (2005)
		Have acquired the luxury culture in infancy from parents	Old money	Demographic, Socio-behavioral	Income, Status	Solomon et al. (2017)
		Luxury consumption is a day-to-day consolidated habit	Inaccessible luxury	Socio-behavioral	Product category	Allérès (1991)
		The luxury consumption happens in a specific cultural context	Traditionalists	Socio-behavioral	Values	Hemzo and Silva (2009)
		Brand preference is part of a family tradition				
		They master the luxury signs, the semiotic contents				
		Prefer sports like golf, equestrianism, and yachting				

(continued)

Table 6.1 (continued)

	Metasegment	Common key characteristics	Statistical segment	Variable category	Segmentation variable	Authors
7	Luxury tourists	Have low, sporadic annual luxury consumption, as their income doesn't allow more	Luxury Coconners	Socio-behavioral	Motivation	Danziger (2005)
			Get Set	Demographic, Socio-behavioral	Income, Status	Solomon et al. (2017)
		Can consume luxury as they wished	Almost rich	Socio-behavioral	Motivation	Gardyn (2002)
		They "can't have the luxury kitchen so they buy the luxury brand's knife"	High medium class	Demographic, Socio-behavioral	Income, Status	Geargeoura (1997)
		They mix luxury brands with fashion brands	Accessible luxury	Socio-behavioral	Product category	Allérès (1991)
		Are afraid not to be dressed as well as their pairs or clients	Luxury Aspirers	Socio-behavioral	Values	Hemzo and Silva (2009)
		Don't belong to the universe of luxury, but know the top five brands				
		Possible consumers of thrift shops and counterfeits				
		Consumers of accessible luxury: perfumes, cosmetics, and entry luxury clothes				

(continued)

6.8 Summary

Table 6.1 (continued)

	Metasegment	Common key characteristics	Statistical segment	Variable category	Segmentation variable	Authors
8	Oriented to technology	They value technology and modernity Technical aspects are predominant in the product evaluation and selection Associate technology with luxury	Technomoderns	Socio-behavioral	Motivation, Values	Hemzo and Silva (2009)
			Addicted to technology	Socio-behavioral	Motivation	Brun and Castelli (2013)
9	Luxury democrats	They believe that "luxury should be accessible to everyone", without prejudice See luxury consumption as a good thing that should be shared with family and friends Luxury is a fair reward for those that worked hard Luxury are the best things in life and should be lived without excesses	Democratics	Socio-behavioral	Semiotic repertoire	Dubois et al. (2005)
			Transferrers	Socio-behavioral	Motivation	Castarède (2006)
			Discreets	Socio-behavioral	Values	Hemzo and Silva (2009)
			Materialists	Socio-behavioral	Values	Wiedmann et al. (2009)

(continued)

Table 6.1 (continued)

	Metasegment	Common key characteristics	Statistical segment	Variable category	Segmentation variable	Authors
10	Social Wearer	Value sustainability, innovation, and charity. Do a lot of research before buying a brand, and can be very loyal to them	Social Wearer	Socio-behavioral	Motivation, Values	D'Arpizio (2017, 2018)
		Typically consumes clothes, bags, food, and wine	Green consumers	Socio-behavioral	Motivation, Values	Kang et al. (2012)
11	Little Prince	Children of well-succeeded parents, from the generation Z, cosmopolitan, digital natives, connected, frequent users of social media	Little Prince	Socio-behavioral	Motivation, Values	D'Arpizio (2017, 2018)
		Value fun, hedonic, innovative, and cool products	Generation Z	Socio-behavioral	Motivation, Values	Mabuni (2017)
		Consumers of esthetics and lifestyle products, clothes, accessories, and leather goods				
		Insecure, anxious, impulsive				
		The brand is more important than quality, demand esthetics and design				

(continued)

6.8 Summary

Table 6.1 (continued)

	Metasegment	Common key characteristics	Statistical segment	Variable category	Segmentation variable	Authors
12	Fashionistas	First to know new brands, new trends, new designers, value details Motivated by the fashion and sexy side of luxury Trendsetters, strong and defined opinions Like to go out, look at window shops and hunt novelties Emotional, impulsive, value art and design Consumers of personal luxury: perfumes, clothes, bags, shoes, and cosmetics	Fashionistas	Socio-behavioral	Motivation, Values	D'Arpizio (2017, 2018)
			Fashionistas	Socio-behavioral	Motivation, Values	Jin and Ryu (2019)

Bibliography

Allères, D. (1991). *Luxe...stratègies.* Economica.
Brun, A., & Castelli, C. (2013). The nature of luxury: A consumer perspective. *International Journal of Retail and Distribution Management, 41,* 823–847.
Castarède, J. (2006). *Apresentação Seminários sobre o Luxo ESPM* [Presentation Seminar on Luxury]. São Paulo.
Chan, W. W. Y., Chester, K. M. T., Chu, A. W. C, & Zhang, Z. (2014). Behavioral determinants that drive luxury goods consumption: A study within the tourist context. *Research Journal of Textile and Apparel. 18*(2), 84–95.
Churchill, G. A., & Peter, J. P. (2017). *Marketing.* Saraiva Educação SA.
Danziger, P. G. (2005). *Let them eat cake: Marketing luxury to the masses—As well as the classes.* Dearborn.
D'Arpizio, C. (2017). Bain & Co. luxury goods. *Worldwide Market Study.*
D'Arpizio, C. (2018). Bain & Co. luxury goods. *Worldwide Market Study.*
Dubois, B., Czellar, S., & Laurent, G. (2005). Consumer segments based on attitudes toward luxury: Empirical evidence from twenty countries. *Marketing Letters, 16*(2), 115–128.
Egger, M., & Smith, G. D. (1997). Meta-analysis: Potentials and promise. *British Medical Journal, 315*(7119), 1371–1374.
Gardyn, R. (2002). Oh, the good life. *American Demographics, 24*(10), 31.
Geargeoura, L. J. (1997). *Marketing para Bens de Luxo. Um estudo exploratório no setor de objetos de viagem, couro e acessórios de moda – o caso Luis Vuitton* [Master's thesis, Faculdade de Economia e Administração da Universidade de São Paulo, São Paulo].
Hemzo, M. A., & Silva, A. P. de O. (2009). *Um Estudo Exploratório do Novo Luxo: Fatores e Segmentos de Valores e Motivações dos Consumidores.* XXXIII ENANPAD – Encontro da Associação Nacional de Pós-Graduação e Pesquisa em Administração, São Paulo.
Jin, S. V., & Ryu, E. (2019). Instagram fashionistas, luxury visual image strategies and vanity. *Journal of Product & Brand Management, 29*(3), 355–368.
Kang, K. H., Stein, L., Heo, C. Y., & Lee, S. (2012). Consumers' willingness to pay for green initiatives of the hotel industry. *International Journal of Hospitality Management, 31*(2), 564–572.
Kotler, P., & Armstrong, G. (2016). *Principles of marketing* (16th Edn.). Pearson.
Mabuni, L. (2017). *Exploring the meaning of luxury to Gen Z.*
Marck, L. M. (1967). *Metanalysis* [Dissertation, New York University].
Martinez, E. Z. (2007). Metanálise de ensaios clínicos controlados aleatorizados: aspectos quantitativos. *Medicina (Ribeirão Preto. Online), 40*(2), 223–235.
Robertson, T. S., Zielinki, J., & Ward, S. (1984). *Consumer behavior.* Scott, Foresman and Company.
Schlüssler, F. (2000). *Geomarketing: Anwendung geographischer Informationssysteme im Einzelhandel* [Zugl.: Gießen, Univ., Diss.]. Tectum-Verl.
Semenik, R. J. & Bamossy, G. J. (1995). *Marketing principles: A global perspective.* Makron Books.
Solomon, M. R., et al. (2017). *Consumer behavior: Buying, having, and being.* Pearson.
Tappert, W. (2007). *Geomarketing in der Praxis.* Harzer.
Vigneron, F., & Johnson, L. W. (2004). Measuring perceptions of brand luxury. *Journal of Brand Management, 11*(6), 484–506.
Wiedmann, K.-P., Hennigs, N., & Siebels, A. (2009). Value-based segmentation of luxury consumption behavior. *Psychology & Marketing, 26*(7), 625–651.

Developing Strong Luxury Brands for Products and Services

7.1 Introduction

Chapter Objectives
In the next two chapters it is described the processes related to designing luxury brands and products and services attributes: Creating strong brands, Developing Brand Equity, New product development, Innovation, and Creativity, and includes a new discussion on the role of the creative director, how it evolved and the new demands he has to fulfill. It is discussed the main aspects of defining branding strategies and brand logos (fonts and colors) and the importance of Packaging, its functions, and strategies.

7.2 Creating Strong Brands

Brands are of fundamental importance to the financial success of a company. The brands represent the memories and associations that consumers have developed in their experience with the product, and that they use as a reference for their future relationships with it, generating the repetition of the purchase and loyalty.

The creation of the brand equity of a product is a careful and long-term process that results in a monetary value equivalent to a non-tangible equity of the company, which can be evaluated according to different methodologies.

A strong brand, in addition to the value of its brand equity, also allows the possibility of line and category extensions, with savings resulting from the use of existing knowledge of the brand.

Companies that want to work with various markets need to develop a set or portfolio of strong brands, which results in high brand equity.

7.3 Creating Brand Equity

The positioning work, together with the support of marketing actions, makes the brand known and establishes strong associations between it and its attributes and benefits, through long-term commitment, careful planning, and creative execution.

One brand, according to the American Marketing Association (Kotler & Armstrong, 2016) is:

> ... a name, term, sign, symbol or design, or a combination of all of this, intended to identify the goods or services of a supplier or group of suppliers to differentiate them from those of other competitors.

The brand, therefore, is the element that represents the functional, rational or tangible, symbolic, emotional or intangible characteristics, and differentials of an offer for a given need. It is a way of distinguishing one product from another, identifying the origin of a product, and associating a certain performance with it.

The trade mark performs valuable functions for the consumer. If it did not exist, consumers would have to evaluate dozens of seemingly equal products to find out on what they differ, and best meet their needs, and which ones do not meet their expectations. When he wants to make another purchase, he would have to start this process again, from scratch. In this way, the brand stores a lot of information and useful experiences that help and simplify consumer choice.

The brand is also important for the company. They allow you to identify your offer, simplify its handling, inventory, tracking, and distribution, offer legal protection for your exclusive use, create customer loyalty, facilitate negotiation with distributors, allow you to obtain premium margins on your prices, etc.

This process of establishing a brand for a product (Kotler & Armstrong, 2016) is called branding. It consists of installing a differentiated image in the consumer's mind, convincingly, through marketing actions. The brand now has a market value, which can be traded, and which in certain cases exceeds the value of the physical goods of the company.

Kotler and Armstrong (2016) defines this value as brand equity:

> ... the added value attributed to goods and services. This value can be reflected in the way consumers think, feel and act in relation to the brand, as well as in prices, market share and profitability generated by the brand.

If we consider that products that are perceived as equal are sold at the same price, as is the case of commodities such as beans, coffee, and sugar, sold on the stock exchange, brand equity represents how much the consumer is willing to pay more to have the specific benefits of a brand.

The work of building brand equity consists in communicating the promise of brand value, providing the appropriate and satisfactory experiences of the consumer with the product, and creating in their perception strong, positive, and exclusive associations between them.

7.4 Evaluating Brand Equity

As the brand has high intangible value, it became increasingly important to consider this value in the total value of a company.

According to Kotler and Armstrong (2016) and Keller and Machado (2005), there are three main models of brand equity valuation: BRANDASSET VALUATOR, BRANDZ, and Brand Resonance.

7.4.1 *BRANDASSET VALUATOR*

The BRANDASSET VALUATOR (BAV) model was developed by the advertising agency Young & Rubican, based on a survey of nearly 800,000 consumers in 51 countries, offering comparative brand equity measures of thousands of brands in hundreds of categories.

The key components of this assessment (Keller & Machado, 2005), are:

- **Potential differentiation**—degree with one brand is seen as different from the other
- **Relevance**—adequacy and breadth of brand appeal
- **Esteem**—perceptions of quality and fidelity and degree with which it is reputed and respected
- **Knowledge**—degree of knowledge and familiarity of consumers with the brand.

BAV's analysis has shown that consumers focus their devotion and purchasing power on a reduced group of special brands.

7.4.2 *BRANDZ*

The BRANDZ model was created by consultants Millward Brown and WPP (Keller & Machado, 2005), and models the brand's strength through five stages representing the growing sequence of its brand equity:

- **Presence**—active familiarity based on past experience, evidence, or knowledge of the brand promise
- **Relevance**—relevance to the target audience
- **Performance**—believes it delivers acceptable performance
- **Advantage**—believes you have an emotional or rational advantage over competitors
- **Link**—preferred rational and emotional connections with the brand.

7.4.3 Brand Resonance

In this model it is also assumed that the brand is built through a progressive process of steps (Keller & Machado, 2005):

- **Identity**—Ensure that customers identify the brand and associate it with a specific category or need; aims at deep and broad brand recognition
- **Meaning**—Establish with solidity the meaning of the brand in the minds of customers, strategically linking to it a series of tangible and intangible associations; aims to work points of parity and difference
- **Response**—Get the appropriate customer responses regarding brand-related assessments and sensations; aims to create positive, accessible reactions
- **Relationship**—Convert customers' brand response into active and intense loyalty; aims to create intense, active loyalty.

The steps in the rise of equity are:

- Brand **prominence**—represents the frequency and ease with which it is evoked in consumer situations
- Brand **performance**—indicates the degree to which it meets the customer's functional needs
- Brand **image**—extrinsic properties of the product, including the degree of social and psychological needs
- Brand **judgments**—represent consumers' personal opinions and assessments
- Brand **sensations**—customer responses and emotional reactions to the brand
- Brand **resonance**—degree of harmony in the relationship of the brand with the client.

7.4.4 Brand Equity Boosters

All brand contacts can help build a brand equity (Kotler & Armstrong, 2016), but it can be highlighted three main groups:

- Initial choices of brand elements or identities—in general, brand elements (brand names, logos, slogans, jingles, packaging, etc.) should be short, easy to memorize, refer to benefits, and be understandable within consumer culture
- The product and all its marketing activities and marketing programs associated with it—there must be harmony and synergy between the different programs and marketing activities, so that they reinforce a unique message and are consistent with the positioning and promise of brand value
- Other associations indirectly transferred to the brand, linking it to some other entity—the brand may seek external associations, with other people, places, or things, that can leverage your image perception.

7.5 Developing the Brand Elements

Brand elements (Kotler & Armstrong, 2016) are features, such as signs, names, and phrases, that can be registered and serve to identify the brand.

There are six criteria for choosing a brand element:

- **Easy memorization**—short, audible, easy-to-association names are usually easier to remember
- **Significant**—is credible, represents an effective brand promise
- **Captivating**—humorous names that arouse positive feelings
- **Transferable**—names that can be used in new categories, other segments, and other countries
- **Adaptable**—easy to change and update
- **Protected**—must be within legal regulations so that it can be protected properly; cannot be generic, nor similar to the point of indicating competitor copy.

The less tangible the benefits of the brand are, the more important it will be to have brand elements that capture these tangible characteristics.

The development of brand equity results not only from the elements of the brand, but from all integrated marketing actions. There must be coherence and synergy between the meanings conveyed by the elements of the marketing mix, such as the point of sale, the price, the product, and the communication tools.

7.6 Internal Branding

Employees play an important role in the branding process, to the extent that many will have contact with the consumer, as a brand may have hundreds of interface points with their customers, and will convey the image and value of the brand through their attitudes and actions. The company needs to make sure that its employees and partners are prepared to reinforce the correct features of the brand image.

Internal branding (Kotler & Armstrong, 2016) consists of a set of activities and processes that help inform and inspire employees about brands.

Well-trained sellers help give credibility to the promise of brand value and show that they value their work and your company.

Mitchell (2002) presents three principles of successful internal branding:

- **Choose the right time**—identify moments where the brand's internal image is still confusing or uncertain, so actions and internal branding help align perceptions and motivate employees.

- **Link internal to external marketing**—internal messages must have the same content as external ones, so that there is harmony in the company's communication effort. The internal audience must be prepared when the external message begins to occur, so that they can work in synchrony.
- **Keep the brand alive for employees**—communication must be rational and emotional, be informative and energizing, to generate pride and passion.

7.7 Measuring Your Brand Equity

The brand equity of a specific brand (Keller & Machado, 2005; Kotler & Armstrong, 2016) can be measured through an indirect approach or direct approach.

The indirect approach evaluates brand equity based on brand knowledge and associations. The direct approach assesses the real impact of brand knowledge on consumer response. These two approaches are complementary and can be used together.

To understand brand equity sources, we can use brand auditing. To track their evolution and growth we can use brand tracking studies.

A brand audit assesses consumer relationships with the brand to identify opportunities to improve and leverage their value.

Brand tracking studies collect historical series of quantitative information to evaluate brand marketing actions and programs.

7.8 Managing Brand Equity

Brand equity, as well as other financial assets, have a natural depreciation that must be managed. If a brand stops investing, the public gradually forgets its characteristics and the associations weaken.

The brand must constantly invest in communication messages that reinforce its attributes, benefits, and needs that meet, and in justifying and maintaining its differentials in relation to its competitors.

Eventually, the brand can go through a period of difficulties and even crises, if its competitive environment suffers changes that harm or weaken its differentials, and may weaken associations, generate negative associations, or lose credibility. It may then be necessary for a strategy of the revitalization of the brand, when it can seek to return to its original core values, which have somehow been lost over time, or go through a repositioning, where it develops a renewed and updated image with its consumers.

7.9 Branding Strategies

The branding strategy or branding architecture (Keller & Machado, 2005; Kotler & Armstrong, 2016) describes the brand elements of the company's product suite and its specific products, considered from the point of view of a portfolio of brands.

Branding a brand creation can be done in three branding alternatives:

- Create new brand elements for the new product
- Use some brand elements of other existing products
- Make a combination of new and existing elements.

7.10 Brand Extensions

A brand extension is the use of an established brand to launch a new product. It can be a line extension when you launch a new product in the same category as an existing brand, or a category extension, when the new product is launched in a new category.

An example of line extension is when a juice brand launches a new flavor in the same category, while the category extension, is when launching a bike with the same brand as a motorcycle manufacturer.

According to Kotler and Armstrong (2016), 80–90% of new products launched on the market are actually line extensions.

The main advantages of brand extension are:

- **Greater chance of success of the new product**—upon noticing the launch of a new product as a brand extension, the consumer creates expectations based on their knowledge of the parent brand and experiences with other products of the company. If you create positive expectations, the extension is acting to offer information that reduces uncertainty and perceived risk by the consumer, leading to a faster consumption decision-making process. This consumer behavior can also be used as a positive argument when negotiating with the distribution channel, as it will have less difficulty getting the final consumer to adopt the product and develop fidelity. In this way, you can facilitate channel acceptance by placing the product on your offer list and reserve shelf space for it. One can also achieve channel requirements, such as promotion and events at the point of sale. This reduction in communication and distribution allows the launch of the product with less money, without reducing its chance of success in the market.
- **Positive feedback effect**—brand extensions can help clarify a brand's meanings and values, and improve the level of consumer loyalty to the parent brand. They can renew their interest and taste for the parent brand, and help expand their market coverage.

The main disadvantages of brand extension are:

- The brand may have a greater difficulty in creating an identity of its own, which Ries and Trout (2001) calls the "line extension trap". The identity of the extension can become very tied to that of the parent brand, or the extension gradually assume its own identity and dilute the identity of the parent brand.
- The launch of an inappropriate extension can create uncertainty and confusion in the consumer, which can affect the parent brand.
- Channels, especially supermarkets, do not have room for a large number of extension launches and may reject this strategy.
- The extension can make the brand portfolio too large to be manageable.
- Brand extension can be a failure and affect the parent brand.
- The brand extension can cannibalize part of the parent brand's sales.
- The brand extension may be taking away the company's chance to develop an entirely new brand, which could generate other extensions in the future.

How to assess the success potential of a brand extension? Volckner and Sattler (2006) propose six basic questions to assess the success potential of a brand extension:

- Does the parent brand have a strong brand equity?
- Is there a strong connection base?
- Does the extension have the ideal parity and difference points?
- How can marketing programs improve the brand equity of the extension?
- What implications will the extension have on the brand equity and profitability of the parent brand?
- How can feedback effects be better managed?

The three main branding strategies (Keller & Machado, 2005; Kotler & Armstrong, 2016) most used today are:

- **Family name of individual or distinct brands**—each product of the company has a different brand, particular to its market. It can be interesting for companies operating in various markets, without large associations with each other. The main advantage of this strategy is to be able to sell the brand in case of failure, without the company having its image negatively affected. On the other hand, developing brand equity brand is the most expensive option as it requires the greatest marketing effort.
- **Corporate umbrella or company brand name**—the company has a unique corporate brand for all its products and has the advantage of a faster and cheaper launch. The corporate brand is already known in the market, and its image is transferred to the new product, taking advantage of the learning already existing among consumers. This also implies spending less on communication, generating savings. On the other hand, there is a risk that a product that

has poor performance or image problems will contaminate the corporate brand, negatively affecting other existing products.
- **Sub-brand name**—the sub-brand combines the corporate brand with another individual brand. There is a corporate brand that endorses the new brand, but it also has its own brand that highlights its individuality. It can have the advantages or disadvantages of the previous two strategies.

7.11 Brand Portfolio Management

A company that owns many brands must have a brand portfolio management strategy. A brand portfolio (Kotler & Armstrong, 2016) is the set of all brands and brand lines that a company offers to a particular segment.

One focuses on a specific segment, and in order to grow, the company often needs to develop several brands focused on different segments. The greater brand variety allows the company to occupy more shelf space in retail, serve less reliable consumers seeking variety, better serve different segments with different needs, and achieve savings in communication and distribution.

The ideal portfolio is one that maximizes the brand equity of all the brands that make up it. It should cover the market well in order to take advantage of most potential customers, but without overlap that generates cannibalization between brands.

Brands in a portfolio often play one of the following roles:

- **Combat brands**—or flankers, are brands created to be positioned directly against competing brands of the flagship brands, which are the most important and profitable. They tend to be simpler brands, with lower prices, but they focus on offering part of the competitors' differentials, fighting with them for market share installments.
- **Dairy cows**—are already-consolidated brands, usually in markets that have already reached lower growth rates, but have loyalty from their audience, without the need for much marketing investment. They usually have a significant market share, allowing the company to offer a flow of financial resources without major investments.
- **Entry at the entry level**—also known as entry brands, are brands with lower prices, relative to the portfolio, but that are more accessible to potential customers, who can enter the market and have a consumer experience that leads to a future migration to other brands positioned higher in the portfolio. In the luxury motoring industry, this practice is common, as in the case of the series 1 BMW, and A-class Mercedes-Benz.
- **High prestige, and high level**—are the relatively more expensive brands, and are associated with the company's greater prestige and credibility. They are

brands that demonstrate the skills and potentials of the company, and this prestige tends to extend also to the other brands in the portfolio. They do not always have high profitability, but they leverage the profitability of other brands.

7.12 Luxury Branding Strategies

Luxury brands (Seo & Buchanan-Oliver, 2015) convey unique sociocultural and individual meanings to their consumers. These meanings (Kapferer, 1997),

> ...*implicitly convey their own culture and way of life: hence Saint Laurent is not Chanel. They offer more than mere objects: they provide reference of good taste.*

The brand strategy, as consequence, should be developed based on phenomenological experiences and sociocultural influences, in order to create a strong brand image.

A frequent challenge (Kapferer, 2016) for the luxury brand manager is to conciliate this need of creating a distinctive, unique brand image and at the same time, reach corporate goals that demand volume, rentability, and in many situations, be accessible to a greater public, spread over the world, without becoming just a fashion item and losing the appeal it is supposed to have.

Other specificities of luxury brands (Kapferer & Bastien, 2012) are that the communication should also be directed to the non-target public, in order to create distinction and differentiation of the target. The role of the communication is mainly to sell, but to create the desire and the glamour of luxury, and the perception of scarcity. It is also important to create associations with the arts in general.

7.13 Summary

> Brands are fundamental to a company's financial success. They represent the memories and associations that consumers have developed in their experience with the product and their marketing actions, and that they use as a reference for their future relationships with it, generating the repetition of the purchase and loyalty.
>
> The creation of the brand equity of a brand is a careful and long-term process that results in a monetary value equivalent to a non-tangible equity of the company, which can be evaluated according to different methodologies.
>
> A strong brand, in addition to the value of its brand equity, also allows the possibility of line and category extensions, with savings resulting from the use of existing knowledge of the brand, and time at launch in the market.

Companies that want to work with various markets need to develop a set or portfolio of strong brands, which results in high brand equity. The ideal portfolio should be one that maximizes the total brand equity of the brand set.

Brand extension, however, also has its disadvantages, such as the risks of cannibalizing or diluting brand equity, confusing and weakening the image, and even contaminating the perception of the parent brand.

Luxury brand has specific characteristics that demand a different approach from traditional products, and they are more associated with social differentiation and lifestyles.

Bibliography

Kapferer, J. N. (1997). Managing luxury brands. *Journal of Brand Management, 4*(4), 251–259.

Kapferer, J. N. (2016). The challenges of luxury branding. In: F. D. O. Riley, J. Singh & C. Blankson (Eds.). *The Routledge companion to contemporary brand management* (pp. 505–523). Routledge.

Kapferer, J. N., & Bastien, V. (2012). *The luxury strategy: Break the rules of marketing to build luxury brands*. Kogan Page Publishers.

Keller, K. L. & Machado, M. (2005). *Strategic brand management*. Pearson Prentice Hall.

Kotler, P., & Amstrong, G. (2016). *Principles of marketing* (16th Edn.). Pearson.

Mitchell, C. (2002, January). Selling the brand inside. *Harvard Business Review*.

Ries, A., & Trout, J. (2001). *Positioning: The battle for your mind*. McGraw Hill.

Seo, Y., & Buchanan-Oliver, M. (2015). Luxury branding: the industry, trends, and future conceptualizations. *Asia Pacific Journal of Marketing and Logistics, 27*(1), 82–98.

Volckner, F., & Sattler, H. (2006, April). Drivers of brand extension success. *Journal of Marketing, 70*(2), 18–34.

Creating Competitive Products

8.1 Introduction

Chapter Objectives

Consumers change their preferences over time, as they get new information, competitors launch different and better products, interact with influencers, and their culture changes. Companies have to develop new products in order to remain competitive in the market, but on the other hand, studies show that up to 80% of new products fail when entering the market, due to several reasons, making the introduction of a new product very risky for any company. Managers have to find a balance between these two needs, innovating without failing.

The development of a product is the materialization of benefits and differentials that will be offered to the market, through its attributes. There are several types of products, with specific characteristics for the markets to which they are directed. These products are placed on the market and exhibit distinct behaviors throughout their life cycle, directing marketing efforts to each stage, according to their evolution.

In general companies have more than one product, and therefore should also develop a strategy for their product suite or portfolio, as seen in the previous chapter. This product portfolio may have greater or lesser variety, depending on the company's market coverage strategies, and should be managed in order to bring the best possible profitability to a given portfolio.

Packaging and labeling are also important elements of the product, performing communication, sales, and protection functions of the product.

8.2 Defining Product Strategy

After defining positioning and branding strategies, we have a concept that needs to be translated into an offer for a specific segment. For this, we will have to turn this concept into a product.

A product (Kotler & Armstrong, 2016), in addition to physical goods, can also have other forms, such as services, ideas, places, people, events, etc. It is all that can be offered to a market to meet needs.

8.2.1 Product Levels

One product (Churchill & Peter, 2017; Kotler & Armstrong, 2016) can be conceptualized into different levels, each adding value to the final offer, in a hierarchy of value for the customer. The main levels are:

- **Central benefit**—it is constituted by the main benefit that the product offers. If it is a car, it can be the transport between two locations, to a hotel, a quiet place to spend the night. It is a generic benefit, which will be offered by all products in the category.
- **Basic product**—is the result of creating the product that will deliver the benefits. In the case of transport, for example, it will be the car.
- **Expected products**—are the attributes of the product, within the level of expectation of quality and satisfaction that the target audience desires. In the case of an automobile, for example, comfortable seats, efficient brakes, low maintenance, etc.
- **Expanded products**—are additional attributes, in addition to those expected, that help to positively surprise customers.
- **Potential products**—are all potential attributes that can be added in the future. They are alternatives to make the product more competitive in your market.

8.2.2 Product Classification

Considering the variety of products that can be offered to the market, it is useful to divide the categories based on similarities, facilitating their understanding and management, and helping to define strategies for each of them.

There are several classifications (Kotler & Armstrong, 2016):

- **By durability and tangibility**:
    - *Non-durable goods*—are products that are consumed quickly and purchased frequently. Usually work with low margins, gaining from turning, require extensive distribution and mass communication.

- *Durable goods*—are tangible goods, usually more complex and used for a longer period of time. They are complex, depend on personal sales with well-qualified sellers, offer larger margins, and require guarantees.
- *Services*—are characterized by being intangible, inseparable, variable, and perishable. They require attention to quality control, credibility building, and adaptability management.
- **By the habit of buying, for consumer goods**:
  - *Convenience goods*—products purchased frequently, usually low risk and low involvement, where the consumer makes little effort in the sales decision process. They must have extensive distribution and with a lot of exposure, usually bought on impulse, such as bullets and chocolates, and in emergency cases, such as umbrellas when it starts to rain.
  - *Comparative purchasing goods*—are more complex goods that require more information to compare acquisition alternatives. These goods should offer variety to meet different needs and qualified personal sales support to give detailed information and give advice to the customer in their comparison.
  - *Specialty goods*—are products with exceptional characteristics, which the consumer is willing to make a greater effort for their acquisition. Usually, the consumer knows where the point of sale is and is willing to travel to it.
  - *Unsought goods*—are products that the consumer usually does not know or that does not usually think about buying, such as life insurance, cemetery properties, and deposits. One must make intense communication efforts to create awareness and interest in acquisition.
- **For the relative cost and participation in the production process, for industrial goods**:
  - *Materials and parts*—can be raw materials and manufactured parts, which will make up manufactured products. Raw materials will generally undergo some transformation through different processes, while manufactured parts will make up manufactured products.
  - *Capital goods*—are those that have a long duration, being generally used for the production or management of the finished product. They can be facilities (factories, offices, generators, presses, elevators, etc.) and equipment (portable tools and machines). They are expensive, complex products that require the monitoring of specialized sales personnel.
  - *Business supplies and services*—short-lived goods, used in the production and management of the finished product.

8.2.3 Product Differentiation

To varying degrees, all products in their creation process seek to develop a differentiation within their target market, to avoid becoming a commodity, and be forced to compete in terms of prices.

There are several ways of differentiating (Kotler & Armstrong, 2016) that can be used in the creation of a product:

- **Shape**—size, and physical structure. Different volumes can be targeted to users with different frequencies of use, such as the six-beer package for heavy users, or to different numbers of users, such as individual packaging for one person's consumption to family packaging, for all family members.
- **Features**—varied attributes that goods be offered in conjunction with the basic benefit, increasing the perceived value of the product by the consumer.
- **Customization**—the construction of a specific offer for each consumer, based on the knowledge of their profile and preferences.
- **Quality of performance**—indicates the level of operation of the basic characteristics of the product. The company must identify the appropriate level to act with its target market and competitors.
- **Quality of conformity**—all product units meet a minimum performance standard, ensuring the consumer that this minimum quality will be delivered to any unit he acquires.
- **Durability**—product life, and should be adjusted to not last much longer than its operational life, which would increase costs, nor have early obsolescence, with short life and environmental impact.
- **Ease of repair**—the easy availability of repair services, or if possible, self-repair capability by the consumer.
- **Style**—visual, aesthetic, visual sensations aroused by the product.

Differentiation is not limited to product characteristics, in today's world where there is the ease of reproduction of attributes, companies have increasingly resorted to differentiation in terms of services:

- **Ease of order**—speed and clarity in order processing, if possible aided by dedicated systems connecting customer and supplier.
- **Delivery**—agility, precision, care, and guarantees in product delivery.
- **Installation**—most important for more complex products and customers with less knowledge.
- **Training**—provide the necessary training to operate the product or services being purchased.
- **Guidance**—provide advice so that the customer can use the product in the best possible way.
- **Maintenance and repair**—technical support that ensures that interruptions from problems will be small or non-existent.
- **Returns**—to return an unsatisfactory product generates frustration in the customer, who has to wait longer to be able to use the product, in addition to having to incur extra effort in re-packaging and reshipping the product to the manufacturer, and eventually even having additional costs.

Another recent alternative is differentiation through design. The design (Kotler & Armstrong, 2016) is:

> ... the set of characteristics that concern the appearance, feel and functioning of the product from the consumer's perspective.

The design seeks to offer rational and emotional benefits, acting on decisions of form, attributes, performance, compliance, durability, reliability, ease of repair, and style.

8.3   Product Lifecycle Management

Products (Churchill & Peter, 2017; Kotler & Armstrong, 2016) have a limited life span, as their sales go through stages with different dynamics, and require different marketing strategies for each cycle.

The product life cycle model presents a bell-shaped curve, which goes through four distinct phases: introduction, growth, maturity, and decline.

In the introduction phase, the market is still relatively small, and the product is unknown, so you should focus on creating a first product that works well, or quickly make the most critical adjustments, and put it at key points of sale that reach your users, usually people who like novelties and have the income to acquire it. The price can be higher, within the strategy of skimming the market, asking an initial high price and maintaining it until competitors enter the market, or the penetration strategy, of practicing a more affordable price that allows rapid growth of sales and market share.

In the growth phase, competitors generally appear, sales volume and the number of consumers are rapidly increasing, and the company must release new models and versions to meet the growing variety of desires in the expanding market. Distribution should increase its coverage to serve its customers more closely, communication intensifies and starts using more mass tools, and the price can be reduced to become more competitive, or offer promotions, or add product attributes that add value to the company's offering.

In the maturity phase, practically the entire market is being served by the company or its competitors; the company should evaluate whether some models and versions are really competitive and eventually keep the most profitable; the price should be decreased or added more value, and points of sale should be revalued to identify whether they actually cover the target market.

In the declining phase, the market is shrinking and some competitors have already withdrawn; the company should assess whether it remains or also withdraws from the market and reinvests in other more profitable options; if it stays, you should reduce product options, take advantage of savings to reduce prices without losing margin, reduce communication by focusing on remaining consumers, and eliminate unnecessary points of sale.

8.4 Product Line Management

8.4.1 Categorization of Product Lines

Products (Kotler & Armstrong, 2016) can be grouped in several ways, based on their relationships:

- **Family of needs**—a central need in common to products, e.g., food.
- **Product family**—all products that meet a central need, e.g., savings.
- **Class or category of products**—subgroup of the product family, brings together those with a certain functional coherence, e.g., financial instruments.
- **Product line**—subgroup of the product class, has a similar function, is sold to the same markets, and marketed by the same channels.
- **Product type**—subgroup of the product line, which shares one of several possible forms of the product.
- **Item**—a distinct unit within a brand or product line.

Another way to aggregate products is through the product system, a group of products that work in a compatible way, such as an mp3 player and headphones, cables, covers, batteries, chargers, and speakers.

A mix of product assortment (Churchill & Peter, 2017; Kotler & Armstrong, 2016) is the set of all the items that a company decides to put up for sale, and that can range from a single one to a wide variety.

The product mix can have as characteristics:

- **Comprehensiveness**—is the number of product lines offered by the company
- **Extension**—is the total number of items in the product mix
- **Depth**—is the number of options offered within each product
- **Consistency**—is the degree of relationship between the various lines, in terms of their final use, production processes, distribution channels, etc.

The company can therefore expand its business within these above four dimensions.

8.4.2 Evaluation of Product Lines

When offering a product line, the company must develop a management of its set of options, evaluating several aspects:

- **Sales and profits**—the products of the line that represent the largest share of sales and the largest share of profits must be identified and protected, with investments suitable for them to grow and exploit their full potential. Those who make a small contribution should be analyzed considering whether there

is potential for future growth, or if the best option would be to discontinue them and redirect their resources to other more profitable products.
- **Market profile**—the company must evaluate the offers it has, through its different products, identifying which markets are positioned, and which are its competitors. From this analysis, it can verify whether in the most attractive markets, it finds strong competitors that make these markets highly competitive and where high investments will be needed, or whether it is relatively only and can better exploit the profitability that the market offers; it can also identify products that are not associated with potential markets, or markets with potential that are not being met.

Successful products create the potential for product line extension (Kotler & Armstrong, 2016), and the company should analyze opportunities such as:

- **Up-selling**—create extensions that meet different market levels, causing the consumer to purchase an entry product, and as it develops and refines its taste, and increases its purchasing power, starts to acquire the following products, such as Mercedes-Benz, with the A-Class as the entry product, the E-Class as the executive sedan, and the S-Class as the top-of-the-line sportsman.
- **Cross-selling**—create extensions that form a system and that further outsell each other, such as personal computers and printers of the same brand.
- **Lines of protection against the variation of the economy**—create extensions focused on the different levels of the economy—low, medium, and high—so that there is always demand for part of the line, regardless of variations in the economy, since in periods of recession increases the trend of buying cheaper products, while in periods of heating consumers start to prefer more sophisticated products.

The manager should also analyze the possibility of expanding the line (Kotler & Armstrong, 2016), starting to act in new market price ranges:

- **Down-market expansion**—the company starts to operate in lower price ranges than normally it does. It can occur due to three basic reasons:
  - *Emergence of opportunities for growth in popular markets*, such as was seen in the construction market, which with the increase of purchasing power of class C, began to offer popular housing.
  - *Launching products to occupy markets where potential competitors operate*, in order to divert their resources from a possible attempt to enter its superior market.
  - *Loss of potential or reduction of the higher market* where it operates.
- **Up-market expansion**—the company starts to operate in higher price ranges, seeking greater growth, greater profitability, offer a more complete line, or seek the prestige that the premium segment offers. Often the extension adds to the original brand the words Ultra, Extra, Super, Plus, etc.

- **Double magnification**—the line is extended up and down, seeking to make your offer more complete and different sources of profitability.
- **Complementation of line**, with the growth of products in the same range, in order to offer a more complete line and meet new segments or niches.

All products tend to lose competitiveness over time as consumers learn about new technologies and offerings from competitors, so the company should evaluate its line modernization and innovation strategies. If not done within an appropriate timing, it can, if done too early, lose revenues that could still have been obtained with the old product, lowering its profitability; and if they are made too late, it runs the risk of losing market share, or market share, to its competitors.

In rapidly changing markets, such as technology, there is not much time to wait, and modernization must be planned to take place virtually continuously. In slow-moving markets, such as cement, there is time to test changes with customers before making deeper changes, and identify reactions to them.

Throughout their life, products may show a fall in their sales, and one should analyze, within the lines, which are showing a fall, and seek their reasons. Seasonal falls may occur, where this fall is expected, and falls may occur due to increased aggressiveness of competitors, which may show the need to do promotions and other point-of-sale actions to recover the line. Eventually, the line may be reaching the end of its life, and it may be necessary to analyze the possibility of its withdrawal from the market.

8.5 Product Mix Pricing Strategies

The price determination of the product mix differs from the pricing of an individual product (Kotler & Armstrong, 2016; Nagle et al., 2008), in that a price combination is sought that maximizes the profitability of the product mix as a whole, which should consider cost structures, demands, and competitors that can be interrelated but different.

There are six situations that involve pricing a product mix:

- **Price for product line**—prices are set within ranges for different levels of product groups, and prices are usually associated with quality, such as a low-priced popular line, mid-priced executive line, and luxury line at a high price.
- **Price for optional features**—the company defines which accessories are offered as standard and which are offered as optional, and establishes a pricing policy within its strategy of attracting specific target markets.
- **Prices for captive complementary products**—in cases where one product is required for the use of another, such as the razor and razor blade. The company can offer at low prices the appliance, so that consumers use the blades, sold at higher prices. In some cases, the device may even be offered free of charge, to stimulate the use of the set.

- **Compound price**—this is the case of the payment of an initial fixed amount plus a monthly variable amount, depending on consumption, such as when joining a club, the registration fee plus the monthly fees is paid.
- **Price for by-products**—when the company is able to develop by-products of its main product, it has two sources of revenue, which can be used together to optimize its results.
- **Price for product package**—when the company negotiates a set of products for a special price.

8.6 Co-Branding

Co-branding, also called a double brand or combined brand (Keller & Machado, 2005; Kotler & Armstrong, 2016) consists of the marketing of a product with two or more known brands. It can be through the combination of brands of the same company, or different companies brought together in a joint venture, or other types of alliance. It has advantages such as reducing costs, when using known brands, and if a correct combination is made, one brand can leverage or complement the attributes of the other.

Ingredient branding is a particular form of co-branding, in which the brand of the product combined with the brand of one of its components is used, such as the Dolby system in sound equipment, or the Intel processor in a given laptop.

To succeed, an ingredient brand must have:

- Consumers who realize that the ingredient is important for the performance and success of the final product.
- Consumers are convinced that the ingredient performs better than their competitors.
- The final product has some indication, such as a symbol or logo, that signals the presence of the component in the product.
- The ingredient must communicate to reinforce its differentiated image and communicate its presence at the point of sale.

8.7 Packing

Packaging (Kotler & Armstrong, 2016) is the set of container design and production activities that involves a product. It is an important element that contributes effectively to the success of the product. It acts as an element of communication with the customer, attracting and stimulating the choice of the product. It is the customer's first element of contact with the product and can be part of the consumer experience, acting as a product support or exhibitor.

The packaging can be developed in up to three levels:

- **Primary**—it contains the product, such as the glass bottle of perfume. The attractiveness of this packaging can contribute to the brand equity of the brand and is even collected.
- **Secondary**—is a protective packaging from the exposure of the product, allowing it to be placed, for example, on supermarket shelves, disclosing the characteristics of the product without exposing the primary packaging to scratches.
- **Tertiary or shipping**—is a packaging used for storage and transport of batches (half a dozen, a dozen, two dozen, etc.) of secondary packaging units. It is usually made of corrugated paper.

The use of packaging has grown due to factors such as:

- **Self-service**—packaging has become sophisticated to perform various sales functions, such as attracting consumer attention, describing the product, and convincing of its advantages and benefits.
- **Consumer purchasing power**—increases the willingness to pay for packages that offer convenience, appearance, reliability, or prestige.
- **Brand and company image**—enable an instant company or brand recognition.
- **Innovation opportunity**—can offer new ways to facilitate the use of the product.

The main objectives of the packaging should be (Kotler & Armstrong, 2016):

- Identify the brand
- Transmit descriptive and persuasive information
- Facilitate transport and product protection
- Provide guidance on home storage
- Provide guidance on product consumption
- Be sustainable and environment-friendly.

The packaging should combine functional and aesthetic factors. The main aesthetic factors to be analyzed are size, shape, materials, colors, text, and illustrations.

8.8 Labeling

The label is a packaging element (Kotler & Armstrong, 2016) that can range from a label attached to the product to a complete graphic design. Its main functions are:

- Identify the product and brand
- Indicate product classification or category
- Describe the product
- Promote the product
- Include mandatory information such as ingredients and alerts.

8.9 Competitive Products in Luxury

In luxury, products have some peculiarities (Kapferer, 1997).

As an artisanal product, it is not expected to be without flaws, although it should express all creativity and uniqueness of the brand, providing the emotional appeal and the social recognition of the status of the owner. A mechanical luxury watch, that can reach prices of hundreds of thousands of dollars, is less precise than a ten-dollar quartz watch, but the intricacy of the mechanisms and the craftsmanship involved more than compensate for this flaw. A luxury sports car may not be comfortable, as it has to remove comfort equipment to reduce weight and reach higher performance. Most of the Ferrari models don't come with air conditioning or even a sound system.

Luxury brands tend to have long life cycles, with most of the famous ones being centenary. There may be many models and variations in a brand line, but there is no introduction phase, a luxury brand is carefully brought to the market as it spreads through the clients' lives. Even when discontinued for financial reasons, the strong brand equity can allow the brand to return, even decades after.

The brand Fabergé, for instance, founded in 1842 by Gustav Fabergé, was nationalized by the Bolsheviks in 1918. In 1924 his grandsons Alexander and Eugène Fabergé opened Fabergé & Cie in Paris, with the brand FABERGÉ, PARIS and they closed down in 2001. In 2007, it was announced the reunification of the Fabergé brand and the Fabergé family, with Tatiana Fabergé and Sarah Fabergé, both great-granddaughters of Peter Carl Fabergé, as founding members of the Fabergé Heritage Council, a division of Fabergé Limited. In 2013, Fabergé Limited was sold to the gem mining company Gemfields for $90 million, and the brand lives on.

Co-branding (Bragatte et al., 2021) can have a positive impact on attitude toward the brand (in fashion), and, mainly, on purchase intention, that is, there is evidence that the brand obtained advantages in terms of aesthetic perception and differentiation due to the presence of a second brand, in a study of co-branding between luxury and streetwear brands.

Brand combinations, uniqueness, and price (Yu et al., 2020) significantly impact consumer desirability of luxury co-branding combinations. The luxury brand and sportswear combination results in the highest desirability when the price is more similar to the sportswear constituent and participants perceive that the collaboration is exclusive.

When Missoni, a luxury Italian knitwear brand (Luck et al., 2014) partnered with Target in September 2011, releasing a large, one-off, mass-market collection that ranged from apparel to homewares, the collaboration received extensive media coverage and the online sales site crashed within hours of opening while shelves were cleared in stores minutes after trading began, and just a few hours later, many pieces were being offered on eBay for premium prices. The lack of available stock, despite the enormous hype created, reinforced Missoni's luxury image, as the brand gained massive awareness, despite not employing any of its own communication channels in the promotion of the collaboration. However, the co-branded collaboration was distinctively Missoni, potentially inciting comparison and confusion with the signature line.

Co-branding strategies can offer a viable opportunity for luxury brands to increase their market share, while they maintain their market position.

Packaging in luxury demands special attention to all aspects, that have to both reinforce the position of the brand and keep the same level of luxury in all components. The cognac Louis XIII, for instance, comes in a box made of noble woods, with details in rose gold, and the bottle is made of Baccarat crystal.

When (Hammers et al., 2020) customers' expectations on packaging are surpassed, the customer experience is affected positively. Packaging containing tissue paper and gifts enhances the unboxing experience. Satisfaction is affected by expectations and packaging can contribute to a better overall experience.

Logistics questions also have to be considered, as shipping costs vary according to weight and volume, and sometimes adjusting dimensions can result in significant cost reduction. The use of plastics, although with environmental impact, many have to be considered, when the product is exposed to moister, rain, or heat.

8.10 Summary

The product is the materialization of benefits and differentials that will be offered to the market, through its attributes. There are several types of products, with specific characteristics for the markets to which they are directed. These products are placed on the market and exhibit distinct behaviors throughout their life cycle, directing marketing efforts to each stage, according to their evolution.

Usually, companies have more than one product, and therefore should also develop a strategy for their product suite or portfolio. This product portfolio may have greater or lesser variety, depending on the company's market coverage strategies, and should be managed in order to bring the best possible profitability to a given portfolio.

Packaging and labeling are also important elements of the product, performing communication, sales, and protection functions of the product. Packaging in luxury is extremely important to endorse the luxury characteristics of the brand.

Bibliography

Bragatte, G. D., Hemzo, M. A., & Hemzo, L. F. (2021). Impacts of collab between streetwear and luxury brands on attitudes and intention of purchase of consumers. In: *Tópicos de Marketing no Século XXI* (vol. I).

Churchill, G. A., & Peter, J. P. (2017). *Marketing*. Saraiva Educação SA.

Hammers, K., Herrlin, A., & Johansson, A. (2020). Customer experience through packaging in an online context: Creating value to neo-luxury customers in Generation Y.

Kapferer, J.-N. (1997). Managing luxury brands. *Journal of Brand Management, 4*(4), 251–259.
Keller, K. L., & Machado, M. (2005). *Strategic brand management.* Pearson Prentice Hall.
Kotler, P., & Amstrong, G. (2016). *Principles of marketing* (16th Edn.). Pearson.
Luck, E., Muratovski, G., & Hedley, L. (2014). Co-branding strategies for luxury fashion brands: Missoni for Target. *Global Fashion Brands, 1*(1), 41–56.
Nagle, T. T., Hogan, J. E., & Zale, J. (2008). *The strategy and tactics of pricing.*
Yu, Y., Rothenberg, L., & Moore, M. (2020). Exploring young consumer's decision-making for luxury co-branding combinations. *International Journal of Retail & Distribution Management, 49*(3), 341–353.

Place Strategies for Luxury Brands

9.1 Introduction

Chapter Objectives
In this chapter it is discussed the main aspects related to the Place mix: Channels, Logistics decisions, flow management, distribution centers, and customs management. It is presented how to analyze macro and micro store location decisions, how distribution strategies should be considered for luxury brands, and the concepts and theories on foreign market entry strategies, and its application to luxury companies. The role of the Flagships, as temples of luxury and the place for experiences with the brand is presented.

9.2 Channels

The channels fulfill several important functions for the consumer, in a specialized way, such as transport, storage, security, and communication of products, allowing companies to direct their resources to their productive and innovation activities, where their competitive skills are.

The channel project includes defining the types, levels, and channel formats to use. Channel management tracks performance, supports through training, and manages channel conflicts.

Retail planning involves defining the type of store, target market, channel structure, product assortment, procurement, prices, services, store atmosphere, in-store activities and experiences, communication, and location.

Wholesale planning involves defining the type of wholesaler and offering and organizing its business functions.

Market logistics planning involves the analysis of the value proposition for the customer, the selection of the best channel system and network strategy, operational excellence in sales forecasting, warehouse management, transport and materials, and implementation of the solution.

9.3 Channels and Value

The decision of marketing channels is of great importance for the company, because they contribute a substantial portion of the perceived value of the product, by offering variety of choice, practicality, convenience, and customer service.

The company is at the center of a value network (Kotler & Armstrong, 2016):

> ... *a system of partnerships and alliances that the company creates to supply, increase and deliver its offerings.*

It includes direct and indirect suppliers, direct and indirect customers, and third parties, such as academic researchers and government regulatory agencies.

Demand chain planning, which is the analysis of the target market and the planning of its supply chain, provides several information:

- Estimate whether there is a greater possibility of making money at the top or bottom of the chain, deciding whether it is better to integrate forward or backward, assuming these new functions.
- Identify problem points in the supply chain that may result in sudden variations in costs, prices, or supplies.
- Evaluate internet usage as a way to improve your communications, transactions, and payments, reduce costs, and streamline information.

On the client side, companies have invested in CRM—Consumer Relationship Management—the concept of managing their relationship with their customers.

While there are people who criticize intermediaries as "middlemen" who only make products more expensive for the end customer, these intermediaries and marketing channels perform a variety of functions that add value to the consumer, filling the gaps in location, time, and ownership that break the company from their customers (Churchill & Peter, 2017):

- **Transport of physical products**—invests in the assembly and operation of the fleet.
- **Transfer of ownership between company and customers**—oversees and formalizes ownership transfer processes.

- **Marketing communication**—develops persuasive messages at the point of sale.
- **Issuance of orders**—formalization and delivery of orders to manufacturers.
- **Payments**—handles large volumes of payment-related documents.
- Information in general—monitors and informs about the competitive environment and competitors in the market.
- **Market information**—being closer to the market, intermediaries are better able to get information about customers.
- **Negotiation**—definition of prices, payment terms, and ways of transfer of ownership.
- **Financing**—evaluates credit conditions and provides the necessary financial resources for installment payment.
- **Risk management**—assumes the risks, such as theft, losses, and obsolescence in the operation of the channel.
- **Storage**—invests in the creation and structuring of specialized sites such as distribution and storage centers.
- **Breaking large batches into smaller batches, up to the unit**—for companies, it is more economical to sell their products in large batches, while for the customer, it is more interesting to buy one or a few units.

Transferring these functions, in whole or in part, from the company to its intermediaries, allows it to focus on its productive activities, taking advantage of its specific competencies.

These are strategic decisions that have to be analyzed under the light of added perceived value, and not as some people do, based on misconceptions, like the intermediate adds costs to the total price. Depending on the location distribution and value perception of the consumers, they may be mandatory and will add more perceived value than perceived costs.

9.4 Marketing Channels

9.4.1 Marketing Channel Systems

A system of marketing channels (Kotler & Armstrong, 2016) is

> ... the set of specific marketing channels used by a company.

Marketing channels (Kotler & Armstrong, 2016):

> ... are sets of interdependent organizations involved in the process of putting a good or service available for use or consumption.

Marketing channels are made up of intermediaries who take goods and services from the factory to the end user.

Intermediaries can be merchants, such as wholesalers and retailers, who buy and resell products, or facilitators, who support but do not market, such as carriers, advertising agencies, stores, etc.

Channels also represent an important portion of the price. In an American survey, it was estimated that the channels correspond from 30 to 50% of the total price, while advertising corresponds only to 5–7% of the final price.

9.4.2 Hybrid Channels

Hybrid channels (Kotler & Armstrong, 2016) is the strategy of using two or more marketing channels to reach a particular segment. For example, the company can use its sales team to serve its largest customers, telemarketing for average customers, direct mail for small customers, and an ecommerce website for special customers.

Each channel has features that allow them to better serve different groups in the market. It is important that each channel complements itself, operating with synergy, taking into account the preferred form of consumer channel, to avoid channel conflict, where two channels of the same company fight for the requests of the same customers.

Channels must act in an integrated manner, so that actions on one channel may be sequenced in another, such as being able to order by catalog, withdraw in physical store, and cancel the order via online, if this is the preferred form of the consumer.

9.4.3 Channel Levels

Every channel has at least one manufacturer and one final consumer. The channel level or extension (Churchill & Peter, 2017; Kotler & Armstrong, 2016) is the number of intermediaries we find between manufacturer and consumer. For instance:

- **Zero-level channel or direct marketing**—the manufacturer does not work with intermediaries, and sells directly to the end consumer, through its own stores, telemarketing, direct mail, infomercials allied to telemarketing, sales TV channels, Internet, etc.
- **Level one channel**—there is a single intermediary, the retailer that buys from the factory and sells to the final consumer.
- **Level two channel**—there are two intermediaries, usually a wholesaler who buys from the factory and sells to a retailer, who sells to the final consumer.
- **Level three channel**—there are three intermediaries, for example a large wholesaler who buys from the factory and sells to a smaller wholesaler, who can specialize in a particular market segment, which sells to a retailer that serves the end consumer.

There may be more levels of intermediaries, but with the increase in the number, the complexity of the channel and its costs increases, and therefore one should evaluate whether this increase is bringing additional value to the end customer.

9.4.4 Channel Design

The design of a channel can be developed in four stages (Kotler & Armstrong, 2016):

- **Analyze the needs and desires of customers**—consumers can choose a channel based on price, assortment, convenience, and purchase objectives. The same consumer, however, can choose different channels for different functions during the purchasing process. Channels can offer five levels of services:
  - *Lot size*—the consumer may want different batch sizes, from one unit to a large quantity
  - *Waiting and delivery time*—time to receive the goods
  - *Spatial convenience*—ease of access to the point of sale, allowing lower spending and faster
  - *Product variety*—the number of products offered
  - *Type of intermediaries*—the different types of channels, such as direct sales, own stores, representatives, resellers, retailers, etc.
- **Establishment of objectives and limitations of the channel**—vary according to the characteristics of the product, such as bulky products should use channels that minimize distances, to reduce costs; complex products are usually sold directly by the company with specialized support of own personnel.
- **Identification of the main channel options**—a channel option can be described by three elements:
  - *Service support*—options offered, such as creative, delivery, installation, maintenance, etc.
  - *Number of intermediaries*—the company can opt for exclusive distribution, where intermediaries work exclusively with the company; selective distribution, when working with a restricted but not exclusive group of distributors, and intensive distribution, when working with a large number of distributors, aiming at wide market coverage.
  - *Rights and responsibilities of channel members*—the business relationship must be defined, in terms of pricing and discount policy, conditions of sale and payment, territorial divisions, services, and mutual responsibilities.
- **Evaluation of the main channel alternatives**—each alternative should be evaluated in terms of three criteria:
  - *Economic*—sales volumes designed for different price levels
  - *Control*—rules and performance incentives
  - *Adaptation*—flexibility and ability to adapt to competitive change

9.4.5 Channel Management

Selected the channel, the company must develop a relationship with it, and establish support processes so that it has the expected performance. The main channel management activities (Kotler & Armstrong, 2016) are:

- **Selection of channel members**—definition of the ideal profile, such as time of experience in the business, other products marketed, indicators of growth, profitability, and solvency, degree of cooperation, and reputation.
- **Training and motivation of channel members**—develop training and training programs, establish motivation programs, and conduct behavior and consumer satisfaction surveys.
- **Evaluation of channel members**—the company must establish performance metrics in different indicators, such as sales, inventories, service time, satisfaction with service, etc.
- **Modification of the channel structure**—evaluation of modifications and expansions of the channel, and needs to adapt to these new demands.
- **Channel change decisions**—performance assessment and corrective measures when performance is not at the planned level.

9.4.6 Integration of Channel Systems

Channel systems can take on complex configurations (Churchill & Peter, 2017; Kotler & Armstrong, 2016) when we have several interrelated companies operating. The three main types of channel systems are vertical, horizontal, and multichannel systems:

- The **vertical** marketing system is formed by a manufacturer, several wholesalers, and retailers, all acting as a unified system. Usually, one of the members owns or franchisors the other and holds most of the decision-making power in the channel.
- The **horizontal** marketing system consists of two or more unrelated companies that bring together resources or unify programs to explore a particular market opportunity. A retail company, for example, can team up with a bank to offer better financing conditions to its customers. This union may be transitional or permanent, usually in the form of a joint venture.
- In the **multichannel** marketing system, the company operates through various types of channels, seeking this variety to obtain a wide coverage of the market.

9.4.7 Channel Conflict, Cooperation, and Competition

A channel conflict (Kotler & Armstrong, 2016) occurs when a channel member's actions prevent another channel member from achieving their goals by competing with for same customers.

Three types of channel conflict can occur:

- **Horizontal** channel conflict—between members of the same channel level. It occurs, for example, when a store reduces its quality of service to control its costs, damaging the image of other stores in the network.
- **Vertical** channel conflict—between them from different levels of the channel. For example, creating an ecommerce site can take customers away from a wholesaler, who sees their customers being served directly by the company.
- **Multichannel** conflict—between two or more channels selling to the same markets. For example, the effect that creating stores in shopping malls could have on another channel of the same company, door-to-door sales.

There are four root causes for channel conflicts:

- **Incompatibility of goals**—the manufacturer wants high margins, while retailers prefer to gain with spin and volume.
- **Unclear rights and roles**—lack of clarity in the definition, for example, of sales territories, or customer portfolios.
- **Differences in perception**—for example, when the company evaluates the market optimistically and insists that the channel replenish its inventories, while channel members evaluate the market with pessimism and think about reducing inventories and lines offered to the market.
- **Dependence of intermediaries on the manufacturer**—especially when the channel member is exclusive, he can become very dependent on the decisions that the manufacturer adopts, and may be impaired by its evaluation errors.

A certain degree of conflict can encourage a wholesome competitiveness, but too much can bring a lot of problems. The main forms of conflict management (Kotler & Armstrong, 2016), so that they do not exceed these acceptable limits, are:

- **Strategic justification**—show that strategically the channels are focused on different objectives, if possible developing specific versions for the different objectives.
- **Double compensation**—in addition to the normal commissioning of a channel, it will receive a second commission for the results of the conflicting channel.
- **Over-ordered goals**—setting common goals that meet channel needs.
- **Exchange of employees**—exchange between employees of conflicting channels, so that they know the other side of the operation.

- **Joint participation in associations**—allowing the discussion of problems in a more independent external forum.
- **Co-optation**—open the participation of conflicting channel members in the other channel, so as to allow it to also make part of the decisions.
- **Diplomacy, mediation, and arbitration**—we use third parties who will represent the interests of each side and evaluate alternative solutions.
- **Judicial proceedings**—may lead to a legal decision, or to an agreement negotiated between the parties during the proceedings.

9.5 Success Factors in Ecommerce

Ecommerce sites have become increasingly common, either through a solely virtual presence strategy, or in combination with other channels.

Several cares are needed (Kotler & Armstrong, 2016) in the creation and operation of ecommerce sites:

- Definition and criteria of customer service training
- Make the site easy to navigate, quickly, simply, and easily
- Creating a pleasant shopping experience
- Facilitate customer iteration—seller
- Offer alternative online chat
- Ensure security and privacy
- Investment in design
- Investment in technologies and equipment that ensure speed.

9.6 Marketing Channel Strategies for Intermediaries

Intermediaries, whether wholesalers, retailers, or logistics companies, are also companies operating in a given market, and therefore need well-designed strategic marketing planning to succeed.

9.7 Retail

Retail (Kotler & Armstrong, 2016) includes all modes of sale directly to the final consumer, for final consumption. The retailer is the company that gets most of its retail sales revenue.

The main types of retailers (Churchill & Peter, 2017; Kotler & Armstrong, 2016) are:

9.7 Retail

- **Retail stores**—are retail establishments with a physical presence, through the store that can present several formats.
- **Specialty Stores**—work with a restricted line of products, but within it, has a variety of brands, ample stock, and specialized personnel, offering a high degree of service.
- **Department stores**—a large area is divided into several departments, each serving a category of products; offers an average level of services.
- **Supermarket**—self-service in a wide area, working with low margins and high volumes, mainly focused on the food, hygiene, and household cleaning sectors.
- **Convenience Store**—relatively small, located near residential areas, operates at extended times, works with convenience and turnover product lines, coffees, and snacks.
- **Pharmacy**—specialized in medicines, toiletries, and beauty.
- **Discount shop**—practices lower prices, operating with low margins and high volumes
- **Off-price retailer**—offers lower prices for non-standard products such as stock tips, leftovers, and defective products.
- **Superstore**—occupies a large area and offers, in addition to supermarket items, such as food, hygiene, and household cleaning, various services such as laundry, banking, tailoring, repairs, etc.
- **Retail without store**—the formal physical store, the sale can take place in four formats:
  - *Direct sales*—the sale is made directly by the company's sales team to the end customer, usually through visits, door-to-door modalities, and sales meetings.
  - *DirectMarketing*—the company makes communication and sale directly to the customer, through media such as direct mail, catalog, websites, telemarketing, and television marketing.
  - *Vending machines*—machines that through payment automatically release the purchased product. The older ones operate with coins, today many already accept credit card, and is in the test phase of the use of mobile phone, via Bluetooth.
  - *Purchase Service*—companies that sell products from retailers with special discounts, often purchased as benefits of companies to their employees.
- **Corporate retail and franchise**—large corporations focused on retail, and can be composed of cooperative networks, voluntary networks, retail cooperatives, consumer cooperatives, franchises, and marketing conglomerates.

A retailer's strategic marketing planning should address the following decisions:

- **Target market**—the company needs to gain a deep knowledge of its segment, identifying its profile within the various segmentation variables.
- **Distribution channels**—it will probably be a multichannel strategy, where you will create a set that offers synergy for the consumer buying process.

- **Product assortment**—must be tailored to the wishes of the target audience, in terms of breadth and depth, offering the categories and lines that best meet your demand.
- **Procurement or purchasing strategy**—define suppliers, establish purchasing criteria and practices, predict demand, select goods, track inventory, allocate store space, and define product exposure criteria at the point of sale.
- **Prices**—the pricing policy should be associated with retail positioning; generally exclusive and specialized stores work with higher margins and lower volumes, while mass stores work with large volumes and low margins, earning in turnover.
- **Services**—define the services of pre-sales (communication and point of sale), sale (level of service), after-sales (deliveries, adjustments, etc.), and auxiliaries (parking, changing room, restaurants, etc.). It is a strategic decision, as services add perceived value, but also costs.
- **Store atmosphere**—psychological impact of environmental perception, layout organization, and distribution of space and circulation.
- **Activities and experiences in the store**—fun actions and contact with the brand identity of the retailer, transmitting his personality.
- Communication—tools to generate traffic and purchases at the point of sale, such as promotions, sales, tastings, discount announcements, etc.
- **Location**—location definition, based on the potential attraction of the target audience, within a given region. Information such as people traffic, cost of rent or acquisition, flow restrictions, and location of competitors are used.

9.7.1 Shopping Center

The main alternatives are

- Large shopping malls
- Small neighborhood shopping malls
- Commercial galleries
- Units within a larger store
- Independent stores.

9.7.2 Wholesale

Wholesale (Kotler & Armstrong, 2016) covers all activities related to the sale of goods or services for resale or commercial use.

The main types of wholesalers are:

- **Commercial wholesalers**—independent companies that purchase the goods they work with.
- **Full-service wholesalers**—in addition to buying and stocking the merchandise, have sales team, finance, and delivery orders.
- **Wholesalers of limited service**—act in a specialized way in the offer of chosen product categories, through selected channels.
- **Brokers and agents**—work in a specialized way, through commission, mediating sales, without incurring possession of the good.
- **Branches and offices of manufacturers and retailers**—perform wholesale operations between manufacturer and retailer.
- **Specialized wholesalers**—cooperatives, warehouses, oil terminals, auction companies, etc.

Wholesalers efficiently perform (Kotler & Armstrong, 2016) the following functions:

- Sales and promotion
- Procurement and supply training
- Fractionation of purchase lots
- Storage
- Transportation
- Financing
- Risk management
- Survey of market information
- Retail management and consulting services.

9.7.3 Logistics

Market logistics (Kotler & Armstrong, 2016) involves:

> ... infrastructure planning to meet demand and subsequent control of physical flows and implementation of materials and final products between points of origin and points of use in order to meet the demands of customers making a profit.

Physical distribution has expanded (Kotler & Armstrong, 2016) to the broader supply chain management concept, which means strategically supplying the right supplies, efficiently converting them into finished products, and dispatching them to the final destination.

Market logistics planning consists of four steps:

- Decision of the value proposition for the client.
- Selection of the best channel system and network strategy to reach the customer.

- Development of operational excellence in sales forecasting, warehouse management, transport, and materials.
- Implementation of solutions with the best information systems, equipment, policies, and procedures.

The objectives of market logistics should be based on the needs of its customers and the offer of its competitors, and design a system that minimizes the costs to achieve them.

The main market logistics decisions are:

- **Order processing**—management of the request-payment cycle, which corresponds to all the necessary activities from the generation of the order, to its payment.
- **Storage**—making two main decisions:
  - striking a balance between the number of storage points and the distance between warehouse and customer; more warehouses reduce distance but increase storage costs and vice versa.
  - setting the maximum and minimum stock size; maximum inventory determines the size and cost of the warehouse, while the minimum stock defines the replacement level.
- **Transport**—the main means of transport, with different advantages and disadvantages, are rail, air, road, naval, and pipelines.

It is important that logistics planning is done always taking into account the needs of the customer, in order to add value to the company's offer. Excessive concern about costs can lead to cutting important sources of value to the customer.

9.8 Location Decisions

The decision of location of a store is taken at two levels:

- Macro level—based on data about the market potential of broader regions, those with better numbers are selected to go to the next stage.
- Micro level—the focus reduces to smaller areas, links blocks and roads, considering other factors like natural barriers, circulation restriction, and distance to the consumers. A few of the best options should be selected for visits and final loco evaluation.

9.9 Luxury Channels Strategies

One relevant question is the decision on physical or digital channels. Luxury is traditionally associated with full service in physical stores, but as the internet penetrated in every level of society, even luxury consumers incorporate the digital channel in their purchasing habits. As digital channels only appeal to two of our senses, in comparison to the five senses in the physical store, in order to offer the same level of shopping experience, luxury digital channels have to find ways to compensate for these limitations. The advantages of the digital channel are that they are faster, more comfortable, allow to reach brands all over the world, and access greater stock offers that a single physical store can't provide. But is important that the digital channel offers the same level of service, through direct contact with the salespeople, using video, chat, email, WhatsApp, and other digital tools. The exclusivity has to be maintained by by-invitation-only access, and personal passwords that maintain the exclusivity of access to the brand.

Depending on the level of luxury (Brandao et al., 2021), performance goals and configuration elements assume different importance and different characteristics. An understanding of these differences is relevant for defining strategies and managing luxury supply chains properly. Differences in the level of importance of supply chain performance goals and the critical success factors for each luxury supply chain configuration, which are called accessible, aspirational, and absolute.

As luxury tends to be a global business, in order to better reach most consumers, brands have to enter and grow in foreign markets. There are many ways of the entrance with different levels of risk.

The easiest way is to authorize a dealer to represent the brand, being responsible for defining lines and quantities of price, under strict control of the practiced price, location, communication, store decoration, etc. They can be exclusive or multibrand and will have to use his knowledge of the local market to reach defined goals. It is also to establish joint ventures, or taking more risk, open own stores.

An interesting strategic approach to market entry (Moore et al., 2010) is to open luxury flagship stores, employed to support, enhance, and develop distribution activities within a foreign market.

Flagships, as seen before, are temples of luxury and can be a place for experiences with the brand, allowing learning and experimentation for the consumers, and also learning about this consumer, for the brand.

A study of six luxury brands (Son & Jin, 2013) identified that these luxury brands' entry decisions are positively related to the country's disposable income per household, purchasing power, land size, and masculinity. That is, more luxury brands entered countries with wealth and masculine cultures.

Considering all these specificities (Thomas & Mizushima, 2005), luxury logistics demand well prepared and trained professionals, that understands international laws, and customs rules in different worlds, and processes that speed delivery without increasing costs.

Shen et al. (2020), in a special issue on logistics and supply chain management in the luxury industry, point many relevant points to luxury logistics, as the impact of COVID-19 in reducing the availability of global logistics, the use of blockchain to increase privacy in the transactions, different levels of control in different countries, the value of the supply chain and the impacts on sustainability.

9.10 Summary

We have seen that channels, by specializing in several functions important to the consumer, such as transportation, storage, security, and communication of products, allow companies to direct their resources to their productive and innovation activities, where their competitive skills are.

The channel project includes defining the types, levels, and channel formats to use. Channel management tracks performance, supports through training, and manages channel conflicts.

Retail planning involves defining the type of store, target market, channel structure, product assortment, procurement, prices, services, store atmosphere, in-store activities and experiences, communication, and location.

Wholesale planning involves defining the type of wholesaler and offering and organizing its business functions.

Market logistics planning involves the analysis of the value proposition for the customer, the selection of the best channel system and network strategy, operational excellence in sales forecasting, warehouse management, transport and materials, and implementation of the solution.

Logistics is fundamental for luxury brands, as most of the business is global, and there is an increased complexity of dealing with different law systems, custom procedures, and local uncertainties.

Bibliography

Brandao, M. S., Godinho Filho, M., & Da Silva, A. L. (2021). Luxury supply chain management: A framework proposal based on a systematic literature review. *International Journal of Physical Distribution & Logistics Management*.
Churchill, G. A., & Peter, J. P. (2017). *Marketing*. Saraiva Educação SA.
Kotler, P., & Amstrong, G. (2016). *Principles of marketing* (16th ed.). Pearson.
Moore, C. M., & Doherty, A. M., & Doyle, S. A. (2010). Flagship stores as a market entry method: The perspective of luxury fashion retailing. *European Journal of Marketing, 44*(1/2), 139–161.
Shen, B., et al. (2020). Logistics and supply chain management in the luxury industry. *Transportation Research Part E: Logistics and Transportation Review, 143*, 102095.

Son, J., & Jin, B. (2013). Identifying factors related to luxury brands' international market selection. In *International textile and apparel association annual conference proceedings*. Iowa State University Digital Press.

Thomas, A., & Mizushima, M. (2005). Logistics training: Necessity or luxury. *Forced Migration Review, 22*(22), 60–61.

Managing Pricing and Value of Luxury Brands

10.1 Introduction

Chapter Objectives
In this chapter it is discussed the main topics related to pricing, as how to define full-pricing strategies, how to work properly with dynamic-pricing strategies, how to set operational pricing decisions, as promotions and discounts, as well as credit and installment decisions.

Price formation has a fundamental strategic function for the company when defining its revenues. If not calculated properly, the company's financial health can be seriously affected and may even fail.

Usually, the pricing decision is made by a specialized team, with the monitoring of senior management, and can be developed in six stages. When the reference price is defined, it can be changed depending on the specific context of each sale.

10.2 The Strategic Importance of Pricing

The company's pricing decisions are fundamental to its financial success, since they define the revenue volumes that the company will receive and that, after covering its expenses, will result in its profit and define its profitability.

Pricing (Belke & Berto, 2009; Nagle & Hogan, 2008) is a complex and dynamic process that continuously involves factors related to the company, its customers, its competitors and the macroenvironment. These factors can be discussed from the point of view of:

- marketing, where the price allows to obtain competitive advantages, through the offer of value perceived by the consumer; in the market, the price represents, for the consumer, the monetary disbursement that will be necessary, to in return receive the feeling that a certain set of needs was satisfied, within the best ratio between cost and benefit. Finding the price that offers this best ratio is what will determine the profit and profitability of the company, and a healthy relationship with the market, in a competitive way.
- finance, where the price guarantees the profitability of the company's investors; within the company, the price must allow a positive margin on costs, so that its investors are remunerated. The costs establish the minimum that the company needs to cover its invested resources, but it is necessary to look out, to the competitive environment, to identify the largest margin that the consumer is willing to pay, considering the alternative offers of competitors.

Of all strategic marketing decisions, only price results in revenue input (Belke & Berto, 2009; Kotler & Armstrong, 2016); the other defines how to direct the company's resources—financial, human, technological, etc.—to obtain returns in the future. They are outflows of resources with the promise of return at a future time, within a certain degree of risk.

The intensification of international trade (Nagle & Hogan, 2008) makes markets more competitive and increases pressure by reducing margins of return, as well as by creating new attributes of value for the consumer. This forces companies to know more deeply their costs, to optimize their use, and to eliminate what is not valued by the market.

These decisions can be highly complex, as pricing must be continuously assessed and should be changed quickly to take advantage of the competitive environment. It is a more dynamic process than the definition of the other elements of the marketing mix, since developing products, conducting promotional campaigns, and establishing distribution channels involve an extensive process, with a sequence of activities over a long period of time.

For example, upon receiving the news of the entry of a new competitor into the market, the company can evaluate and establish a new pricing policy appropriate to this new situation in a matter of hours.

Although the same business strategy (Nagle & Hogan, 2008) is maintained, we may have variations in marketing strategy based on this competitive dynamic.

- Consumer behavior changes over time due to cultural, economic, technological, and competitive actions.
- Moments of recession in the economy lead to greater restraint in consumption, while with the warming of the market these consumers feel more confident to consume.
- New technologies can make an existing technology obsolete, as in the case of digital media that have replaced analog ones.

- And the greater or lesser degree of aggressiveness of competitors in competition for the market can lead companies to change their price to improve the perception of their cost–benefit ratio.
- The company itself can change its positioning, and change its price range to reinforce this new image.
- The emergence of new channels, especially digital channels, brings new cost structures, with different distribution processes.
- Entry into new markets or launching new products can also lead to the evaluation of the marketing strategy, and its alignment with the company's overall strategy.
- Innovation and process management can also contribute to changing the cost structure, either through optimization that reduces cost or production time, or the adoption of new technologies that add value to the consumer.
- Some customers may have a demand for bespoke products, which represent significant financial results, and justify their service. The price should also be appropriate to this specific offer.
- We can have regional differences in purchasing power, not allowing us to practice a single price.
- There may also be differences in bargaining power, usually higher in large clients, which can lead to lower prices to close the deal.
- Tactical changes in price can occur when specific opportunities are identified to reduce inventories or take advantage of seasonal demands.
- And finally, the government market can lead to specific prices, depending on the specifications of public competition notices.

10.3 Who Determines Prices in the Company

Pricing is a function that we find in all companies. In small businesses (Kotler & Armstrong, 2016), it is usually the owner of the business that determines the price. He can participate in purchases or have another person take care of this function, and based on market analysis and competitors, sets the prices to be practiced.

In large companies (Kotler & Armstrong, 2016), prices are usually determined by division and product managers, based on objectives determined by senior management, which approves the prices suggested by managers of the lower levels.

Companies where price is of great importance may have a specialized department, subordinated to marketing, finance, or presidency.

Sales managers, production managers, financial managers, and accountants can also participate.

10.4 The Pricing Process

To establish its pricing policy, the company (Kotler & Armstrong, 2016) needs to evaluate a complex set of factors, which can be synthesized in a six-step process:

- Selection of the price determination objective
- Demand determination
- Cost estimation
- Analysis of costs, prices, and offers of competitors
- Selection of a pricing method
- Selection of the final price.

10.4.1 Selection of the Price Determination Objective

The pricing strategy (Nagle & Hogan, 2008) can be defined according to the specific strategies of competition in the market:

- The company can opt for a strategy to achieve market leadership quickly, which brings advantages to the possibility of erecting barriers against the entry of competitors and achieving economies of scale. In this case, it may choose to adopt prices that attract consumers more quickly, sacrificing margins in exchange for rapid growth in market share.
- Another alternative may be to seek to maximize profits in the short term, even losing market share. In this case, it seeks to quickly obtain the highest possible profitability, which can make the company attractive to potential investors, and satisfy existing investors.
- In times of crisis or economic recession, it may be interesting to adopt a survival price policy, when giving up profitability, in exchange for ensuring enough cash flow to cover its operating costs, spin inventory, keep employees, and thus allow the company to continue existing until it is possible to return to the normal strategy and repay investors.

There are also pricing strategies for the specific marketing objectives (Nagle & Hogan, 2008) of a product or a product line.

- Price can be oriented toward a specific strategy of maximizing profitability, or achieving a minimum profitability target, established for specific cases.
- It can also be oriented toward sales-related strategies. One can seek to maximize sales volume, and the value of revenues, offer lower prices to conquer more price-sensitive segments, prices to increase inventory turnover, exploit seasonal demands, seize new market opportunities, or defend market share threats by more aggressive competitors.

10.4.2 Demand Determination

The demand for a product is a function of the price practiced (Kotler & Armstrong, 2016). In general, the higher the price, the lower the amount demanded, following a curve, known as the demand-price curve.

In the case of prestigious items, however, the curve may lean upward, indicating that the price increase attracts higher demand, which can be caused by a perception by the consumer that the price increase implies higher quality. However, this usually occurs in a certain price range, which if exceeded can lead to a further fall in demand.

The demand curve shows the behavior of demand in relation to price variation for a given market. This curve may have different inclinations, depending on each market.

In some markets, the curve has a gentle slope, while in others it has a sharp slope.

This slope indicates the speed at which demand changes, for a given price change, indicating that consumers have different sensitivities to price variations. This sensitivity is a characteristic of a market and is called elasticity.

Elastic markets are those where for a given price change, the variation in demand is more than proportional, while in non-elastic markets, the variation in demand is less than proportional.

This means that in elastic markets the sensitivity to price variations is large and has a strong effect on demand, while in non-elastic markets the price change does little to affect demand.

In general, customers are less price sensitive in the markets for low-cost products or infrequently purchased, or products with few substitutes or competitors. For example, basic food products like beans, rice, salt, and sugar.

The main factors that lead to lower price sensitivity are:

- The product is unique
- Buyers are less aware of the existence of substitutes
- Buyers cannot easily compare the quality of substitutes
- Price is a small part of the customer's total income
- Price is small relative to the total cost of the final product
- Part of the cost is assumed by third parties
- The product is used in conjunction with previously purchased goods
- The product is currently of the most quality, prestige, or exclusivity
- Buyers cannot stock the product.

There are different methods (Kotler & Armstrong, 2016) to estimate demand curves:

- **Surveys**—through interviews with potential users who would estimate whether they would buy for different price levels. Care should be taken because consumers tend to exaggerate the amount they would buy and the price they would be willing to pay.
- **Experiments**—the most common format is to establish groups of clients of two types: experimental and control. In the experimental groups, the price varies and the corresponding demand is averaged; in the control group, the price is maintained and demand variations are compared. On the Internet, it is possible to make systematic variations in the price and quickly measure the reaction in demand.
- **Statistical price analysis**—through the analysis of historical series and the use of econometric and multiple regression models, it is possible to identify the correlation elements between price and demand, if the data are available.

Demand establishes the maximum price that the consumer wants to pay, within his analysis of the cost–benefit that results in the perceived value of the offer.

This value represents the ceiling for the price to be practiced.

10.4.3 Cost Estimate

The costs of a product or service will serve as a parameter for the floor to be practiced in the definition of the price, since prices below the cost represent a loss to the company, which will not be able to survive long in this way.

The company must establish its price (Kotler & Armstrong, 2016) in order to cover its production, distribution, and sale costs, and generate a margin that will repay its investment and business risk.

There are three basic costing systems (Nagle & Hogan, 2008):

- **Full or absorption costing**—There are two basic types of costs:
  - **Fixed or indirect costs**—are those that do not vary by production; think of all the costs that must be paid even if the company does not produce a single unit. For example, rent, energy, interest, wages, etc.
  - **Variable or direct costs**—are costs that vary according to production volume, such as raw material, packaging, components, etc.
- The total cost of a product is the sum of its fixed and variable costs. The main difficulties in this system are related to the allocation criteria, when costs are fixed, or when costs are indirect, and why they need to be apportioned between products or cost centers that have absorbed variable costs or direct costs. Several apportionment criteria have been proposed, each with advantages and disadvantages, which generates discussions about the justice of its application. The main apportionment criteria involve the distribution proportional to the percentage weight of the revenue, the area used, time of use, the intensity of use, etc. Each criterion can result in different weights in the allocation of indirect or

fixed costs, and should be carefully analyzed to avoid improperly overloading a product line, which can decrease its competitiveness in the market. If a product has higher costs, its managers will have to practice higher prices to maintain the desired margins. This criterion is the most traditional, adopted by most companies, and used for legal purposes in Brazil.

- **Marginal or variable costing**—The marginal or variable costing system considers only variable costs and expenses generated by a specific product, that is, costs that only exist due to the existence of the product, without including fixed or indirect expenses, which are considered as structural costs, the responsibility of the company as a whole, and which must be absorbed by the contribution margins. The contribution margin is the difference between the price and the marginal cost. It expresses the potential that a given product has, to cover the structural costs of the company, which is the sum of fixed costs and expenses. In this system the price management of a product portfolio becomes more flexible than in the system of full cost or absorption, since different margins can be established according to the strategic needs of each product and the company, with products of greater margin allowing existence and making competitive others with smaller margins, but also important for the company. This system requires integrated vision, greater organization, monitoring of the entire product portfolio, more complex information systems, and greater knowledge of managers.
- **Activity-Based Cost or ABC**—Traditional apportionment criteria bring discussions about the justice with which they distribute fixed or indirect costs. They can create errors and uncertainties in data collection and apportionment criteria, those in the criteria for covering structural costs by margins. The "Activity-Based Cost" or ABC, assumes that products consume activities, that consume resources; divides the production processes into activities; and appropriates to each product all expenses and direct costs (both fixed and variable) of each activity. The goal is to fix the cost (and price) based on the value of the activities performed to deliver the product or customer service. Allocating costs to each activity allows you to identify costs in more detail, and more accurately. The evolution of information technology contributed to the more intense use of this system, which would be too complex for manual implementation. Its advantages stand out when working with several market segments of different characteristics and needs, since costs can be allocated according to the activities demanded. And activities that represent costs and do not add value can be identified and eliminated. It also allows greater flexibility and speed in pricing decisions in cases of products that have a short life cycle, and higher fixed costs.

10.4.4 Analysis of Competitors' Costs, Prices, and Offers

Defined the floor by cost and ceiling by customer demand, price-positioning within this range should be done based on the analysis of the strategy of its competitors.

It is necessary to identify, for a given market range (Kotler & Armstrong, 2016) the costs, prices, and possible price reactions of competitors. The company should also evaluate differences in offers and the possible perceived value of them, and from this mapping, decide how it will position itself, whether above, equal to, or below its competitors.

This information can be obtained through different forms of research, from literature consultation, brochures, internet sites, and other sources of secondary information to surveys with selected customers in the market and suppliers.

10.4.5 Selection of a Pricing Method

There are basically six pricing methods (Kotler & Armstrong, 2016):

- **Mark-up price**—is the simplest method, where you add a mark-up, or multiplier, to the cost of the product; for example, the small retail trade, for certain fabrics, usually practices the mark-up of 2.5, that is, the price is 2.5 the cost. It is not a very efficient system, as it does not take into account factors related to demand, perceived value, and competition.
- **Target return price**—the company determines, for a given production volume of a product with known cost, what price leads to a rate of return established in its strategy.
- **Price of perceived value**—the company establishes the price based on the evaluation of the value perceived by the customer, for the various factors of its offer, such as image, channels, reputation, reliability, durability, services, guarantees, etc. It is necessary an intense communication work with the client for him to recognize and value the different elements of value that are being offered.
- **Pricing based on the ideal value**—the company establishes relatively low prices, without losing quality, while redesigning its operations for cost reductions in development, manufacturing, distribution, service, and sales.
- **Determination of market prices**—the price is determined based on those practiced by competitors. It is more common in oligopoly markets, where there are few competing companies, and there are not much incentives to raise prices in relation to competition, because the others would not rise and the company would lose sales, nor incentives to lower prices compared to competition, since all others would be forced to lower their prices, causing everyone to lose financial margin.
- **Price determination by auction**—prices are displayed as bids, and the highest value is the winner.

10.4.6 Selection of Final Price

Until the previous stage, it was possible to analyze the competitive environment and reach a range of price values to be practiced (Kotler & Armstrong, 2016).

The final selection should take into account the additional factors:

- **Influence of other elements of the marketing mix**—all marketing compounds can add perceived value, and should be considered in pricing (the price itself can be associated with quality), the location and environment of the point of sale, the quality and content of the communication, the attributes of the product, its packaging, labeling, and guarantees.
- **Company pricing policies**—The company may have policies for specific situations, such as exception cases such as delays, cancellations, and misuse of services, when additional fees and fines may be charged.
- **Pricing by sharing earnings and risks**—in addition to the price itself, the company offers performance guarantees, and can bear losses if performance is not achieved; another option is to establish a price level, but to condition greater performance to pay fees on the additional gain.
- **Price impact on third parties**—finally, should third-party reactions be considered—will the price be accepted by sellers or distributors? Can the government intervene? Can consumers feel harmed?

10.5 Tactical Pricing Decisions

The price set out in the process described above is a reference value for trades, which is called in the practice of full price or list price.

Based on it, sellers start sales negotiations with their customers, and can change this value depending on each context. We may have the following situations (Kotler & Armstrong, 2016).

10.5.1 Geographic Price

There is the practice of geographically differentiated prices, when customers are located in different regions with their own market characteristics, purchasing power, distribution structure, storage, transportation and sales, currency differences, etc.

10.5.2 Discounted Prices and Promotions

Discounts can be offered by prepayment, large volumes, off-season purchases, etc.

10.5.3 Promotional Price

Special prices charged to stimulate increased sales:

- **Price-bait**—generally used by supermarkets, consists of reducing the prices of some of the most popular products to attract customers to the store, generating traffic and the possibility of display and sale of other products with normal prices.
- **Price of occasion**—reduction of prices associated with specific dates, such as holidays and commemorative dates.
- **Price for special customers**—prices for selected customers, usually classified as VIPs within a loyalty program, and who often buy in larger volumes and more often.
- **Cash rebate**—used for example in car sales, the purchase financed by the list value entitles you to receive a cash value.
- **Low-interest financing**—reduced rates are offered compared to those normally practiced.
- **Payment in longer terms**—longer term leads to reduction of the value of the monthly installment, making the good more accessible.

10.6 Pricing Strategies in Luxury Markets

The main factors to be considered in the pricing of luxury products (Fiske & Silverstein, 2005) and that should be identified through research are:

- Consumers are becoming more aware of luxury alternatives in the market, and this perceived growing value should be added to the price.
- In specific categories, consumers are willing to pay a premium for excellence and differentiation, which should be reflected in price, not just incremental advantages.
- Identify, from the consumer's point of view, what are the specific benefits that he recognizes, not just what innovation is.
- Consider the value of the product purchase and consumption experience.
- Deliver benefits across the entire value chain.
- Increase value by referring brand ambassadors to increase their reliability.

Differently from mass products, luxury products are associated to high prices, that signals both quality and exclusivity. Luxury prices have to be significantly above mass prices, and as luxury brands extend their product lines with entry products that are more accessible, they also have to increase price of their top product lines frequently in order to preserve the exclusivity of the brand.

10.7 Summary

We have seen that pricing has a fundamental strategic function for the company, when defining its revenues, and determining whether it will offer the desired profitability. If not calculated properly, the financial health of the company can be seriously affected, and may lose competitiveness and even reach its bankruptcy.

Usually, the pricing decision is made by a specialized team, with the monitoring of senior management, and can be developed in six stages. When the reference price is defined, it can be changed depending on the specific context of each sale.

In luxury, price can also affect (Gutsatz & Heine, 2018) the perception of luxury itself, and the positioning of the brand.

Traditional pricing procedures (Fassnacht et al., 2012, 2013) do not equally apply to luxury brands. In luxury more than in any other segment, prices are an indicator of the finest quality, prestige, rarity, and hedonic value. To enhance and preserve this image prices for luxury brands should not only be highest in the relevant market but also kept stable over time. Many luxury brands never offered price discounts throughout their history. They even may buy back its products from licensed retailers to prevent sales at reduced prices during the financial crisis or burn excess stock not sold. Any volatility in prices jeopardizes the luxury brand image. First, pricing luxury brands requires specific procedures that largely differ from traditional pricing procedures in four integral parts of the pricing process framework:

- **Strategic direction**: before actually determining prices, luxury firms should precisely define price objectives and the brand's price-positioning. Subsequent brand extensions and other marketing mix instruments should be aligned to this price-positioning.
- **Analysis**: internal cost structures, competitor prices, and customer's willingness to pay should be analyzed taking into account that, in luxury, price increases do not necessarily go along with decreasing demand (known as Veblen effect).
- **Decision**: based on the strategic direction and analysis luxury firms should follow predefined rules to determine prices. Specifically, prices should be stable in the short run by employing a rigid price promotion and price discrimination policy. In the long run luxury firms should slightly increase prices to retain the distance from the mass.
- **Implementation**: finally, luxury firms should centralize the pricing authority and distribute through their own stores and carefully selected retailers only to control sales prices and how they are communicated.

Bibliography

Beulke, R., & Berto, D. J. (2009). *Precificação: Sinergia do marketing e das finanças.* Editora Saraiva

Fassnacht, M., Kluge, P. N., & Mohr, H. (2012). Do luxury pricing decisions create price continuity? In *Identitätsbasierte Luxusmarkenführung* (pp. 121–137). Springer Gabler, Wiesbadenp.

Fassnacht, M., Kluge, P. N., & Mohr, H. (2013). Pricing luxury brands: Specificities, conceptualization and performance impact. *Marketing ZFP, 35*(2), 104–117.

Fiske, N., & Silverstein, M. J. (2005x). *Trading up-why consumers want new luxury goods and how companies create them* (pp. 1–15, 47–53). Boston Consulting Group.

Gutsatz, M., & Heine, K. (2018). Is luxury expensive? *Journal of Brand Management, 25*(5), 411–423.

Kotler, P., & Amstrong, G. (2016). *Principles of marketing* (16th ed.). Pearson.

Nagle, T. T., Hogan, J. E., & Zale, J. (2008). *The strategy and tactics of pricing.*

Communication Strategies and Tools for Luxury Brands

11.1 Introduction

Chapter Objectives

> This chapter presents the main concepts and specific characteristics of Advertising, Sales promotion, Events, Experiences and Live Marketing, Promotion, Publicity, and Public Relations, Digital tools, Social Media and Influencers, Mobile Marketing, Direct marketing, and Personal Selling.
>
> Communication is one of the most powerful components of the marketing mix, because it allows to create images and perceptions that contribute to the formation of positioning and product identity.
>
> There is a wide variety of communication tools, with their strengths and weaknesses, and they should be used in sync to communicate the desired message in a unique way.
>
> The eight main communication tools, both mass and personal, are presented, and the main decisions for them to act efficiently.

11.2 Integrated Marketing Communication

11.2.1 Marketing Communication

If the company simply creates a product, sets its price, and sets its sales channels, it will likely have few results, as its consumers will not be aware of its attributes and benefits. For this, it is essential that marketing communication tools are used.

They allow you to inform and remember that the product exists, persuade the consumer of the advantages and value offered, help choose among other alternatives, guide how to go to the point of sale, inform how to make the purchase, how to use the product, and how to manifest your satisfaction or dissatisfaction with it. Strengthening loyalty contributes to the growth of brand equity of the brand.

The communication mix consists of eight communication tools (Kotler & Armstrong, 2016; Shimp, 2010):

- **Advertising**—any form of payment for presentation and non-personal promotion by an identified advertiser.
- **Sales promotion**—several short-term incentives used to stimulate experimentation or purchase.
- **Events and experiences**—activities and programs aimed at creating interactions between customers and the brand.
- **Public relations and advertising**—a variety of programs aimed at promoting or protecting the image of a company and its products.
- **Direct marketing**—communication actions developed directly from the company to its customers.
- **Interactive marketing**—online communication activities and programs.
- **Word-of-mouth marketing**—direct communication of one person with another, which can be influenced by the company.
- **Personal sales**—personal interaction between seller and customer aiming at dissemination and sale of products.

All these tools, when used, represent different facets of the company's voice, and must be coordinated in an integrated way (Shimp, 2010) to convey the same message. When consumers hear the same message from different channels, they reinforce and increase their credibility, but when these tools emit different messages about the same company or product, they create confusion in the consumer's mind, and the likelihood of them being filtered or forgotten by the consumer increases.

Each tool has advantages and disadvantages, depending on its characteristics and forms of operation. But they all act as marketing processes, which can be modeled from macro and micro points of view.

The macroprocess of marketing communication presents the interaction as a whole between sender and receiver and the elements of communication.

This first model is composed of nine elements (Kotler & Armstrong, 2016; Shimp, 2010):

- **Sender**—is the person who creates the message
- **Receiver**—is the person who receives the message
- **Message**—is the information you want to transmit
- **Medium (or media)**—is the element that contains the message
- **Coding**—is the sender's process of transforming the meaning that is in your mind into a message

- **Decoding**—is the receiver's process of turning the message into meaning in your mind
- **Answer**—is the reaction that the message awakens in the receiver
- **Feedback**—is the interpretation by the receiver response issuer
- **Noise**—random and competing messages that can affect communication.

Marketing communication micromodels focus on consumer-specific responses to communication.

Communication occurs through three stages, cognitive, affective, and behavioral.

There are four basic templates. In all of them, initially the customer is aware of the message when receiving and processing its meanings. In the second stage, the affective stage, he evaluates the message received and takes a position, acceptance or refusal of the proposal of the message, if this evaluation is negative, it ends here the process, but if it is positive, it passes to the third behavioral stage, where it takes the necessary steps for the acquisition of the product.

It is a complex process, where the customer needs to absorb, assimilate, and accept the message, recognizing the product as a solution to their desire, while in parallel we have several other competing messages diverting their attention.

11.2.2 Steps for the Development of Effective Communication

To develop effective communication, eight steps (Kotler & Armstrong, 2016) are required:

- **Identification of the target audience**—communication should be directed to a specific profile of consumers, defined in the process of strategic marketing planning, along with its positioning. This profile helps you understand your behavior in the consumption decision process by identifying the main factors that influence this behavior.
- **Determination of objectives**—every communication action must be clear from the outset what objectives it wants to achieve. The main ones are:
  - *Category need*—presents why that category is a viable solution to the customer's need
  - *Brand awareness*—shows the consumer that the brand exists, and make them recognize it, spontaneously or stimulated
  - *Attitudes toward the brand*—make the consumer understand that the brand is a relevant alternative to the solution of their problem, creating a positive predisposition toward it
  - *Intention to purchase the brand*—induces the consumer to make the decision to acquire the brand.

Communication should consider three aspects:

- **Message strategy**—what is meant to be decided, generating ideas, appeals, and themes that convey positioning and points of similarity and difference.
- **Creative strategy**—establishes the way in which to say what is desired, in an informative way, where the focus is on solving the problem through the attributes and benefits of the product, or in a transformational way, based on lifestyle and emotions generated by the use of the brand.
- **Source of the message**—defines who should say the message; the source must have credibility, expressed by mastery of the subject, perceived image of reliability and honesty, and attractiveness and sympathy. Messages are usually transmitted by celebrities, industry professionals, and ordinary consumers who have the same profile as the target audience.

11.2.3 Selection of Communication Channels

—The main communication channels are:

- **Personal channels**, which involve two or more people communicating directly with each other, and may occur in person or via telephone, mail, email, or chat. They are most often used for the communication of more complex, sophisticated, risky, and subjective products.
- **Non-personal channels**—are channels aimed at multiple people, and cover media, sales promotions, events, and public relations.

11.2.4 Budget Establishment

There is no single rule, which can vary considerably in different segments; consumer products usually invest higher percentages than organizational products. The four most common methods are:

- **Method of available resources**—the company uses only what it currently considers available, without assessing the impact and efficiency of the communication effort, being more subject to communication failures and failures.
- **Sales percentage method**—the value is set based on a percentage of sales in the last period, or forecast for the next. It does not allow the company to establish the effort according to the market need, the competitive situation against its competitors, or according to the position in the product life cycle.
  - **Method of parity with competition**—the value is established as a proportion of the competitor's budget. It does not take into account the specific needs of the moment and market.
  - **Method of objectives and tasks**—is the most recommended. The company establishes a distributed planning over time, for example, in a year, where it defines all the actions necessary to achieve its communication objectives and

establishes budgets for each of them. Allows effort to be focused on results and objectives.

11.2.5 Decision on the Communication Mix

The communication mix should be defined as the communication effort will be distributed among the eight communication tools: advertising, sales promotion, public relations and advertising, events and experiences, direct marketing, interactive marketing, word-of-mouth, and sales force.

Each presents advantages and disadvantages for certain competitive contexts and segment profiles, which must be evaluated in each case. The main factors to be considered in the analysis are:

- **Type of product market**—in the consumer market, mass advertising, and promotions are more common, while in the organizational market personal sales and events are more used.
- **Buyer's disposition stage**—advertising tends to be more interesting in the early stages, to generate awareness and interest, while personal sales and promotions are more efficient to influence attitudes and generate predisposition to purchase.
- **Product lifecycle stage**—advertising, and events are usually better in the early stages when the product is not yet known and there are greater doubts, while personal sales and promotions stimulate sales in the following phases. In the declining phase, promotions are generally maintained and the use of other communication tools is reduced.

11.2.6 Measurement of Communication Results

The evaluation of the communication results should be made in terms of revenue sums and achievement of objectives, verifying whether the impact was compatible with the pre-established goals. The main metrics are memory and recognition, attitudes, purchase intent, and effective purchase.

11.2.7 Integrated Marketing Communication Management

The variety of communication tools available requires the company to make use of them in an integrated manner, with a "360-degree view", ensuring that all customer communication contacts are made in a relevant and consistent manner.

It is expected that with the adoption of this process and its steps, the company can efficiently allocate the resources needed to achieve its communication objectives.

11.2.8 Creative Communication Strategies

- **Informative**—the product appears as a solution to the problem, when the character is faced with a problem derived from a need, but the product, as a hero, prevents him from having problems.
- **Transformational**—in this second creative strategy, the product is presented as a way to show its owner as a person who had a successful life and the product is the symbol of his lifestyle.

11.3 Mass Communication

The communication tools that make up the communication mix can be grouped into two large groups, mass communication and personal communication. In this topic, it will be covered in greater detail those of the first group, and in the next topic, those of the second.

11.3.1 Advertising

Advertising (Kotler & Armstrong, 2016) is an important tool for the communication of persuasive and informative messages, although it has been losing effectiveness over time, but it can still be effective, provided that it is used in a coordinated way with other tools of the communication mix.

An efficient advertising plan (Kotler & Armstrong, 2016; Shimp, 2010) should consider the five Ms:

- **Mission**—must define the objectives of communication, in terms of a specific and quantified task, in a given audience and within a certain time frame; for example, to increase the degree of brand knowledge from 10 to 60% among executives seeking sporting goods in the next six months.
- **Money**—you must define the necessary budget, depending on the stage in the product life cycle, market share, degree of competition, frequency of advertising, and degree of product replacement.
- **Message**—creation of the propaganda campaign, from the creation and evaluation of the message to the creative development and execution.
- **Media**—the main media decisions are:
  - *Coverage*—is the number of customers who must be exposed to the media at least once during the delivery period.
  - *Frequency*—is the number of times, on average, that the customer is exposed to the media during the delivery period.
  - *Impact*—is the qualitative value of an exhibition in a given media, evaluating the degree of attention and interest that it arouses in the target audience.

- **Measurement**—is the evaluation of the effectiveness and efficiency of advertising. Before carrying out the advertising campaign, the research identifies the current situation and establishes quantitative objectives to be achieved with advertising. Once the campaign has begun, it is already possible to conduct research to assess whether the results are compatible with planning. The first surveys may already indicate trends of success or failure, allowing changes to be made in the conduct of the campaign, aiming at better results.

11.3.2 Sales Promotion

The sales promotion (Kotler & Armstrong, 2016):

> ... Consists of a Set of Incentive Tools, Most Short-Term, Designed to Stimulate Faster or More Purchase of Specific Products by the Consumer or Distribution Channel.

The concept of promotion includes (Kotler & Armstrong, 2016) a wide variety of actions:

> ... consumption promotion tools (samples, coupons, refunds, discounts, giveaways, prizes, rewards, free trial, guarantees, combined promotions, cross promotions, point-of-sale displays and demonstrations); promotion of distribution channel (discounts, advertising and exhibition bonuses and free goods); and promotion of business and sales team (trade fairs and conventions, sales contests and gifts).

The main sales promotion decisions (Kotler & Armstrong, 2016) are:

- **Goal setting**—promotions aim, for the consumer, to generate experimentation, attract new consumers, and increase sales volume, and for retail, encourage the acceptance of new items, increase inventory, equate promotions of competitors, and retain the retailer.
- **Selection of promotion tools for the consumer**—according to the profile of the market segment, communication and promotion objectives, efficiency, and costs.
- **Selection of promotion tools for retail**—and according to negotiation with retailers, to meet the above objectives.
- Selection of business promotion tools for the sales force—aiming to generate new business and motivate salespeople.
- **Development of the program**—definition of the minimum volume to be reached, the conditions of participation, the duration of the program, and the means of distribution.
- **Implementation and evaluation of the program**—definition of schedule of actions and evaluation metrics

11.3.3 Events and Experiences

Events and experiences are planned moments (Kotler & Armstrong, 2016) to cultivate the relationship between the brand and its customers.

The main reasons for using events are:

- Create identification with a specific market or lifestyle segment
- Increase brand exposure to your target audience
- Create and reinforce perceptions of associations between event characteristics and brand identity
- Strengthen corporate identity
- Create experiences and generate emotions
- Join community and social causes
- Offer entertainment to customers and employees
- Leverage other promotional actions.

The main sponsorship decisions are:

- **Choice of events**—select the ones that fit the brand image and your target audience.
- **Preparation of sponsorship plans**—presentation of the profile of the event and target audience, possibilities of image association, and expected results.
- **Evaluation of sponsorship activities**—the most common way is to estimate the value of advertising generated with the association of the brand with the event.

The experience seeks to create unique moments for the client, through visits to factories, museums, and exhibitions.

11.3.4 Public Relations

The work of public relations (Shimp, 2010) is to develop and protect the brand, through relationships with opinion-makers, in order to generate free and positive coverage. Can be used in various marketing tasks (Kotler & Armstrong, 2016):

- Product launches
- Repositioning of mature products
- Generating interest by product category
- Influence on specific audiences
- Management of problems and public product crises
- Construction of corporate and product image.

The main public relations tools are publications, events, sponsorships, news, presentations, and activities to provide services of public interest and management of visual identity.

The main public relations decisions are the establishment of objectives, choice of messages and vehicles, implementation of the public relations plan, and evaluation of results.

11.4 Personal Communication

The main tools of personal communication (Kotler & Armstrong, 2016) are direct marketing, interactive marketing, word-of-mouth communication, and personal sales.

11.4.1 Direct Marketing

Direct marketing (Kotler & Armstrong, 2016; Shimp, 2010) is the use of direct channels, without intermediaries, to deliver products and services to the consumer.

The main channels are direct mail, catalog marketing, telemarketing, interactive TV, sales kiosks, websites, and applications for mobile phones and tablets.

Its great advantage is the speed of measurement of the customer's response, being able to make quick adjustments in its actions, depending on the results. Works well when integrated with other communication and distribution channels.

Direct mail (Kotler & Armstrong, 2016) consists of sending, from a list or mailing list of pre-classified, offer, ad, reminders, or other items.

Its advantages are the ease of targeting specific segments, customization, and flexibility. However, due to its intense use in recent decades, it has generated a negative reaction from customers due to the excess of correspondence it generates, which leads part of the containers not to read the messages, even discarding the envelope still closed.

To develop a successful campaign, objectives, target audience, message, and offer elements, efficiency testing mechanisms, and result indicators should be selected.

Catalog marketing (Kotler & Armstrong, 2016; Shimp, 2010) works with a publication or catalog that lists all your products on offer, in print or digital form.

Its success depends on the development of a focused and updated mailing list, good inventory management, selection of the appropriate product mix, and the creation of a strong brand that represents credibility.

Telemarketing (Kotler & Armstrong, 2016; Shimp, 2010) consists of customer service and sales through a team of operators or telephone centers. It usually has lower costs and allows agility and speed in customer service. It can be active, when used to contact customers, or receptive, when it acts only in response to customers' demands.

Other forms of direct marketing are the publication of advertisements in newspapers with the indication of how to place the order, the TV infomercials, and the sales TV channels.

11.4.2 Interactive Marketing

Interactive marketing (Kotler & Armstrong, 2016) is what uses electronic means that allow dialogue with the customer, for sales and relationships.

Its main advantage is the possibility of customizing the interaction, to the specific profile of each consumer.

It also allows the creation of virtual communities, on websites, blogs, and social media, where customers can interact with the brand and others like it.

Some disadvantages are the possibility of electronic filtering, the difficulty of assessing the difference between presence and interest, and vulnerability to hackers.

11.4.3 Tips for Creating Effective Websites

Kotler & Armstrong, 2016 cites Rayport and Jaworski's study, which relate the 7 Cs to creating effective websites:

- **Context**—layout and design.
- **Content**—text, images, sound, and video.
- **Community**—communication mechanisms between users.
- **Customization**—ability to adapt the site by the company and the customer.
- **Communication**—communication mechanisms between the website and company.
- **Connection**—site connectivity to other sites.
- **Commerce**—ability to allow the marketing ads on search engines to work by buying space via online auctions of keywords that trigger the display of the ad.
- Generally, the use of more generic keywords is better for creating marketing awareness, while the use of the brand is more appropriate for the effect of the purchase.

Mobile marketing is the use of messages on mobile devices, usually targeted to specific profiles. It can be done through SMS messages, ads on websites, and specific applications for smartphones.

11.4.4 Word-of-Mouth Communication

Word-of-mouth communication (Kotler & Armstrong, 2016) is the informal exchange of information between people about brands and their attributes and benefits, having a great influence on the customer's consumption decision.

Positive word-of-mouth can be stimulated through communication, in particular by social media, communities, blogs, and online forums.

Two specific ways are buzz marketing and viral marketing, by creating messages that attract and encourage people to talk about the topic and pass on the message to their network of friends.

11.4.5 Personal Sales

Personal sales are an important tool, due to the social interaction that happens between customer and seller. However, its cost is high and should be used with the proper follow-up to ensure that it will be efficient.

The main tasks of the sales team (Kotler & Armstrong, 2016) are the prospecting of customers, allocation of time between potential and effective customers, communication about the company's goods and services, realization of the sales process, from the approach to the closing of the sale, after-sales support, and allocation of products in case of production shortage.

11.5 Communication Strategies in Luxury

Digital technology (Mosca & Gallo, 2016) …

> *has brought about a radical change in the dynamics of marketing, and it is becoming increasingly important. The spread of social media and mobile media offers firms new business opportunities; these firms have the potential to create viral communication campaigns and to reach, thanks to the potential of new media, multiple market segments, providing the ability to customize messages.*

Luxury firms thus address their system of offerings to consumers with a view of producing any number of functional benefits. With this in mind, the physical quality of the goods, while important, is instrumental in the creation of the emotions that are sought and shared. This can enhance a new concept called "reverse multichannel marketing". What has primarily been a communication platform thus far is now transforming into a selling place, while what has always been a selling platform is now becoming a "showcase" where people can gather information and experiment with what they can buy online. This represents an interesting and fruitful area for future research for both "academics and managers".

Luxury brands (Bhanot, 2012), after a period of caution, fully entered the internet and the digital media, increasing the brand present in most relevant social media, using them as a way to maintain dialogues with their clients and promote their brands, and to instill word-of-mouth about them.

A distinct challenge (Ramchandani & Coste-Manière, 2012) that brands face in digital communication is the global profile of their consumers, and the need to communicate in several languages. It can have an impact in their positioning, as it can affect the brand whether a French or Italian brand uses the English language as the main one in their communication. The number of available language options is fundamental to allow proper communication with consumers in different countries, with different languages and dialects.

11.6 Summary

> Communication is one of the most powerful components of the marketing mix, because it allows to create images and perceptions that contribute to the formation of the positioning and identity of the product, and by its power of information and persuasion.
> The eight main communication tools, both mass and personal, which must be used consistently, are presented, and the main decisions for them to act efficiently.
> Luxury brands have challenges to integrate their communications and offer language options to cover sometimes hundreds of different speakers.

Bibliography

Bhanot, S. (2012). Application of social media to word-of-mouth marketing and promotion of luxury brands. *FIIB Business Review, 1*(2), 9–15.

Kotler, P., & Armstrong, G. (2016). Principles of marketing (16th ed.). Pearson.

Mosca, F., & Gallo (Ed.). (2016). *Global marketing strategies for the promotion of luxury goods*. IGI Global.

Ramchandani, M., & Coste-Manière, I. (2012). Asymmetry in multi-cultural luxury communication: A comparative analysis on luxury brand communication in India and China. *Journal of Global Fashion Marketing, 3*(2), 89–97.

Shimp, T. A. (2010). *Integrated marketing communication in advertising and promotion*.

Managing People for the Luxury Market

12.1 Introduction

Chapter Objectives
In this chapter it is discussed the main topics related to managing talented people for excellent services in luxury: How to get the best employees for the best clients; Recruiting to attract the best; Selecting the best; Training the best for excellence; Motivating the best for high performance; Evaluating exceptional people; Managing people in luxury.

12.2 Managing People

People, in particular those working in the interface of the company with the client, are fundamental for great experiences (Kotler & Amstrong, 2016, Wirtz & Lovelock, 2016). But to deliver experiences at that level of excellence, a thorough process is required. When someone recalls a particularly good experience, most of the time it was offered by a knowledgeable, likable, attentive person that go beyond the expectations. Not all people are like this. Some people have naturally these skills, while others will need extensive training to enhance these abilities, and some others just don't have what it takes.

Good service can increase clients' loyalty and improve the brand image. They are seen by the clients as representatives of the company, that is evaluated based on how good or bad the shopping experience was.

The background employees are also very important, as they provide the support for those in the foreground to better perform their work. Even in low-contact services, as in some cases in ecommerce, there are moments when the clients have to contact someone in the company, particularly in case of problems, when the employee has to do his best to recover the service.

In consequence, we present six elements of the process to manage people that can deliver great experiences. A strongly motivated team can be a sustainable competitive advantage, hard to imitate and compete with.

12.3 Recruiting

Recruiting is a crucial step, not just because it is the first one, but also because is the first filter to find the right person for the right place. So, the first decision is to define the profile of the professional in need. That implies in specifying both soft and hard skills that will be demanded for the specific position.

Hard skills are the technical skills that the candidate will have to master in order to best perform the job activities, as understanding the fiscal laws, if for a position in the accountancy department, or which glass is more appropriate for the wine ordered by the client, if for the position of waiter.

Soft skills, on the other hand, are those interpersonal skills that help create a good working environment and develop empathy with clients. People that treat clients cheerfully are good listeners, focused on anticipating clients' needs, creative to the detail level, interested in the job and in ways to improve it, appreciative of learning, collaborative, pride of her skills, etc.

They both have to be specified in detail, in order to create check lists of comparison of different candidates, and ask the support of the human resources department for the best tools to be used in the next step of selection.

Usual recruiting tools could be ads in social media, recruiting fairs, recruiting agencies, and employees' network. An interesting case is the luxury hotels chain Carlton-Ritz, where employees are encouraged to give his business card with a message on the back, recommending to the HR someone that offered a good experience and he considers suited for a position in the hotel.

Company branding, the process of creating a good reputation in the job market, can be of great importance in attracting the best candidates to the company. This can be achieved by communicating to the job market information on being a good employer, such as a company that recognizes merit, incentive learning, and invests in growth of their employees, among other actions.

The objective of this step is to gather a reasonable number of candidates that present or have potential to offer the desired skills, so one can extract quality from quantity.

12.4 Selecting

Based on the desired profile of soft and hard skills, selecting tools and techniques can be selected to help evaluate and classify the candidates. Psychological tests can be used to identify desired personality traits. Group dynamics help evaluate how the candidates interact with other people, the degree of competitiveness and collaboration, skills of time-keeping, leadership, rapport, confidence, etc.

From a great range of tools, HR professionals can be of great assistance in selecting the most appropriate ones. The profile defined previously is very important to decide what criteria to use in the evaluation and identification of the right candidate. A wrong selection decision can have long-term impact on the company, as this employee will have to be dismissed, with additional costs, not considering the time and money spent in training, adapting, waiting for an increase in performance that never comes, and the costs involving in starting over the process to find another adequate candidate.

At this stage, is very important that both sides ask as many questions as necessary. The candidate must have a fair and realistic perspective on the job, apart from what is available in the company's site, in order to assess if he will be able to fit well. Apart from the salary and fringe benefits, candidates usually are interested in companies that invest in training and development, possibilities of ascending in the company, and details of the company culture. The company, on the other hand, has to make sure that the candidate is bringing the right skills in and will adapt well to the company culture.

In the selection process, a combination of tools should be used, as multiple interviews, with those involved with the position, group dynamics to observe behavior in different situations, various psychological and personality tests, communication tests, confidence and self-image tests, reports of real-life previous experiences, etc.

A final point to remember is that it is not easy to find the perfect candidate, and the company should be prepared to also consider hiring candidates that present part of the desired traits, as long as the missing ones can be trained—mostly the hard skills. Previous experience in similar areas, good interpersonal skills, work ethics, attention to details, etc., and a good fit with the company culture should be considered enough in case other candidates don't excel in all areas, as these are usually areas that are hard or not at all possible to be taught.

Some companies have cultures where a slow rate of growth in promotions is valued, so the candidate will have to wait an "acceptable" period in a position before being promoted. This could be too slow for those that are attracted for a position where he can ascend quickly to higher positions, what could cause insatisfaction with the job, due to company's values.

The final aim should be to bring in and put the right person in the right position.

12.5 Training

Training is a continuous process for two reasons: no new employee will arrive 100% prepared for the job, or knowing the details of the culture of the company. And over time, as consumers change their behavior and preferences, employees have to be trained on the necessary adjustments in service processes that will substitute those that became outdated or obsolete.

With the support of the appropriate training, employees will feel valued and motivated, perceiving the company as an employer that believes and invests in the improvement of their people.

On the strategical level, training should start with presentations from the CEO level, about the company culture, values, history, purposes, mission, goals, strategies, etc. This information will define general procedure rules to help decisions, according to what is acceptable or nor by the company. Core values like comradeship, honesty, responsibility, excellence, commitment to the company and the client, team spirit, client satisfaction, etc., could be presented as exemplary stories of the right behavior in the past, or how the founder would or did react to different situations.

On the operational level, training covers the processes and skills necessary to better serve the clients. Product and service characteristics and options, benefits and advantages that they may provide, use situations, demonstration skills, service values, etc.

Coaching is an interesting option, as more experienced people could work with new employees, sharing their experience, evaluating their work, and counseling on how to better perform their tasks.

Internal communications are fundamental to spread information over the company, about new strategies and products, marketing actions, new policies, employees' achievements, etc. An intranet can make available detailed documentation, training videos, CRM databases, etc.

12.6 Motivating

People are not like machines. Machines can be connected to an energy source and immediately, and almost indefinitely, start producing at the optimal level, 24 hours a day, 7 days a week. People, on the other hand, need emotional energy to perform well, and that depends on personal and social factors, like health, relationships with family and friends, enough hours of leisure and sleep, feeding, etc. As a result, people often work at levels of productivity between 50% and 80%, and if forced to increase above this level, the quality of the work may decrease dramatically.

The word motivation has the same roots as movement, and is the study of the factors that motivate, or move people, to do things. Some of the main theories of motivation are the one proposed by Freud Sigmund (2021) where drivers of personality explain human behavior; Maslow's hierarchy of needs (Healy, 2016) proposes five levels of needs, that people try to fulfill in a hierarchical way, and many others.

Managers have to follow and support their employees, identifying the need of offering motivational actions to help their subordinates perform better.

There are many situations that can reduce the level of emotional energy of an employee.

Work in the frontline can be stressful and presented with conflicts. One has to smile continuously, sometimes for hours, as part of the job role, no matter how you are really feeling. Smiling is very important to gain and retain the confidence of the client. Sometimes clients are not as kind as one is supposed to be, becoming arrogant or belligerent. Employees should be trained to support this stress, but it cannot be comfortable.

Role conflicts when there are different expectations and the salesman has to take sides. The manager wants him to be effective and productive, reaching goals of sales and profit, while the client may want to bargain a better price or a discount, or to have a complain solved by the company. He has to be both fast and efficient, but also courteous and helpful. Personal behavioral traits may make it more difficult for some people to handle rude or aggressive clients. Sometimes may be necessary to deal with conflicts between clients, like husband-and-wife discussions, smokers in non-smoking areas, or louder-than-usual clients.

Several studies have shown that employees can be motivated both by monetary and non-monetary incentives.

Monetary incentives include salary, bonuses, and prizes in money.

Non-monetary incentives can vary, from encouragement words to good working conditions, opportunities to travel, to promotions, better job contents, diverse, challenging, relevant to others and society, flexibility, positive feedbacks, etc. Simple things, like being selected as employee of the month, a trophy for good performance, gifts, etc., can be good motivators.

Motivation is contagious, and appeals to the competitiveness of others, and can result in better performance for the whole team.

Goals are important to drive efforts to a desired level, and to gauge personal performance against company's expectations. They can be perceived, when achieved, as rewards themselves.

The demand of a goal has to be finetuned, as if they are too low, they will be easy to achieve, and will not be motivating. On the other hand, if it is too high, it can be discouraging, and will also not be motivating. A good starting reference in setting goals is to base on previous years, adjusted by 5% to 10%, and discussed considering the context of the current year with the employee. It has to propose a reasonable challenge, perceived to be achievable, with some reasonable effort. Higher levels of goals are better accepted when discussed in public, and should be followed periodically, in order to verify if it is going in the right direction.

12.7 Evaluating

Regular evaluation and feedback are important to keep employees motivated. A fair evaluation can be an opportunity for corrections in actions, processes, or even strategies. The expectations previously agreed have to be remembered, and used to compare against actual performance. In case of results below the goals, it is very important to discuss the reasons, not just excuses, identify adjustments, eventual chances in the goals, or simply demand better levels for the next period. The manager should discuss together possible ways of improvement, pointing inefficiencies and mistakes, and making clear what will be the consequences for the future.

12.8 Dismissing

Being dismissed can be a strong shock for anyone. A position in a company becomes a part of the extended self of an individual, and losing a job can be akin to losing a part of the self. People miss the status of the position, the benefits, the power of his position, the confidence of being the provider for him and his family with his work, a feeling that his skills are no longer relevant in the market, and fear of the uncertainty that these months ahead will present without a salary, having to use his savings without knowing for how long, missing the work routine he was used to, a sense of betrayal from the company he made so many sacrifices not recognized, etc. It can also imply in changing the life style of the family, reducing shopping expenses, changing children to a more accessible school, having to chance to a cheaper car, or even a cheaper house. All these factors can have a strong impact on someone's self-image, confidence personal and social life.

For the company, if the employee has any complain of injustice in the dismissal process, like not having the attention and respect he deserves, not enough information to understand the decision, or the feeling that he lost his job because of a jealous boss or some other unfair reasons, he may leave with a bad image of the company, that may result in negative word-of-mouth in the work market, affecting the company brand image as employer.

The company must understand that it is common for candidates to contact friends and colleagues in the market, and if possible, working in that company, to gather information on a potential employer, and if this information is not positive, it will have an impact on the number of possible recruits. Particularly the best candidates, those that tend to have more offers and options, may choose to go to another company with better references.

Companies also have to remember that the market for certain jobs with specific talents is limited, and maybe five to ten years later the dismissed candidate can be an interesting option for hiring for a different situation, because of maturity or experience acquired over this period, and a bad experience may reduce his interest.

12.9 Managing People in Luxury

Luxury demands a different employee profile from different sectors. But attracting and retaining talents (Larkin & Burgess, 2008) is a common concern with all other sectors.

When the LVMH group initiated his consolidation (Son, 2005), he faced a scarcity of managerial talents in luxury. The solution was to hire and train talents from other sectors, particularly retail, art schools, engineering, and former MBAs, that had "good taste", and taught them their ethics of work, the importance of the search for excellence, the taste for an exceptional art of living. In 1991, LVMH partnered with the Parisian business school ESSEC to create a luxury brand marketing chair.

12.9 Managing People in Luxury

On-the-job training and brand immersion seminars complemented the formation of these new luxury managers.

Henry Royce, one of the founders of Rolls-Royce, once said:

Strive for perfection in everything. Take the best that exists and make it better. If it doesn't exist, create it. Accept nothing nearly right or good enough.

People that think in this way are ideal to be selected to work in luxury. They should know very well the importance of always looking for perfection, for excellence, in all details, and never accept just the "good enough".

Candidates to work in the luxury sector (Batt & Berghaus, 2014) seems to be attracted to brands that position their image with drivers like conspicuousness, uniqueness, association, hedonism, and quality.

A possible obstacle (Gutsatz & Auguste, 2013) to attracting talents is that most of the luxury companies, even the great groups, are at least partially owned by families, and some talents prefer not to work for these companies, as the possibilities of reaching the upper positions, as well as the decision power, are somewhat limited to members of the family.

Another restriction is that usually 80% a 90% of the staff works in the stores, in sales positions, and managerial positions are limited to a small office staff, rigidly controlled by the headquarters. This can be not attractive for those that prefer office positions with more autonomy and liberty to make decisions, and don't favor starting a career in sales before reaching the office.

On the other hand, a good formation in luxury manager can be a strong asset for those wishing to open his own business, applying concepts and values of luxury to other excellence businesses.

Usually, the main positions (Gutsatz & Auguste, 2013) in a big luxury company are:

- *Executive*: Country Manager, Marketing Development Director, Production Director
- *Creative*: Collection Director, Senior Fashion Designer, Visual Merchandiser Manager
- *Manufacturer/Workshop*: Manufacturer Director, Department Managers, Artisans
- *Retail*: Store Director, Sales Staff, Sales Expert.

The possibility of an employee (Mohsin et al., 2013) to leave a job in luxury (in this study, the results are from a luxury hotel) is: first, directly related to the employees' enthusiasm for the profession and organization, the nature of the work and its impact on social and family life. Secondly, to the level of satisfaction with the job in terms of organizational loyalty, relationship with supervisors, job security, earnings, and additional benefits.

Those wishing to enter this market should notice some points:

- Glamour is related to the client, not the employee. Be prepared to carry heavy boxes, perform repetitive tasks, and service demanding clients. If the brand offers a party, and they are quite frequent, you will be there after a working day, still working, not enjoying yourself.
- You should feel at ease, not guilty for working in luxury. Prices are high because of the intellectual and creative work of artisans, the use of expensive raw materials, the cost of the store, logistics and communication. Luxury creates jobs, activates the economy, contributes to arts and social causes. There is no correlation, as some argue, that this high value spent should be used elsewhere, for charity, to mitigate hungry or inequality in the world, as those are caused mostly by inefficiencies and corruption in dictatorships.
- Enthusiasm for the brand and the creator is essential to present the heritage and symbolic content of the brand, as it is very difficult to sell something you don't believe in.
- Understand that you work in luxury, you don't live in luxury. You are the professional, not the client. You should remain always in a position of service, not an equal to the client.
- Luxury is global, brands sell for the world, be prepared to deal with other cultures, other languages, for instance, today China and Japan are among the greater clients of luxury brands, and they may consume for different reasons than those you are used in your country.
- Travels are common for managers, but most of the time is spent in airports and meetings.

What leaders (Gutsatz & Auguste, 2013) in the luxury industry have in common? A comparison of four successful CEOs found:

- All three have strong cultural backgrounds, acquired through their families and their education, which provided them with international exposure to cultural and business diversities. These early experiences provided them with a strong sense of self, highly sociable personalities, and very positive mindsets which made them comfortable with the people who "play and spend" in the luxury environment.
- All of them have demonstrated great sensitivity to family business heritage and real passion for the craftsmanship factor.
- Their leadership sense, which would score highly in terms of emotional intelligence (EQ), cultural intelligence (CQ), and social intelligence (SQ), demonstrates their capacity to inspire passion and trust among all the people they met and/or worked with, all over the world.
- Each of them, as businessmen, have initiated new ways to address the luxury business, that are now acknowledged as standard in the industry.

Considering the characteristics of luxury's Top 100 board members (Gutsatz & Auguste, 2013) and the analysis of luxury leadership competencies, these authors suggest that the luxury industry must find leaders that:

- Present a balanced leadership profile that blends intelligence with relevant competencies (creative, intuitive, rational, and social) in order to be efficient;
- Have operated in different key geographic regions, such as Asia or America, to understand the different cultural characteristics both of employees and of customers;
- Switch easily between different time frames, from long-term thinking to short-term operating;
- Bring change management skills to an organization in order to reinvent the business model, while preserving the "mystery" of a brand's DNA;
- Have great attention to retail and customer issues, acknowledging the central role of sales staff;
- Have the talent to represent a brand as its ambassador and a great cultural ability to interact well with a very demanding international clientele;
- Develop specific leadership skills to work efficiently with creatives and designers;
- Fit in with the founder's vision of the world and those of the family members who are inevitably involved in the business;
- Understand the characteristics of the brand's organizational culture; and
- Possess the cultural background (from their family values and their education) that allows them to master the intricacies of a very "cultural" business.

12.10 Summary

People are fundamental in today's competitive world to create sustainable advantages that satisfy needs and offer magic experiences.

These people are special, not easily found, and a proper process should be adopted to increase the chances of attracting and retaining these talents.

Recruiting is fundamental to attract a reasonable number of qualified candidates, so the company can select those that better fit to their needs. The selection has to use objective tools to identify present or potential characteristics, appointing the qualified. Even the best candidates need training, as industry characteristics, company's values and culture, and changing consumer behavior and habits, demand continuous preparation to better adjust to these influences. Motivation helps achieve the necessary levels of emotional energy to create empathy and the proper rapport in service to the client. Dismissing is a stressful situation for the employee that can affect the image of the company as employer in the job market.

A luxury job demands special characteristics for those willing to enter, to those wishing to leader.

> It is a very demanding and professional market, but still marked by some characteristics of family business, and there is a need to adapt to these circumstances to reach success in this profession.

Bibliography

Batt, V., & Berghaus, B. (2014). *Luxury brands as employers.*
Freud, S. (2021). *Edição standard brasileira das obras psicológicas completas de Sigmund Freud.* Imago Editora.
Gutsatz, M., & Auguste, G. (2013). *Luxury talent management: Leading and managing a luxury brand.* Palgrave Macmillan.
Healy, K. (2016). A theory of human motivation by Abraham H. Maslow (1942). *The British Journal of Psychiatry, 208*(4), 313–313.
Kotler, P., & Amstrong, G. (2016). Principles of marketing (16th ed.). Pearson.
Larkin, R., Burgess, J. (2008). Staff retention in the luxury hotel sector in Australia: Essential, but not necessary! *In Proceedings: 8th Annual Pacific Employment Relations Association Conference.*
Mohsin, A., Lengler, J., & Kumar, B. (2013). Exploring the antecedents of intentions to leave the job: The case of luxury hotel staff. *International Journal of Hospitality Management, 35*, 48–58.
Som, A. (2005). Personal touch that built an empire of style and luxury. *In European Business Forum* (pp. 69–71).
Wirtz, J., & Lovelock, C. (2016). *Services marketing: People, technology.* World Scientific Publishing Company.

Process Management and Operations for Luxury Brands

13.1 Introduction

Chapter Objectives
Managing processes has become an important part of marketing management, as its control can guarantee homogeneous high-quality performance and consumer satisfaction. In this chapter, it is discussed the main aspects of how to evaluate and improve processes: Process mapping techniques, Process analysis, failure analysis, process reengineering and the use of Process manuals, and the importance of processes for luxury services.

13.2 The Importance of Process Management

If consumers see services as experiences, the company sees processes behind services.

A process (Kotler & Amstrong, 2016; Wirtz & Lovelock, 2016) is a sequence of activities with a common objective, in the case of services processes, a sequence of actives to deliver a magic experience. Great processes are agile, focus on the client and his needs, are lean, and waste no time or effort. To work properly, they have to be planned and designed based on the understanding of all necessary steps and their contribution to the clients' satisfaction.

But even the best processes may become obsolete over time, as clients' expectations change, and new ideas and technologies can offer best alternatives to the steps of the process. This means that processes have to be periodically reviewed and adjusted whenever necessary.

13.3 Process Mapping Techniques

The first step in the management of services processes is to map it in detail. Usually, this is done graphically, what allows to better visualize the activities, the sequences, and the performance.

Three of the main graphic process representations are the flowcharts, blueprints, and the consumer journey.

13.3.1 Flowcharts

A flowchart is a graphic representation of a process, with arrows and boxes, where the arrows indicate the sequences and the boxes, the activities. It is a good way to start mapping a process, from the larger view, in order to understand the process as a whole, and the main connections between the activities. It can be conducted through a series of interviews with all involved, to understand the tasks, skills, and actions that each participant of the process has to perform. It can be used in discussions on the performance of the process, helping all to understand what is going on and the impacts and implications of each one in the process, as well as understanding points of delay and failure, and how they happen.

13.3.2 Blueprints

A blueprint is a more detailed and complex representation, that add to a flowchart much more information. It divides the process in acts, sequences of actions that perform different stages of the total process. It allows one to follow step by step all the activities, in as much detail as desired and demanded, to fully understand the process. It can be more detailed in those steps identified as critic, and less detailed where it seems to be working fine. To be built, one has to conduct extensive interviews with all personnel involved, in order to faithfully represent all the necessary details and information to be represented.

A blueprint is more detailed, as it separates the process into activities performed by clients, employees (foreground and background), and supporting systems, and represents the interaction interfaces between these players.

First, one has to identify all key activities involved in delivering the experience, and then specify how they are connected.

The main elements of design in a blueprint are:

- Foreground activities
- Images (photos, drawings, or other graphic representations of the panorama where the stage is performed)
- Dividing lines between visible and background activities
- Background activities

13.3 Process Mapping Techniques 173

- Support systems (information technology, security, maintenance, valet, cleaning, catering, etc.)
- Possible failure points
- Bottleneck points
- Details of desired performance metrics for the activity
- Other service delivery services.

In a first moment, the representation should be kept relatively simple, in order to show the main picture, and then, when necessary, stages of the process that may demand more attention can be presented in more detail.

13.3.3 Consumer Journey

A recent technique that has proved to be of value is the consumer journey.

Its origins are from digital services, and is related to the fact that consumers today use the omnichannel strategy to make their consumption decisions.

The consumer journey represents the places that consumers access to support his consumption decision. He transits from digital to physical places to perform the actions related to each stage of the process.

The first stage is to become aware of a need, and that usually happens when he realizes he has a need, through internal (physical sensation, memories, etc.) or external stimuli (advertising, mouth-to-mouth, etc.). It is important to identify these external sources of stimuli, as they may be ideal communication tools to present the services as good solutions for their needs.

The second stage is to search for information about possible alternative solutions. The client can do a search on the internet, or visit a shopping center and look at the physical stores and talk to salespeople. In this stage, the consumer looks for available brands and products, their specifications and prices, and evaluation from trusted people. This stage should result in a set of possible alternatives.

The third stage is to evaluate and select these options, based on the information collected from different sources. The evaluation criteria will depend on which attributes the client considers more relevant in a possible solution. The two main ways of evaluation are by elimination and by compensation. Evaluation by elimination means that the consumer will eliminate any alternative that doesn't perform at a specified minimum standard. Evaluation by compensation, on the other hand, is when a weak specification in an alternative may be compensated by another of higher performance. For instance, elimination will be the case of a client looking for a French restaurant, so all other gastronomical options will not be considered. Compensation will be a restaurant where the location may not be convenient, but the food is great and the restaurant has a Michelin star.

The next stage is to decide where to buy, in ecommerce sites or at the physical stores, based on price and paying conditions, and the level of service provided. For more complex purchases, people might prefer a physical store, where a salesman can provide more information, while for repetitive purchases, the convenience of the ecommerce might be more appealing.

Over this journey, the consumers go from digital to physical and back to digital places. Mapping the journey, one can identify points of interface of the brand with the client, and understand positive and negative situations that could be explored or fixed.

13.4 Process Analysis

To proper analyze a process, it is important to have feedback information from the client. How the experience flows, if there are problematic steps, bottlenecks, low performance, lack of attention and involvement, disappointments, etc. These problematic steps are identified in the blueprint with an F inside a circle in case of probability of failures, or with a W inside a triangle, to indicate bottlenecks. These are steps that merit being studied in more detail, to understand the motives of failure or delay.

13.5 Failure Analysis

Failure points are usually associated with processes that don't result in satisfactory experiences for the client. For instance, a cold meal in a restaurant, a salesman that seems more interested in selling a specific product than finding the best solution for the client, a reservation that is not available, a missing pillow in a hotel room, overbooking in a flight, etc. These processes should be the object of reengineering, where the sequence and contents of each action of the process will be evaluated and if necessary, corrected, in a way that ensures that the problem will not happen again.

13.6 Delay Analysis

Consumers have an expectation of the duration of each stage in a full process. Usually, they are less willing to accept delays in moments where they are idle, like waiting for a table, for the meal, or for the bill, in comparison with when they are active, like eating or performing actions. It is necessary to conduct research with the target to identify the acceptable delay from his viewpoint. Stochastic methods may help identifying how long a process is currently taking, and considering the expectations, a shorter acceptable duration should be obtained, through the increase of resources, like more people, checkouts, etc., or the identification and elimination of unnecessary actions.

13.7 Process Reengineering

The creative analyses of failures and delays often reveal opportunities to improve the process, reducing or eliminating the identified problems.

Processes can become obsolete over time, as the external environment changes, due to new technologies, new client preferences, new legislation, and new offers from competitors. Internal factors can also be relevant, as routine accommodation, unnecessary bureaucracy, low productivity, actions no longer necessary, etc.

All these reasons may justify changing processes through reengineering processes, aiming to improve the quality of the provided service and its productivity.

One successful method proposed by the Total Quality specialists is to find a fail-safe modification, called *poka-yoke*, that is to devise a solution that even if the operator tries, he cannot make mistakes. An example would be placing a mirror by the door that leads to the frontstage, so employees can always check their appearance before contacting the client.

After modifying the processes, it is important to update standards for each target. A script should be prepared, to instruct operators how to proceed, step by step, with clear specifications of what the client will be expecting, and how long they should take in each step.

Services should start with a strong and warm welcome. In many situations, it is the first time that client and employee may be meeting, so it is necessary to break the ice and gain confidence and trust, in order to create empathy with the client. First impressions are very important, people quickly create an impression based on non-verbal clues, that may take some time be changed. It is fundamental to smile, to dress appropriately for the occasion, speak with a clear diction, and to use a vocabulary similar to the client.

If, on the other hand, the salesman and client have been together before, it is the moment to reconnect, by recognizing the client, if possible, by name, asking how he could be served this time, and showing confidence and expertise in proposing good solutions for his needs, and from there performing the additional steps of service.

One interesting reengineering option is to consider changing the process to self-service. Self-service is a form of customer engagement in service production, where customers are asked to undertake specific activities using facilities or systems made available by the service provider. Customer time and effort replace employee time and effort.

The concept is not new—self-service supermarkets date back to the 1930s, ATMs and self-service gas stations from the 1970s. Today, customers find a huge variety of self-service technologies for the delivery of information-based services, both major and supplementary.

The acceptance depends on cultural factors. Usually, clients are used to be serviced, going to a counter where an employee will ask for his needs and will present some solutions. In the self-service format, the client does all the search and selection and, brings his shopping to the checkout. This seems to be a more demanding option, so he has to gradually be convinced that there will be other compensations, like more convenience, speed, lower cost, more practical processes, etc. In luxury, there is a strong cultural resistance against self-service, as clients expect personalized services.

Most services are developed considering coproduction, the participation together with the brand, in defining the final characteristics that the service will present. This involvement will be described in the blueprint, and the role and actions to be performed will be specified. The interaction can happen during the production, the consumption, and the delivery of the service. The quality of the service may vary according to how the brand conducts the interaction, and understands the needs of the client, and on how the client performs his role. In many situations, the client has first to be instructed or even trained to perform correctly his role, in order to prevent failures.

Employees should also be trained, as mentioned before, and supporting tools like intranets and handbooks are important to update information and detail processes.

With the increasing development of technology, automatization, artificial intelligence, and robots are more present in services processes.

They are great to execute repetitive or dangerous activities, and in these cases, they are already present, and people don't notice them anymore. Drone robots, for instance, are being used in logistics, creating a new delivery channel. Automated self-service checkouts in hotels, airlines, trains, etc., can save precious time. Today they are getting more involved in support activities where they operate in conjunction with human beings, helping to access great databases and conducting fast searches to provide information. When stores are connected to the internet, they allow hybrid or Phygital experiences, accessing the ecommerce of the brand, visualization of virtual mirrors, and requesting services.

The area where they will take some time to be more present are those services that involve strong emotional links, like services for elderly people clinics or psychological support.

13.8 Managing Processes in Luxury

Some characteristics of self-service systems can be used to improve experiences in luxury, when they provide quick access to information, comfort, and practicality. Some examples are 24-hour access to databases, reservation systems, product information, store locations, product availability, news about new collections, new services, and details of the brand story and identity.

But they will be accepted only if they work properly, as client complaints usually cite slow connections, confuse navigation, forms that asks for lots of information, and don't give access if the information is not provided in a certain format.

In luxury, the whole chain (Caniato et al., 2011) has to aim for excellence, from production to distribution to retail stores. As they have to supply products related to fashion trends, they have to be flexible to answer to variable demand. Innovation in processes that increases speed and reduce costs can result in competitive advantages, either by the introduction of new methods or improvements of existing ones.

In most cases, processes in luxury will be based on people performing the main tasks, so it is fundamental to train intensively the service people, on the different stages of performing the service, in order to offer homogeneous experiences to all clients.

13.9 Summary

Processes define how brands deliver their experiences. Over time, these processes need to be updated, as the competitive environment changes and some actions may be no longer appropriated to deliver experiences up to the expectations.

The first stage of reengineering of processes is to map all actions and sequences, to fully understand the larger picture. Based on consumer feedback and historical data, points of failure and delay may be identified, analyzed, and modified.

In luxury services, clients are very demanding and processes should be perfect, to deliver experiences that surpass expectations.

Bibliography

Caniato, Federico et al. (2011). Supply chain management in the luxury industry: A first classification of companies and their strategies. *International Journal of Production Economics, 133*(2), 622–633.

Kotler, P., & Amstrong, G. (2016). *Principles of marketing* (16th ed.). Pearson.

Wirtz, J., & Lovelock, C. (2016). *Services marketing: People, technology.* World Scientific Publishing Company.

14 Managing the Luxury Panorama for Great Experiences

14.1 Introduction

Chapter Objectives
The Panorama where luxury services are delivered is very important to create the appropriate mood to favor the social interactions that lead to good services. In this chapter we discuss the luxury Panorama: Physical (The five senses, layout, space and circulation, and visual communication), psychological, and social (salespeople behavior, other presents influence, service training) environment; The luxury panorama and its characteristics and codes; The digital luxury panorama; The ePanorama.

14.2 Managing the Panorama

Many experiences are offered though the contact of the client with the service personal, be it physical or virtual. People have psychological mechanisms that result in quickly forming impressions when first contacting someone else. This impression is formed from cues taken from non-verbal messages received from the other person and the environment where they are.

Recently managers realized that building the right environment and selecting the right people to be there is essential to provide the right client mood, conducive to a better experience. This means that managers have to understand what are the right emotions this combination of people and environment, called the Panorama, should stimulate to propitiate favorable feelings and a better experience: excited, relaxed, at ease comfortable, etc. These stimuli may result in pleasant or unpleasant experiences, more or less money spent, more or less time spent in the place, satisfaction or insatisfaction, etc.

The Panorama comprises every stimulus the client receives (Rosenbaum & Massiah, 2011), both from the physical environment and the service personnel, that is managed and selected to elicit the positive emotions that provide better experiences. The Panorama can make people feel excited or relaxed, according to the proposed experience. Building the right Panorama is an engineering process of composing a set of stimuli that will result in a predefined feeling when inside it. Panorama decisions are strategic, in the sense that they are not easy to change, without cost and image impacts.

Tangible clues and feelings from the Panorama can help clients evaluate quality and brand positioning, stress differentiation and reinforce the brand perception. A high-quality environment communicates the message that the products and services are also of high quality. Apple, for instance, invests in sophisticated design stores, to reinforce their image of specialists in design. In Disneyland, employees in costumes and buildings based on scenarios of popular films contribute to improve the perceived value of their experience. Luxury hotels employ sophisticated architecture to reinforce their image of a luxury experience.

These tangible tools can be divided into three groups: sensory stimuli from the five senses, layout, and visual communication signs.

All these stimuli work together to create a sensation in a holistic way, meaning that a single change in one of them can alter the perception and, in consequence, the experience. The best way to confirm if the resulting sensations are working according to planned is to test the Panorama with the target Persona.

14.2.1 Sensory Stimuli

Sensory stimuli are those received and processed by the five senses: vision, hearing, taste, smell, and tact.

Vision allows to see forms, shapes, colors, and lighting. Research has shown that regular shapes communicate harmony and organization, shapes and sizes can express quantity and weight. Colors can transmit emotions, and can be divided into hot and cold colors. Hot colors, like red (associated with blood) and orange (associated with the sun), can be stimulating, while cold colors, like green (associated with plants and nature) and blue (associated with the sky and the sea) can be relaxing. Strong color tones can be exciting, while pastel colors can be relaxing and sophisticated.

Hearing is associated with rhythmic and music. A fast beat can be stimulating, a slow beat can be relaxing. Some studies suggest that fast beat can induce people to speed their actions, eating faster, for instance, while a slow beat can relax and lead people to stay longer at the table and consume more drinks in a bar or restaurant. Loud noise can be irritating and disruptive to the experience, while low noise can be boring.

Smelling is associated with flavors, that can be stimulating, relaxing, energizing, or balancing. Perfumers can develop custom flavors associating emotions related to the flavors to characteristics of the brand identity and positioning. Research has shown that flavors can improve the evaluation of a store, its environment, and merchandising.

Pleasurable tastes can be associated to the brand, creating a gustatory memory. There are five basic tastes: sweet, sour, salty, bitter, and umami.

The sense of tact can be smooth or rough, soft or hard. Smooth or soft surfaces can be pleasant and help to attract or relax, hard or rough surfaces can be unpleasant and lead to avoidance.

14.2.2 Layout, Space, and Circulation

These are stimuli from the distribution of the space, as distance between furniture or shelves, height of shelves, ease of circulation, counters, machines, etc.

The distribution of space affects the functionality of the Panorama, as in the case of shelves too close in a supermarket, tables too close to each other in a restaurant, reducing privacy and reducing the quality of the experience. Shelves too high or too low can reduce the interest of the client in products placed in them.

The use of focal points can help clients identify relevant products and areas at a glance, when entering or circulating in the store.

The creation of dedicated areas within the store can be used to create scenarios that illustrate the use of products that composes related sets, helping to visualize how the category as a whole works, and how a particular product fits into this set.

14.2.3 Visual Communication Signs

Signs, symbols, and artifacts can be used to communicate the brand's image, help clients find their way in the store, informing how to circulate, where different services and sessions are located, how to behave inside the environment, and strengthen the brand positioning through a uniform corporate visual language.

They are important to facilitate the experience, make quality more explicit, and help increase productivity.

They include signs demanded by law, as places reserved for senior people, pregnant women, people with special needs, identification of hazardous areas, information in case of fire, and so on.

14.2.4 Psychological and Sociological Interaction

All that has been discussed in the previous items comprises the empty environment. Although it has enough stimuli to create an emotional state, one has also to consider the effect of the people present, both employees, clients, and others that might be in the same environment.

Interpersonal interaction processes raise feelings and emotions that, combined by those elicited by the physical store, can be positively or negatively perceived by the client. Client and personnel in different moods can interact in different ways: employees should be trained not to be affected by a client in a bad mood, but to be able to reverse him to a better mood. This can be achieved by keeping a good posture, with professionalism and seriousness.

In order to offer a good servicing, the employee has to show commitment, through attention to what the client is saying, agility in finding and presenting solutions, competence in presenting good options, always with respect and courtesy. He has to stablish rapport, a harmonious relationship with the client with good understanding and communication. The employee has to remain focused, relaxed, hear more than speak, ask questions whenever in doubt about the client's needs, proposing solutions, demonstrating them, and showing their characteristics and value for the client.

14.2.5 ePanorama

Many of these ideas also apply to virtual Panoramas, like sites, ecommerce, social media, etc.

Digital stores are attractive to many consumers because they offer practicality, as a good site is easy and fast to use, saving time and effort that is spent in physical stores.

They allow access from anywhere, as long as one has a connection, operates 24 hours a day, 7 days a week, and as is self-service, there is no pressure to buy, and each one can go at his own pace, return to other options as many times as necessary, access other sites to cross or complement information, and interact with other users that leave positive or negative comments and statements about their experiences with the brand and the product. If the client wishes, he can have a faster experience in finding and buying what he wants. Youtube can provide demonstrations, opinions, and evaluations, complain sites can give information about previous problems other clients had, the brand site can give technical and specification details, offer download of handbooks and other information, and price comparison sites can help find the best offers and conditions. People can send the direct link to a product or an information he wishes to recommend. Sites can offer a much bigger assortment of options, that may not be physically present but can easily be brought from storage sites or ordered from suppliers.

The problem of a digital store is that its experience is based only on two of the five senses, vision and sound, resulting in a poorer sensorial experience, when compared to a physical experience. And even these two senses are limited by the quality of the user's computer equipment, the screen and the speakers, used to access the site.

Having the other three senses, the spatial dimensionality, the non-verbal communication, all these factors help create a much richer experience, that can stimulate better emotions.

It is important to understand the advantages and disadvantages of each option, in order to use the option, the better offer experiences, according to the profile and needs of different clients.

Physical stores can have a reasonable assortment available, allowing the client to choose a product and take it home immediately.

Physical and virtual environments propose a tradeoff to the consumer, he has to choose which experience he prefers, the one that offers a richer personal experience, or the one that offers practicality, convenience, speed, and more options.

14.2.6 Phygital

To avoid this tradeoff, today we observe a trend of convergence between physical and digital experiences, in order to offer the best of both worlds, the phygital experiences.

These are experiences that add technology at the physical store, adding practicality, convenience, speed, and more options through the use of digital interfaces, like apps in mobiles, digital mirrors, touchscreens, radio-frequency tags and client cards, etc.

With high-speed, high-capacity Wi-Fi connection inside the store, the client connects an application in his mobile to the brand system and interacts virtually with it, while enjoying the richer experience of the physical store.

The client can, for instance, access the list of available products, select those interesting to him, get information on each of them, ask a salesman to come and give more information, or consult and AI app to get personalized recommendations, add them to a wish list, have the selected product tried in a virtual fitting room with application of AR, or taken to a real fitting room, in the case of clothes, and when he decides, he can charge it to his credit card, ask to have it packaged and delivered to him, without having to go to the checkout. Pictures of the client in his new purchase can be sent to friends and social media. All the experiences and purchases are stored and available for consulting for both the client and the company. Next time, the AI app can give more precise suggestions based on these previous experiences. The data can be used to create and maintain the relationship with the client, inform about the launching of new products, promotions, new advertising campaigns, and so on.

This phygital experience brings the digital experience of buying via the e-mobile to a physical store.

In this era of COVID, it also allows the client to control the degree of contact or isolation from other people.

14.2.7 Experiential Retail

The store can also be used as a place of interaction and immersive experience with the brand. A place to learn the brand philosophy, relax, and spend time.

Through the use of creativity and technology, a client can try new products before they are introduced in the market, develop a personalized perfume based on interaction with AI the explore the client personality and preferences, try a winter jacket in a simulated snow storm in a subzero environment, have a virtual test drive of a car in the streets of London, use foot scanning technology to help select tennis shoes that best fit his feet, book a Nap Appointment before buying a mattress, visit an art gallery, attend exclusive events, like a seminar on architecture, history or culture, workshops, hosting community and charitable events, co-branding events, etc.

14.3 Managing the Panorama in Luxury

14.3.1 Luxury Panorama and Positioning

The Panorama in luxury has a very important role, of communicating the positioning, the identity, and differentials of the luxury brand, associating the brand to the nine dimensions of luxury seen before: rarity, craftsmanship and symbolic content, status and high perceived value, complexity of acquisition, aesthetic content and lifestyle, and narcissism. The correct combination of these nine factors contributes to the perception of luxury and value of the brand. This perception can be used by engineering the combination of the five senses, using the meanings of each stimulus that reinforce the perception of luxury, like indirect light, pastel colors, light music, relaxing scents, use of wood, metals, stones, refined fabric and carpets, food and drinks service, creating a sophisticated environment.

The employees usually have a uniform, based on suits or long dresses, designed by a known stylist, that helps the client identify himself with the brand.

The generous use of store space, in particular those used for displaying products, with empty spaces between products, helps create a perception of rarity, exclusivity, and value of these products.

The number of salespeople in the store, ready to service the clients, can be another factor to improve the overall perception of luxuosity. Clients should not have to wait for an employee end servicing another client, to get attention.

The overall store should be tidy and organized. When the client is being served, it is all right to bring many products and its packaging, but as soon as the servicing is over, all should be brought back to its original position.

It is important that everything necessary should be at arm's length, as the service experience should not be disturbed or interrupted because the calculator is missing, someone else is using your pen, or the measuring tape is not at its place in the drawer.

14.3.2 Luxury Panorama and the Internet

In the case of the use of the internet (Randon, 2012; Riley & Lacroix, 2003) by luxury brands, it poses a paradox that worried managers of the sector for some time, that luxury brands have to be exclusive, but the internet is democratic and accessible to everyone.

The store as a whole has to be distinctive, but representative of the brand, in particular of its creativity. A common resource is to hire prestigious architects and interior designers, to stress this characteristic of the brand.

A luxury brand website can be used as a persuasive promotion tool to communicate and strengthen the brand identity and the specific points of aesthetic communication, history and dynamic interaction as means of invoking the perception of exclusivity, as luxury brands benefit from communication that reach the greater public, than just the target (Kapferer & Bastien, 2012).

On the other hand, the internet allows to create restricted access and exclusivity by the use of login and password for certain activities, like getting preferential servicing, personalized service, access to special collections, special promotions, special services, special delivery, etc. In this way, the company can select those VIP clients they wish to grant to selective access to special services and remain exclusive.

A physical Panorama (Manlow & Nobbs, 2013) has potential to provide a richer experience, as it can use the five senses, the interpersonal interactions, and the effects of a three-dimensional space. A digital Panorama can only rely on two senses, but is stronger in providing speed, convenience, practicality, and bigger availability of options.

14.3.3 Luxury Panorama and Flagships

One format of store that has a strategic role in the consumer experience (Manlow & Nobbs, 2013) is the flagship store "form and appearance, including architecture, decor, arrangement of space, symbolic elements, location, and its function to better understand the role of the aesthetic environment of the flagship as a means of communicating the brand's objectives, which are mediated by a consumer's perception of the brand and store, the goals he or she brings to the experience, and the situational determinants of the shopping experience".

Within the last decade (Anderson et al., 2010) collaborations have intensified between luxury fashion brands and the most prominent architects and artists, both in stores and in "third spaces" outside of stores, such as the Prada transformer housing various cultural exhibitions and live events. The design of the flagship is a manifestation of the brand's identity, producing what Riewoldt (2002) refers to as a brandscape. The key dimensions of a flagship store have been presented, among others, by Moore (2006), Frings (2008), Kent and Brown (2009). Four main characteristics are evident: first, located in a large outlet in a prominent area; second, offers widest and most in-depth product assortment; third, high-quality store environment; and finally, serves to communicate brand position and values. Luxury shopping allows consumers to fulfill, in a more intensive manner, a dual need for status and a desire to indulge in pleasurable experiences. Luxury flagships are designed to take into account all the senses and create an emotional response in consumers (Riewoldt, 2002). Luxury brands create (Hellman et al., 2007) an emotional branding, a "sensorial universe" capable of reaching different emotional contact points. Luxury fashion brands open flagships in the world's major cities as a way to strengthen and maintain control of their image, to shape it in the eyes of consumers, to promote an identity that enhances the brand, and to provide customers with an enjoyable experience on both a personal and interpersonal level in a branded environment. The function of the luxury flagship has strategic purposes involved being a conduit to market relations, focus of marketing communications, and a blue print for other stores. The flagship is also seen as a branding tool to build and showcase the brand's identity and to position it in the market. Generation of revenue is also a strategic goal.

14.4 Summary

In summary, the Panorama where luxury services are delivered is very important to create the appropriate mood to favor the social interactions that lead to good services. The Panorama is composed by the physical environment where the service experience is delivered, plus the people that take part in the experience, the salespeople, the client, and third people around, creating the psychological and sociological interactions that elicit emotions that contribute to a better buying experience.

Bibliography

Anderson, S., et al. (2010). The motives and methods of fashion designer and architect collaborations. *Journal of Media Arts Culture, 8*(2), 1–11.
Frings, S. G. (2008). *Fashion from concept to consumer*. Pearson Prentice Hall.
Hellman, A., Gobé, M., & Desgrippes, Joël. (2007). *Joël Desgrippes and Marc Gobé on the emotional brand experience*. Rockport Publishers.
Kapferer, J., & Bastien, V. (2012). *The luxury strategy: Break the rules of marketing to build luxury brands*. Kogan page publishers.
Kent, T., & Brown, R. (2009). *Flagship marketing: Concepts and places*. Routledge.
Manlow, V., & Nobbs, Karinna. (2013). Form and function of luxury flagships: An international exploratory study of the meaning of the flagship store for managers and customers. *Journal of Fashion Marketing and Management: An International Journal*.
Mores, C. M. (2006). *From Fiorucci to the guerrilla stores: Shop displays in architecture, marketing and communications*. Marsilio Editori Spa.

Radon, A. (2012). *Communicating luxury brand exclusivity online.* University of Borås.
Riewoldt, Otto. (Ed.). (2002). *Brandscaping: Worlds of experience in retail design/Erlebnisdesign für Einkaufswelten.* Springer Science & Business Media.
Riley, Francesca Dall'Olmo., & Lacroix, Caroline. (2003). Luxury branding on the Internet: Lost opportunity or impossibility? *Marketing Intelligence & Planning.*
Rosenbaum, M. S., & Massiah, C. (2011). An expanded servicescape perspective. *Journal of Service Management, 22*(4), 471–490.

Strategical Satisfaction Management 15

15.1 Introduction

Chapter Objectives

In this chapter we discuss the relationships between productivity, quality, satisfaction, fidelity, and loyalty, all concepts very important to retain the best clients and maintain profitable long-term relationships. We discuss how to attain productivity with quality, how to define quality from the consumer viewpoint, understanding expectations, experiences and satisfaction, managing complaints: listening, solving, and learning, consolidating long-term brand–client relationships, attaining fidelity and loyalty.

15.2 Avoiding Tragic Experiences, Creating Magic Experiences

As seen in previous chapters, what really matters for the client (Wirtz & Lovelock, 2016) is an experience that fulfills or exceeds his expectations, but is never below these expectations. Satisfaction happens when the experience reaches or exceeds expectations, resulting in "magic experiences". But they don't happen by chance, they are the result of a careful process of understanding the client, his expectations, and designing the right characteristics and attributes of the experience that will result in satisfaction. Usually, "tragic experiences" are ill thought, ill designed, and ill executed, resulting in insatisfaction and frustration.

Expectations are created by the brand promises, comments from mouth-to-mouth, reviews from magazines, internet, previous experiences, and contextual situation. Expectations usually result in a minimum level acceptable, and a projected possible maximum level that one could be expected to find for this particular situation. If the experience is perceived to be between these two levels, the client tends to feel satisfied. If is below, it results in insatisfaction, and if above, we have what is called the WOW effect, with surprise and great satisfaction.

In order to obtain positive results and the magic experience, a detailed and complex process has to be developed, the strategic satisfaction management process, as described in the sequence.

15.3 Resources and Productivity

Productivity measures how much result one gets from the use of a certain number of resources. In today's business world, few companies are not aware of the importance of evaluating the productivity of the resources used in any project, and the need to stablish a minimum return on their use.

In marketing, the main metric to analyze is the degree of satisfaction obtained from the used resources, complemented by financial metrics that analyze the monetary return compared to the cost of the actions geared to offer magic experiences.

An important metric is return on investment in satisfaction. The relationship between these two variables is not linear, depending on the stage of investment. Usually, companies that never invested in satisfaction, can get fast and big returns with somewhat little investment. After that, the return will be smaller, as the actions that result in best results are usually tackled initially. Eventually, it reaches the situation when there is the need of great amounts of resources invested, to obtain small gains, and the return doesn't justify further investment.

Companies have to manage the process of using resources to produce consumer satisfaction, through the use of metrics of satisfaction, in relation to the resources utilized.

This process can be divided into three stages: pre-service, service, and post-service.

15.4 Pre-service

15.4.1 Information

Magic experiences depend on good-quality information on the external environment (competitors, macroenvironment, consumers) and the internal environment of the company (strategic corporate decisions like mission, vision, the culture, the organogram, available resources). Today managers can access such overwhelming volume of information that it is becoming humanely impossible to analyze them all, being essential to use computer tools based on Artificial Intelligence and Cognitive Intelligence to fully understand all data, get information, and make decisions.

Till the end of last century, managers got their information from a Marketing Information Service (SIM), that provided organized information through four sub-systems: Internal reports, Marketing research, Marketing intelligence, and Marketing Analytics. Internal reports were responsible for collecting and processing information already available inside de company, as sales, stocks, production costs, financial costs, etc. Marketing research would conduct research outside the company, collecting consumer data, using statistical techniques. Marketing intelligence was based on the military concept, of gathering information from a range of sources, that could not be obtained with the use of traditional techniques, including rumors, to be verified and directed to those in company that might be affected by them. Marketing Analytics try to get new information by crossing different documents and research reports, looking for new insights.

This system could deal with the available volume of information, but managers would complain that they didn't have enough information to make decisions, and would have to use feeling and previous experience to fill the gap.

Today the situation is quite the opposite, the volume of available information is growing exponentially, and managers complain that it is humanely impossible to process them all in a reasonable time, requiring new strategies to deal with information.

The current answer is Data Science, a set of techniques to gather, organize, and analyze great volumes of digital data, the Big Data (Sagiroglu & Sinanc, 2013), stored in the Cloud, extracting information using artificial intelligence and machine learning, and presenting the main relevant information in a concise way.

To be a Marketing Data Scientist, four multidisciplinary skills are required: Math & Statistics (statistical modeling, experiment design, Bayesian inference, machine learning, etc.), Programming & Database (computer science, scripting languages, statistical computing packages, database software, etc.), Marketing Knowledge (business and marketing understanding, curiosity, hacker mindset, creative, proactive, collaborative, etc.), and Communication & Visualization (storytelling skills, translating data into insights, identifying and presenting the main relevant information in a visual, concise, and easy to interpret way, using for instance infographics). There is a strong marketing demand for professionals with these skills.

15.4.2 Customer Experience (CX)

Customer Experience (CX) is the strategic planning of all contacts of the brand with the client, in the three stages of pre-sale, sale, and post-sale, aiming to create a valuable experience for the customer.

In order to create value to the customer (Pine & Gilmore, 1998, 1999), it has been proposed the fourth wave in the economic progression with the emergence of the new economy as the "experience economy".

Customer experience (Jain et al., 2017), a relatively new concept, in both theory and practice, is regarded as a holistic interactive process, facilitated through cognitive and emotional clues, moderated by customer and contextual characteristics, resulting into unique and pleasurable/un-pleasurable memories.

All these contacts of the brand with the client constitute the Customer Journey, that can be mapped, analyzed, and customized according to each persona that goes through the experience. The customization includes products, services, channels, servicing, and the timing of the service to each customer. To optimize this process, it is important that the company adopts a customer-centric culture.

15.5 Service

15.5.1 User Experience (UX)

The term User Experience was created in the human–computer interaction (HCI) field (Hassenzahl & Tractinsky, 2006) and is associated with a wide variety of meanings (Forlizzi & Battarbee, 2004), ranging from traditional usability to beauty, hedonic, affective, or experiential aspects of technology use, resulting in new terms like Funology and Hedonomics, moving the focus of design from just operational support to tasks, to enjoyable and positively emotional experiences in the use of interfaces. The concept, originated in the digital area, proposing the emotional usability (Logan et al., 1994), has been gradually expanded to presential experiences, like stores.

User Experience aims to plan all aspects of the interaction of the customer in the use of products and services.

A good User Experience should provide ease of use, intuitive use, speed, persuasiveness, pleasure (visual and in the use), and usefulness (delivering the task properly).

15.5.2 The Seven Steps to Great Servicing

Service failures are among the main reasons for clients to change to other brands. Good service should give the client attention, commitment, agility, good solutions, respect, empathy, and courtesy. To prepare salespeople to provide these factors, the brand should invest continuously in people management, as we saw in a previous chapter, with good selection, motivation, training, and the creation of a culture of fidelization.

Good service can be provided following good practices based on previous experiences:

- hear more than speak;
- use the right tone of voice and speak paused;
- speak with good diction, use simple words;
- put "warmth" in the voice, that is, speak enthusiastically;
- always ask the customer if he understood what you said;
- if you do not understand what the customer asked, ask him to repeat;
- avoid using slang;

- have the right aptitude for sale;
- know the customer;
- be a partner to the customer;
- sell value.

Good sales can be achieved by following these seven steps:

Preparation
Before starting the sales, the stage has to be prepared. This means cleaning, organizing, and storing tools, products, etc., in the appropriate place. Any tool to be used in servicing should be in its place, products should be positioned in the shelves, calculators should be close to the hand, and so on. Salespeople should have studied the available products, understood their characteristics, history, and benefits, should have been briefed about the different personas that may enter the store, their characteristics, needs, and how to identify them, and to have prepared and trained the seven steps of selling.

Addressing
The first action should be to give a warm reception. Greet the customer with enthusiasm in the voice. Show the customer that he is welcome in the store. Beware that addressing the customer with a comment about a particular item they looked at when entering the store may be wrong. First one should greet, then talk about his needs and the product. Avoid questions that can be answered with a simple word (yes or no), because the chance of developing a relationship from these answers is small. Do not rush to the step of demonstration; sellers who have this custom should slow down; the goods will not run away, nor the customers. People are more comfortable when they are talking to someone who seems sincerely interested in what they have to say. Use this step to build confidence and rapport with client, preparing the stage to start probing when the client allows.

When a customer says he is "just looking", tell him to feel free, tell him your name, and let him know that if he needs any help, he can call you. Move to a certain distance, but don't leave this buyer's field of view. By opening the sale effectively, one can reduce customer resistance and start asking probing questions.

Probing
When the client summons the employee, he should approach the client and start the probing process. Smiling is very effective to create confidence and build rapport. Smiling has many general benefits. Smiling not only helps you appear happier, it actually makes you feel happier. Research has shown that when you smile you release endorphins, opioid neuropeptides, and peptide hormones that inhibit the communication of pain signals, producing a feeling of euphoria. But faking a smile can trick your brain into thinking that you are happy.

Research shows that smiling can also help lower blood sugar and blood pressure, reduce stress, boost immune systems, and release natural painkillers and serotonin, a complex and multifaceted neurotransmitter, that modulates mood, cognition, reward, learning, memory, and numerous physiological processes.

A smile also operates a mirroring effect, putting others at ease, making you more approachable, and easier to relate. As Louis Armstrong used to sing, "when you're smiling the whole world smiles with you".

Probing questions are those questions that help understand the client: preferences, needs, pains, desires, the context of use, customer characteristics in general. Ideally, the salespeople will try to fit the client into a persona that has been studied and detailed by the company, and discussed in training.

The importance of this stage is that the collected information will be very helpful for the salespeople to understand what the client needs, and to use his skills to find the best solution available in stock. It is essential to ask as many questions as necessary to obtain the information he needs to select the right item to be brought to the next stage of demonstration. It is important to ask questions the customer fills are relevant to help find possible options, without tormenting the customer to get answers, but gaining his trust. Trust is developed from the tone of the questions and the empathy established between seller and customer.

An interesting method is to use open questions initiated by WHO, WHAT, WHAT, WHY, WHERE, WHEN, HOW, and HOW MUCH. When the salespeople use open questions effectively, he can help customers clarify their ideas and make the right purchase.

Be careful not to limit the customer's choice before he is ready. Questions should be asked with a choice, such as "this or that", to help filter down relevant options. Do not ask the customer how much they want to spend, but try to understand what product characteristics are more valuable to him. By making appropriate questions and reactions to customers' responses, the salespeople will be able to build trust. Use confirmatory questions to help transition between the presentation of resources and the benefits of their products. Abbreviate probing when you sense the client knows exactly what he wants.

Demonstration
Having selected a few options that may fit the customer needs, based on the probing in the previous stage, now the salespeople have to bring and demonstrate these options. It is not just the case of handling a product, but the two main objectives here to achieve during the demonstration are to establish the value of the product in the customer's mind and create the desire to own the product. He should present the characteristics of the product or service, in conjunction with the benefits that they may provide. To find out what benefits the customer, the seller must remember what he discovered in the survey and offer the benefits of the available product. Customers buy for two reasons: trust and value. Trust should be established in the approach and in the probing stages, so the customer recognizes in the salespeople the respect, the commitment, the will to serve, and to find the best solutions to his problems. The perception of value is built with in the right demonstration, helping the client to perceive benefits (quality, beauty, comfort, etc.) and costs (price, waiting time, risk, etc.) involved in the purchase. Value perception is built

on the relation benefit/cost. As the specialist, the salespeople should be capable of exploring different facets of benefits that the characteristics may provide, that answers the needs identified in the probing stage.

Remember that the seller should be ethical at all times, not criticizing competing companies or manufacturers, but presenting the positive aspects and merits of his solution.

A good demonstration starts with a good preparation. Study beforehand the features, advantages, and benefits of your product. Create and practice a list of words, terms, expressions that you will use. Prepare a script. Rehearse, train, repeat the demonstration. Test with friends and family, ask and include suggestions. Remember to pause during the presentation, to give the customer time to think and absorb. Allow the customer to manipulate, examine, try the product. If it's a service or a project of a product, try to make it tangible. Bring references from other clients, create of model of the future product, use virtual reality to help clients visualize, demonstrate how it works, operation details, movements, etc. Remember to be affectionate with the product, show that it is valuable. Ask questions to confirm that the customer is understanding.

Objections

Objections are part of any selling process, and the salespeople should be prepared to deal with them. In many situations, objections don't mean that the customer doesn't want to buy, but rather that he is in doubt about some aspects and needs more information. Salespeople should also prepare beforehand to deal with objections. Study the different personas that may enter the store, and what objections they usually have. Use the probing stage to ask questions to get to know the customer and his needs. Record key objections and anticipate them (review previous cases, look for patterns, and prepare scripts for them). Break your sales process in stages and follow the steps (diagnostics, proposition, and validation). In the diagnostics stage, the salespeople have to understand clearly what is the objection. The proposition stages present counter-arguments to the objection. The validation aims to get the agreement that the objection has been addressed. If there is no agreement, the three stages of the process should be repeated. One has to be careful with myths, like "every objection is surmountable!", that some managers repeat. No product can satisfy everyone, and sometimes it is necessary to reflect: "does your product really meet the needs?". If not, it is better to be frank and acknowledge the reality than irritate and force the customer. It would be better just to direct this client to another supplier that could best attend his needs.

Closure

Sometimes the customer is decided to buy, but hesitates to take the decision, for some minor reasons, but unconsciously the decision has been taken. It takes some sensitivity to feel the right moment to close the deal. To start closing the sale, there are some possible ways to be tried. The salespeople can ask: "can I separate this piece for you?", or to close the deal by asking closed questions, like "which one will you take: the wooden or the steel one?" Or ask questions presuming closing: "would you prefer the delivery to be this week or next?"

Additional Sales

When the salespeople notices that the customer is inclined to close the deal, he should take advantage of the moment, by increasing the ticket value, offering additional items. There are two techniques, cross-selling e up-selling.

Cross-selling is the case of additional offers of complements and accessories, for instance, when buying a formal suit, also offer a white shirt, a tie, a pair of shoes, a pair of socks, a belt, and so on.

Up-selling is the case of substituting a certain closed product for a superior alternative, for instance, offering a wool suit instead of a polyester suit, that although may be more expensive, it will offer superior comfort, fit, and style.

These two options should be explored as suggestions to increase the ticket value, but phrases that could lead to closing the negotiations should be avoided, like:

- Interrogative phrases that could lead to closure, like "is that all, sir?", a phrase that easily may be answered by a yes.
- Conditional sentences that could lead to closure, like "would you like to see anything else?"
- Negative phrases inducing negative responses "and you sir, will you not get anything for you?"

The new options should offer additional benefits, like practicality, comfort, higher quality, etc.

15.5.3 Expectations and Experiences

After the experience, the customer evaluates if it was satisfactory. Satisfaction results from the comparison of the expectations he had before and what the experience resulted.

The customer expectation is created based on a set of factors. Personal needs define what possible solutions could be effective. Stablished beliefs define what can be expected to be possible. The competitors' offers also affect the expectations, as well as their dynamic responses with innovation and new products over time. Contextual and situational factors influence expectations, as different places and usages may demand different levels of price and attributes. The brand uses different communication tools to promise that the product will perform at a certain level, and this promise is incorporated in the expectation. People also trust closer friends and family, and ask them for their evaluation and opinions on the brand, mainly through mouth-to-mouth communication. Finally, previous experiences of the customer and the information gained in them will also contribute to build the expectation. And it will also mean that every time he has a new experience, he will incorporate new information that may change expectations.

This expectation will be in a range, that goes from a minimum expected experience to the normal reasonably expected experience.

If the experience falls into this range, the customer will feel satisfied. If it is below, he will be unsatisfied, and if it is above, he will be positively surprised.

From this model, one can deduce that expectations depend from many factors, and may change over time, with information and experiences.

It is important for companies to research his clients to identify his expectations, so he can build experiences that reach or surpass these expectations.

15.6 Post-service

Of course, the aim of a company is to have satisfied customers, but this cannot always be possible, as mistakes will always happen. The brand has to be prepared with sound strategies for both situations, satisfaction, and insatisfaction.

15.6.1 Recovering Insatisfaction

Mistakes happen, and the brand has to be prepared to deal with them. Insatisfaction happens when the experience is not up to the expectation, usually because of some kind of failure in the process. Interestingly enough, customers accept that failures happen, but they don't accept that the brand doesn't solve problems quickly. Some research suggests that customers become even more loyal when a problem is solved quickly, compared to those that never had problems. The best way to behave is to be prepared to listen, opening channels of communication, to solve, by quickly finding effective solutions, and to learn, by giving authority to employees to find faulty processes and reengineering them, in order to avoid the problem to happen again.

Listening

Research has shown that most people don't complain, either because they don't trust the brand to solve the problem, don't feel at ease to complain, don't know how to complain, or the cost doesn't justify the effort. The few that complain are those that trust the company, believe the company will try to solve the failure, believe the failure was an exception, or feel confident to complain. They complain because they feel entitled to a restitution or a compensation. They complain because they want to vent their anger and frustration. But they also want to help the company to help improve service and out of altruism, they want to prevent the problem happening to others. The brand has to communicate their customers his willingness to solve problems, facilitate complaining by creating communication channels where problems may happen, and incentive the complaints.

The company should do research to identify the most common complaints, their sources, ask former clients the reasons they left the company, create a mindset that "complaints are opportunities", as they are a great source of information that clients provide for free.

To create this new mindset, it is necessary intensive training, in order to have employees that are proactive, acting immediately and not waiting for the client to complain, the company should have planned and structured failure recovery proceedings, all involved personnel should be taught how to behave and how to develop recovery skills, and given confidence and autonomy to use his judgment and competences to find good recovery solutions.

Solving

It is not enough to listen to the complaints, but the brand has to be prepared to solve them quickly. But in many cases, the company solves a specific problem, but doesn't correct the sources of the problem, or is too bureaucratic and takes a long time to implement a solution. This usually means a culture problem, when management does not recognize evidence that service recovery represents significant financial returns, the company does not invest enough in preventing service errors, consumer service employees do not have the right attitude or the organization doesn't make it easy for the customer to make their complaint.

The brand should aim to be efficient in solving problems, developing systems, and training their employees to solve problems, giving them the necessary autonomy and financial resources.

Training in solving should train employees to act quickly, to admit mistakes but don't get defensive, have empathy and understand the problem from the customer's point of view, recognize the customer's feelings, and above all, never argue with customers.

The right mindset to be built is to give the customer the benefit of the doubt, always clarify all the steps, those responsible and deadlines to resolve the issue. The customer should be kept informed about the progress of the complaint and the steps being taken to the solution, and attendants should always seek to persist in the reconquest of goodwill.

Failures many times results in losses for the customer, so it is important to be prepared to offer financial compensation, which means having a pre-approved budget with authorized limits.

Learning

As seen before, a service is an experience, from the customer's point of view, but a process from the provider's point of view. If the experience is faulty, it should mean a failure in the processes involved, so the processes have to be analyzed and corrected to prevent the failure to happen again.

Processes describe the method and sequence in which service operating systems operate, and specify how they integrate to create the promised value proposition for the client. Poorly designed processes result in lower quality, frustrating the customer, generating dissatisfaction and hindering the work of employees, generating greater risk of failures and reducing productivity.

Flowcharts are important to understand how the service is provided, why failure happens, and what correction in the process should be made.

15.8 Measuring Fidelity and Loyalty 199

This reengineering should result in a more efficient process that will deliver better experiences and reduce complaints.

15.6.2 Managing Satisfaction and Relationship

If solving problems is important, after restoring the confidence and the satisfaction, it is equally important to keep satisfied customers satisfied.

Retained customers spend more over time, make more positive mouth-to-mouth, generate less support cost, and come back to buy more.

Build strong relationships with customers is fundamental to retain them. A relationship means constant contact, that can be obtained by sending messages about news of the brand, offers, differentiated benefits, satisfaction evaluation, suggestions, and rewards for the fidelity.

15.7 Loyalty

Loyalty is the ultimate objective in building relationship with customers. In this stage, the customer not only has positive attitudes in relation to the brand, and a propensity to come back and buy again, but he also has an emotional link with the brand, and is willing to evangelize and defend the brand, spreading good mouth-to-mouth and routinely returning, without considering other competitors.

15.8 Measuring Fidelity and Loyalty

Customer loyalty (Mcmullan & Gilmore, 2003) develops and can be measured in four stages: cognitive, affective, conative, and action. He first gets to know the brand, then develop positive attitudes, then develop intention to buy, and finally he goes into action. A scale to measure loyalty should include items that facilitate measurements of these four stages. For each market, a scale based on these four stages should be developed, validated, and used to measure loyalty.

One should be careful with the use of generic scales, like NPS, as research (Kristensen & Eskildsen, 2014) has shown that the NPS is not what it claims to be, but it is a very poor predictor of both customer loyalty and customer satisfaction. The measure is very sensitive to changes in the underlying distribution, and the precision of the NPS was found to be low compared to other measures of loyalty; it is not possible to predict the NPS categorization and hence it is hard to say precisely, how organizations can influence corporate growth based on the NPS, so it should not be used to base managerial decisions.

15.9 Managing Strategic Satisfaction in Luxury

Satisfaction is based on expectation, so managers should research their customers, finding the main aspects of their expectations, and building experiences accordingly.

Toyota revolutionized the management of quality with methodologies denominated Total Quality Control, with its management principles and philosophies (Sila & Ebrahimpour, 2004) proposed by authors as Feigenbaum, Crosby, Deming, and Juran. The Total Quality Management frameworks were based on the recommendations of Crosby (1979) and his 14-step program to improve quality through, defect prevention, Shewhart and Deming (1986) prescriptions of 14 points encompassing the organizational requirements for effective quality management, Feigenbaum (1991), Feigenbaum & McCorduck (1983) support of the integration of statistical techniques and methodology into the processes of firms to implement company-wide total quality control, and the prescription of the ten fundamental benchmarks as the keys to the successful implementation of total quality control, and Juran (1978) proposition that quality improvement can be attained by applying the breakthrough concept (an improvement to unprecedented levels of performance) to problems of quality. Juran (1989) also offered a framework for Total Quality Management with three sets of processes, including quality planning, quality improvement, and quality control.

The Baldrige National Quality Award became the most prestigious award in the field, and the seven criteria (leadership, strategic planning, customer and market focus, information and analysis, human resources focus, process management, and business results) used to evaluate the candidates could also be used as a framework to evaluate processes and results in quality management of companies in general.

Leadership is important to foster the right culture centered on the satisfaction of the client. Strategic planning is fundamental to incorporate goals based on the satisfaction of the customers. Focus on the customer, and Information and analysis, are related to the gathering and use of information that will help to better understand the customer and design the appropriate experience. Human resource focus helps find the right talents, train them to better perform their functions, and motivate them to fill energized and interested in serving the customers. Process management analyzes current process to verify their productivity, efficiency, degree of failures and delays that might reduce their performance, and the fast and efficient correction of unsatisfactory processes. Business results evaluate performance from a broader view, considering four main business performance areas (customer-focused results, financial and market results, human resource results, and organizational effectiveness results) in order to guarantee that the strategies are balanced and that they do not favor or disfavor any important stakeholders, objectives, or short- and longer-term goals.

Quality management, as seen above is a mindset, a philosophy, a culture that has to be developed in the company and its employees, so they all think in terms of satisfying the client.

This culture has to have both management and guests aligned. A study (Lu et al., 2015) found that in hotels that have this culture there are no fundamental disconnects in the respective understandings of managers and guests, however, the two groups used different language to describe luxury, service quality, and satisfaction; managers evaluated satisfaction in terms of services provided, but the guests conceptualized satisfaction in terms of value received for the price of lodging, and luxury, service quality, and satisfaction were closely related in the minds of the managers and guests and were not independent constructs.

Managers should always consider the specific factors of satisfaction in his sector. A study (Padma & Ahn, 2020), for instance, identified quality of products and services and interaction with employees as the major drivers of customers' word-of-mouth and revisit intentions.

15.10 Summary

In this chapter we discussed how to strategically plan magic experiences, presenting the relationships between productivity, quality, satisfaction, fidelity, and loyalty, all concepts very important to retain the best clients and maintain profitable long-term relationships. To attain productivity with quality, one must define quality from the consumer viewpoint, understand expectations, experiences, and satisfaction, manage complaints, by listening, solving, and learning through errors, to consolidate long-term brand–client relationships, and attain fidelity and loyalty.

Bibliography

Crosby, P. B. (1979). Quality is free-if you understand it. *Winter Park Public Library History and Archive Collection, 4*.

Feigenbaum, A. V. (1991). Total quality control. *New York*.

Feigenbaum, E. A., & McCorduck, P. (1983). *The fifth generation*. Addison-Wesley Pub.

Forlizzi, J., & Battarbee, K. (2004). Understanding experience in interactive systems. In *Proceedings of the 5th conference on Designing interactive systems: processes, practices, methods, and techniques* (pp. 261–268).

Hassenzahl, M., & Tractinsky, N. (2006). User experience—A research agenda. *Behaviour & Information Technology, 25*(2), 91–97.

Jain, R., Aagja, J., & Bagdare, S. (2017). Customer experience—A review and research agenda. *Journal of Service Theory and Practice*.

Juran, J. M. (1978). Japanese and western quality-contrast. *Quality Progress, 11*(12), pp. 10–18.

Kristensen, K., & Eskildsen, J. (2014). Is the NPS a trustworthy performance measure? *The TQM Journal*.

Logan, R. J., Augaitis, S., & Renk, T. (1994). Design of simplified television remote controls: A case for behavioral and emotional usability. In *Proceedings of the human factors and ergonomics society annual meeting* (pp. 365–369). SAGE Publications.

Lu, C., et al. (2015). Service quality and customer satisfaction: Qualitative research implications for luxury hotels. *International Journal of Culture, Tourism and Hospitality Research.*

Mcmullan, R., & Gilmore, A. (2003). The conceptual development of customer loyalty measurement: A proposed scale. *Journal of Targeting, Measurement and Analysis for Marketing, 11*(3), 230–243.

Padma, P., & Ahn, J. (2020). Guest satisfaction & dissatisfaction in luxury hotels: An application of big data. *International Journal of Hospitality Management, 84*, 102318.

Pine, B. J., et al. (1998). *Welcome to the experience economy.*

Pine, B. J., & Gilmore, J. H. (1999). *The experience economy: Work is theatre & every business a stage.* Harvard Business Press.

Sagiroglu, S., & Sinanc, D. (2013). Big data: A review. In *2013 international conference on collaboration technologies and systems (CTS)* (pp. 42–47). IEEE.

Shewhart, W. A., & Deming, W. E. (1986). *Statistical method from the viewpoint of quality control.* Courier Corporation.

Sila, I., & Ebrahimpour, M. (2004). An examination of quality management in luxury hotels. *International Journal of Hospitality & Tourism Administration, 4*(2), 33–59.

Wirtz, J., & Lovelock, C. (2016). *Services marketing: People, technology.* World Scientific Publishing Company.

Culture and Leadership

16.1 Introduction

Chapter Objectives
This final chapter highlights the importance of creating a culture of service and excellence to support this new paradigm, with values that result in satisfaction for the clients and profitability for the company.

16.2 The New Paradigm of Services and Cultural Changes

This book is based on a new paradigm, a new way of thinking business, based on services and their particular characteristics, that should help companies to restore their margins, become more competitive and increase their chances of survival and growth. As a paradigm shift, it implies in a new culture, based by a view centered on the clients and the delivery of magic experiences, supported by lean processes and a well selected, trained, and motivated team. Changing a culture takes time and leadership.

Consumer satisfaction (Wirtz et al., 2020) is fundamental for the financial success of the company, as many studies have shown that consumer satisfaction indexes have high correlation with return on investment. Customer satisfaction is achieved through the deep knowledge of the customer, his preferences, needs, segments, with plenty of information stored in the cloud and analyzed through data science, updated by research and the CRM.

The old paradigm in people management was based on the idea that people were replaceable, not very interested or motivated in their work, not very skilled, and that skill and knowledge were concentrated in the higher levels of management in the company, and workers in general should just follow repetitive and easy processes, supervised by middle managers. A strict hierarchy with several levels. The new paradigm sees people as a source of competitive advantage, based on specialized skills and competences that the company has learned to recruit and manage into high-performance teams, in a lean structure with few levels.

The old paradigm in processes was based on the idea of maximizing productivity, standardization, and quality control of the final product. The new paradigm puts consumer satisfaction and quality at the center of the processes, investing heavily in training, reengineering, and quality control to guarantee final consumer satisfaction.

This means that to implement the ideas presented in this book, it is necessary to introduce many changes in the values and thoughts of the managers in the company. This is a slow but necessary process, that can ensure the future of the company, but depends on a strong leadership to create this new culture.

A strong leader is important to define strategic decisions, decide priorities, and guarantee the implementation. These decisions, in conjunction with a strong commitment to service excellence, can take a company to financial success.

16.3 Leadership in Luxury

Luxury firms have to create value (Jensen, 2017) to leverage financial results while implementing cultural changes, through motivated and committed managers. Some challenges are cultural differences in a global market that have to be integrated in order to collaborate, to quickly act on market opportunities with innovative answers. Collaboration (Jensen, 2017) "and knowledge sharing require consideration of specific organizational routines that interdependently create a common space and environment for innovation". The leader has to be flexible to help these teams, facilitating change and cross-cultural, organizational, and team innovation.

16.4 Summary

> We conclude the book highlighting the importance of creating a culture of service and excellence to support the new paradigm of the service-dominant logic, with values that result in satisfaction for the clients and profitability for the company.

Bibliography

Jensen, K. R. (2017). Global organizational leadership for luxury companies. In *New Luxury Management* (pp. 33–45). Palgrave Macmillan, Cham.

Kapferer, J.-N., & Bastien, V. (2012). *The luxury strategy: Break the rules of marketing to build luxury brands*. Kogan Page Publishers.

Wirtz, J., Hemzo, M. A., & Lovelock, C. (2020). *Marketing de serviços: pessoas, tecnologia e estratégia*. São Paulo.

Index

A
Abarth, 27
Acqua di Parma, 25
Activity Based Cost (ABC), 143
Advertising, 5, 11, 97, 124, 149, 150, 153, 154, 173
Aesthetic content, 12, 15, 16, 184
Age, 62, 77, 85
A. Lange & Söhne, 26
Alexander McQueen, 26
Alfa Romeo, 27
Altuzarra, 26
AMG, 26, 29
Amy Fairclough, 28
Anthropo-zoomorphic metamorphosis, 4
Ao Yun, 25
Apparel, 5, 11, 14, 22, 30, 32, 38, 117
Ardbeg, 25
Armand de Brignac, 25
Arnault, Bernard Jean Étienne, 22, 25
Artisan, 4, 5, 21, 45, 47
Arts of the court, 8
Aston Martin Lagonda Global Holdings PLC, 29
Attractiveness, 41, 75, 76, 83, 85, 152
Audi, 27, 54
Azzedine Alaïa, 26

B
Baby boomers, 79
Bain & Co., 22
Balenciaga, 26
Baume & Mercier, 26
Bayerische Motoren Werke AG, 26, 57, 59, 103
Beauty, vii, 3, 6, 12, 22, 192, 194
Behavioral impacts, 37

Belmond Hotels, 25
Belvedere, 25
Benchmarking, 38
Benefit Cosmetics, 25
Bentley, 27, 29, 59, 60
Berluti, 25
Big data, 35, 38, 191
Bite Beauty, 25
Blueprint, 172, 174, 176
BMW. *See* Bayerische Motoren Werke AG
Bodega Numanthia, 25
Bottega Veneta, 26
Boucheron, 26
Brand, 96
Brand equity, 6, 40, 95–97, 99, 100, 103–105, 117, 150
Brand extension, 14, 29, 101, 102, 105
Brand mantra, 56, 57, 59
Brand tradition, 40
Breitling SA, 29
Brioni, 26
Buccellati, 26
Bugatti, 27
Bulgari, 25
Burberry, 11, 22, 28

C
Caffè-Pasticceria Cova, 25
Calvin Klein Inc., 29
Cantieri Azimut, 29
Cape Mentelle, 25
Cartier, 11, 21, 26
Catalog marketing, 157
Category parity points, 55
Céline, 25
Chandon, 25
Chanel, 11, 28

Charisma, 3
Charles & Keith, 25
Château Cheval Blanc, 25
Château d'Yquem, 25
Chaumet, 25
Cheval Blanc Hotels, 25
Chloé, 26
Chopard, 11, 22
Christian Dior, 25
Christian Louboutin Ltd., 32
Christofle, 11, 21
Christopher Kane, 26
Church'sCar Shoe, 28
Client communication, 39
Cloudy Bay, 25
Coach IP Holdings LLC, 28
Cobra, 26
Co-branding, 115, 117, 118
Communication, 35, 39–41, 46, 48, 53–57, 59, 68, 82, 100, 103, 104, 107, 111, 115, 117, 118, 121, 133, 134, 145, 149, 151, 158, 182, 193
Communication mix, 150, 153, 154
 advertising, 150
 direct marketing, 150
 events and experiences, 150
 interactive marketing, 150
 personal sales, 150
 public relations and advertising, 150
 sales promotion, 150
 word-of-mouth marketing, 150
Competition parity points, 56
Complexity of acquisition, 12, 15, 16, 184
Concept of luxury, 1–3, 10, 13, 16
Concept of money, 7
Consumer Experience, 35
Consumer journey, 172, 173
Consumption decision(s), 53, 61, 67, 69, 72, 158, 173
Corruption of the virtues, 5
Costing systems, 142
 Activity Based Cost, 143
 full/absorption costing, 142
 marginal/variable costing, 143
Craftsmanship, 3, 11, 12, 15, 58, 59, 117, 184
Cruises, 22
Culture, 9, 15, 40, 68, 69
Customer Experience, 191

D
Daimler AG, 26, 29
Database, 38, 164, 176
Data Science, 191, 203

Declericalization of arts, 9
Demand, 8–10, 12–14, 37, 40, 46, 63, 75, 84, 104, 114, 133, 141, 144, 165, 169, 196
Demographic generations, 78
 baby boomers, 79
 Generation Alpha, 78
 Generation X, 79
 Generation Y, 78
 Generation Z, 78
Desacralization, 3
Design furniture, 22, 37
Design Thinking, 35
Determination of market prices, 144
Deus Ex Machina, 25
DFS, 25
Digitalization impacts, 35
Dimensions of luxury, 15, 184
Direct marketing, 149, 150, 157
Discounted prices and promotions, 145
Dismissing, 166, 169
Dodo, 26
Dolce & Gabbana, 29
Dom Pérignon, 25
Dunhill, 26

E
Electric, 26
Entry-price items, 37
Entry products, 41, 146
Era of individualism, 10, 14
Era of magic, the, 3
Era of power, the, 7
Ermenegildo Zegna Group, 33
European cambial crisis, the, 22
Evaluation, 55, 61, 70, 82, 153, 165
Events and experiences, 150, 153, 156
Experience quality, 38
Experiences, 13–15, 22, 34, 35, 48, 49, 66, 96, 121, 133

F
Fabergé, 11, 21
Failure points, 174
False luxury, 11, 12
Fashion, 3, 10–12, 37, 117
Fashion creators, 11
Fast-moving consumer goods, 53
Fear of contamination, 41
Fendi, 25, 28
Fenty, 25
Fenty Beauty by Rihanna, 25

Ferrari S.p.A., 30
Financial impacts, 34
Fine art, 22
Fine food and dining, 22
Fine wines and spirits, 22
Flagships, 3, 121, 133, 186
Flowchart, 172, 198
Fondazione Altagamma, 22
FRED, 25
Fresh, 25
Full/absorption costing, 142

G
Generation Alpha, 78
Generation X, 79
Generation Y, 78
Generation Z, 78
Geographic price, 145
Geomarketing, 77
Ghee, 28
Giampiero Bodino, 26
Giorgio Armani, 30
Girard-Perregaux, 26
Givenchy, 25
Givenchy Parfums, 25
Glenmorangie, 25
Goyard, 11, 21, 30
Gucci, 25, 28
Guerlain, 25

H
Hackett Limited, 30
Helmut Lang, 28
Hennessy, 25
Hermès International S.A., 21, 31
Heterogeneity, 50
Hublot, 25
Hugo Boss AG, 31
Humanitarian feelings, 37
Hypermodernity, 12

I
Industrial revolution, 45
Information collecting and processing, 38
Ingredient branding, 115
Innovation, 28, 40, 46, 47, 53, 95, 114, 134, 177, 196
Inseparability, 50
Intangibility, 50
Interactive marketing, 150, 153, 157, 158
Internal branding, 99

Internal public, 57
Internal structure, 41

J
Jaeger-LeCoultre, 11, 21, 26
Jaguar, 28, 59
JeanRichard, 26
Jil Sander, 28

K
Kate Spade New York, 28
Kendo, 25
Kenzo, 25
Kenzo Parfums, 25
Kering, 25
Krug, 25

L
La Grande Epicerie, 25
Lalique, 11, 22, 31
Lamborghini, 27
Lancel, 26
Land Rover, 28
Lanvin, 11, 22, 31
Learning, 38, 54, 56, 63, 65, 66, 162, 189, 191, 198
Leather goods, 22, 25, 28, 30–32
Le Bon Marché, 11, 25
Les Echos, 25
Lifestyle, 12, 14–16, 31, 39–41, 63, 67, 79, 85, 184
Little affected, 39
Loewe, 25
Logistic processes, 38
Logistics, viii, 39, 41, 118, 128, 131, 132, 134, 176
Loro Piana, 25
Lotus Cars Limited, 31
Louis Vuitton, 11, 22, 25
Lower conspicuous consumption, 49
Lower risk of counterfeiting, 49
Luna Rossa, 28
Luxottica Group S.p.A., 32
Luxury arts, 6
Luxury brands, 3, 6, 7, 11, 12, 21, 22, 25–28, 32, 35, 39, 40, 61, 71, 72, 104, 105, 117, 118, 133, 134, 147, 159, 160, 166, 184, 185
Luxury cars, 22, 26, 27, 38, 49, 59
Luxury consumption behavior, 61
Luxury hospitality, 22

Luxury industry in France, 7
Luxury services, 50, 61, 177, 186
LVMH Moët Hennessy Louis Vuitton, 25

M
Macroprocess of marketing communication, 150
Maison Francis Kurkdjian, 25
Maisons, 12, 21
Make Up For Ever, 25
Marc Jacobs, 25
Marc Jacobs Beauty, 25
Marginal/variable costing, 143
Marketing channels, 123
Marketing communication
  macroprocess of, 150
Market Segmentation, 76, 85
Mark-up price, 144
Maserati, 27
Maybach, 26
McLaren Automotive, 32
McQ, 26
Memory, 54, 63, 66, 70, 194
Mercantilism, 7, 9, 11
Mercedes-Benz, 26, 103
Metanalysis, 75, 84
Metrics, 38, 49, 83, 190
Millennials, 40, 78
MINI, 26
Miu Miu, 28
Mix decisions, 46, 47
Mobile marketing, 149, 158
Moët & Chandon, 25
Monetary incentives, 165
Montblanc, 26
Moschino S.p.A., 32
Most affected, 39
Motivation, 50, 63, 85, 164, 169, 192
Motives, 61, 174
Moynat, 25

N
Narcissism, 12, 14, 15, 184
Needs, 61
Needs of the soul, 10
New conscience of safety, 36
New Luxury, 13–15
Newton Vineyard, 25
Nicholas Kirkwood, 25
Noblesse oblige, 6
Non-monetary incentives, 165
Non ownership, 49

O
Officine Panerai, 26
OleHenriksen, 25

P
Packaging, 3, 15, 58, 95, 98, 107, 115, 118, 184
Panerai, 11, 22
Panorama, 3, 15, 48, 50, 180, 185, 186
Paradigm, 47, 50, 203
Parfums Christian Dior, 25
Pasticceria Marchesi, 28
Patek Philippe, 11, 21
Patou, 25
People, 2, 3, 45, 47, 48, 50, 67, 76, 108, 166, 169
Perception, 41, 57, 58, 64, 65, 104, 117, 123, 141, 147, 160, 184, 194
Perfumes Loewe, 25
Perishability, 50
Persona, 46, 47, 49, 75, 180, 194
Personality, 63, 162, 164, 184
Personal sales, 150, 159
Peter Millar, 26
Phygital, 41, 183
Piaget, 26
Pinarello, 25
Pinault, François, 22, 25
Pinault-Printemps-Redoute (PPR), 25
Places, 3, 4, 48, 98, 108, 173, 174, 181, 196
Points of difference, 55–57
Points of parity, 55, 98
Points of similarity, 55, 152
Pomellato, 26
Porsche, 26, 27
Positioning, 47, 49, 53–56
Prada S.p.A, 27
Prejudice against luxury, 5, 6, 10, 15
Price, 48
Price determination by auction, 144
Price formation, 137
Price of perceived value, 144
Pricing, 137, 139
Pricing based on the ideal value, 144
Pricing policy, 138, 140
Pricing strategy, 140
Princess Yachts, 25
Private jet, 22, 36
Private yatches, 22
Problem solution, 53
Processes, 39, 41, 48, 171, 175, 176
Productivity, 4, 10, 41, 47–50, 85, 164, 175, 190, 201, 204

Index

Products, 3, 5, 11, 12, 14, 15, 17, 26, 33, 45, 47, 48, 55, 59, 62, 68, 76, 84, 101, 107, 109, 112, 114, 143, 176, 201
Professional occupation, 63
Promotion, 15, 46, 48, 114, 117, 137, 149, 185
Promotional price, 146
Protestant Reformation, 9
Protocols, 36, 39, 41, 42
Psychological possession, 49
Public relations and advertising, 150, 153
Pucci, Emilio, 25
Purdey, 26

Q
Qeelin, 26

R
Ralph Lauren Corporation, 32
Ralph Lauren Watch & Jewelry Co., 26
Rarity, 3, 15, 16, 147, 184
Recruiting, 161, 162, 169
Regional and local consumers, 41
Renaissance, 5, 7, 37
Revenge of consumption, 37
Richemont, 26
Rimowa, 25
Ritual, 2, 3
Ritz, 11, 22
Roger Dubuis, 26
Rolls-Royce, 26
Royal Van Lent Shipyard, 25
Ruinart, 25
Rupert, Johann Peter, 22

S
Saint Laurent, 25
Sales promotion, 149, 150, 155
Salvatore Ferragamo S.p.A., 30
SARS epidemy, 22
Satisfaction, 38, 47, 48, 50, 61, 62, 64, 71, 84, 171, 190, 196
Second World War, 28, 37, 46, 79
Sedentary, 4, 15
Segmentation, 46
Segments, 14, 15, 17, 22, 32, 59, 75, 80, 82–85, 103, 203
Selecting, 162
Sensory stimuli, 180
Sephora, 25
September 11 attack, 22
Sergio Rossi, 26

Service-dominant logic paradigm, 50
Shoes, 22, 30, 32, 37, 38, 196
Smart, 26
Social classes, 4, 5, 68
Social position, 4
Social questions, 36
Social responsibility, 14, 15, 40
Sowind Haute Horlogerie, 26
Specialization, 4, 10
Starboard Cruise Services, 25
Status, 6, 7
Stella McCartney, 25
Stellantis N.V., 27
Sumptuary laws, 5, 7–9, 11, 15
Symbolic content, 3, 15, 184
System of marketing channels, 123

T
TAG Heuer, 25
Target and Positioning, 46
Target markets, 54, 75, 76, 85
Target return price, 144
Tata Motors Limited, 28
Technology, 39, 46, 47, 75, 79, 143, 176, 192
Telemarketing, 124, 157
Temple, 3, 4, 11–13, 15, 121, 133
Terrazas de los Andes, 25
The House of Fabergé, 30
Tiffany & Co., 11, 21, 25
Tod's S.p.A., 32
Tomas Maier, 26
Trade mark, 96
Training, 3, 35, 110, 161, 163, 169, 194, 204
Tree-like structure, 54

U
Unaffected, 39
Unique Selling Proposition (USP), 46, 53
User Experience, 35, 192

V
Vacheron Constantin, 26
VALS, 79
Value network, 122
Values, 1, 40, 42, 57, 59, 68, 75, 85, 164, 186
Van Cleef & Arpels, 26
Veuve Clicquot, 25
Volcan de mi tierra, 25
Volcom, 26
Volkswagen AG, 26

W
Watches and apparel, 37
Wenjun, 25
Whistlepig, 25
Woodinville, 25
Word-of-mouth, 153, 157–159, 166
Word-of-mouth marketing, 150
Worldwide luxury market evolution, 23

Y
YOOX NET-A-PORTER, 26

Z
Zenith, 25
Zimmerli AG, 33

The manufacturer's authorised representative in the EU is Springer Nature Customer Service Centre GmbH, Europaplatz 3, 69115 Heidelberg, Germany. If you have any concerns regarding our products, please contact ProductSafety@springernature.com

Printed and bound by CPI Group (UK) Ltd, Croydon, CR0 4YY

23/03/2026

02076748-0001